XcalableMP PGAS Programming Language

Mitsuhisa Sato

Editor

XcalableMP PGAS Programming Language

From Programming Model to Applications

 Springer

Editor
Mitsuhisa Sato
Programming Envt Research Team
RIKEN Center for Computational Science
Kobe, Hyogo, Japan

ISBN 978-981-15-7685-0   ISBN 978-981-15-7683-6   (eBook)
https://doi.org/10.1007/978-981-15-7683-6

This book is an open access publication.

This Springer imprint is published by the registered company Springer Nature Singapore Pte Ltd.
The registered company address is: 152 Beach Road, #21-01/04 Gateway East, Singapore 189721, Singapore

Preface

XcalableMP is a directive-based parallel programming language based on Fortran and C, supporting the PGAS (partitioned global address space) model for distributed memory parallel systems. PGAS is a programming model related to distributed memory system with a shared address space that distinguishes between local (cheap) and remote (expensive) memory access. It provides an easy and intuitive programming model to describe remote data access. PGAS is an emerging programming model for exascale computing.

The XcalableMP project has been started in 2008 as a part of MEXT e-science project, led by Prof. Yutaka Ishikawa, University of Tokyo, Japan. The language specification working group were organized by Mitsuhisa Sato, University of Tsukuba, with members from academia, government laboratories, and industries, who are interested in parallel programming languages. In 2011, version 1.0 of XcalableMP was published. Since 2011, after the e-science project was ended, the specification working group has been managed under the PC Cluster Consortium, Japan. At the same time, the Omni XcalableMP compiler has been developed as a production-level reference implementation of XcalableMP compiler for C and Fortran 2008 by RIKEN CCS and University of Tsukuba.

The XcalableMP project has taken an evolutional approach with the following strategies:

- We focus on migration from existing codes: To facilitate the migration, we took the directive-based approach to enable parallelization by adding directives/pragma in the global view programming. As a local view programming, the coarray feature was supported to replace the MPI communication for the migration from the MPI.
- Learn from the past: In the past, the Japanese HPC language community had a lot of experience on High-Performance Fortran. This experience provided useful insights for the design of the global view programming model.
- Specification designed by community: Programming languages should be shared by many programmers. For the design of the language specification, the specification working group has been organized to collect the idea from the community.

Currently, the working group is organized under the PC Cluster Consortium, Japan.

- Design based on the PGAS model and Coarray Fortran: In XcalableMP, the PGAS model is adopted as the main programming model since it is an emerging programming model for exascale computing. In addition, we extend it with the idea taken from HPF for global view programming. Coarray feature is taken as a local view programming.
- Used as a research vehicle for researches for programming language: As advanced researches, an extension to accelerator, XcalableACC, and global task-parallel programming for XcalableMP 2.0 are explored based on the XcalableMP language.

This book presents XcalableMP language from its programming model and basic concept to the experience and performance of applications described in XcalableMP and some extended research projects using XcalableMP.

Chapter "XcalableMP Programming Model and Language" presents the overview of XcalableMP programming model and language, followed by implementation and performance evaluation of a reference prototype compiler and Omni XcalableMP compiler, in Chapter "Implementation and Performance Evaluation of Omni Compiler". Chapter "Coarrays in the Context of XcalableMP" presents how to design and implement the Coarray feature in the XcalableMP compiler.

XcalableACC is an extended project to integrate the OpenACC with XcalableMP for the programming of the cluster with accelerators. Chapter "XcalableACC: An Integration of XcalableMP and OpenACC" describes the XcalableACC with the implementation and performance evaluation.

Chapter "Mixed-Language Programming with XcalableMP" presents the mixed-language programming with XcalableMP. It demonstrates how to use XcalableMP with other programming languages such as Python. The global view programming of XcalableMP provides very simple and intuitive programming tools to describe a part of program controlled by Python.

Chapters "Three-Dimensional Fluid Code with XcalableMP", "Hybrid-View Programming of Nuclear Fusion Simulation Code in XcalableMP" and "Parallelization of Atomic Image Reconstruction from X-ray Fluorescence Holograms with XcalableMP" present applications experiences, "Three-Dimensional Fluid Code," "Nuclear Fusion Simulation Code," and "Atomic Image Reconstruction from X-ray Fluorescence Holograms" described in XcalableMP.

Chapter "Multi-SPMD Programming Model with YML and XcalableMP" presents the international collaboration with French and German partners. Framework and Programming for Post-Petascale Computing (FP3C) project conducted during September 2010–March 2013 aimed to exploit efficient programming and method for future supercomputers. In the FP3C project, the mSPMD programming had been proposed with the integration of the XcalableMP and YML workflow programming environment. The priority program "Software for Exascale Computing" (SPPEXA) by the collaboration with three countries, Japan,

Germany, and France, had been conducted to address fundamental research on the various aspects of HPC software during 2016–2018 (phase II). The project "MUST Correctness Checking for YML and XMP Programs (MYX)" had been selected. The correctness checking program, MUST is applied to the XcalableMP program.

XcalableMP was taken as a parallel programming language project in FLAG-SHIP 2020 project which was to develop the Japanese flagship supercomputer, Fugaku, for improving the productivity and performance of parallel programming. XcalableMP is now available on Fugaku and the performance is enhanced by the Fugaku interconnect, Tofu-D. Chapter "XcalableMP 2.0 and Future Directions" presents the current status of XcalableMP on Fugaku and a proposal for the next version, XcalableMP 2.0. I conclude this book with challenges for future PGAS models and some retrospectives about XcalableMP.

I hope this book will provide useful information to the XcalableMP programmers. Furthermore, for future exascale computing and beyond, an important role of programming model is to bridge the gap between a new architecture and programmer's view as well as providing a comprehensive architectural view of the system. I believe that the PGAS model and its extensions will be still an important and suggestive model integrating computation and memory.

Finally, I would like to thank the members of the XcalableMP Specification Working Group and all the people who contributed to the XcalableMP project.

Kobe, Japan   Mitsuhisa Sato
July 2020

Contents

XcalableMP Programming Model and Language 1
Hitoshi Murai, Masahiro Nakao, and Mitsuhisa Sato

Implementation and Performance Evaluation of Omni Compiler 73
Masahiro Nakao and Hitoshi Murai

Coarrays in the Context of XcalableMP 97
Hidetoshi Iwashita and Masahiro Nakao

XcalableACC: An Integration of XcalableMP and OpenACC 123
Akihiro Tabuchi, Hitoshi Murai, Masahiro Nakao, Tetsuya Odajima,
and Taisuke Boku

Mixed-Language Programming with XcalableMP 147
Masahiro Nakao

Three-Dimensional Fluid Code with XcalableMP 165
Hitoshi Sakagami

**Hybrid-View Programming of Nuclear Fusion Simulation Code
in XcalableMP** 181
Keisuke Tsugane, Taisuke Boku, Hitoshi Murai, Mitsuhisa Sato,
William Tang, and Bei Wang

**Parallelization of Atomic Image Reconstruction from X-ray
Fluorescence Holograms with XcalableMP** 205
Atsushi Kubota, Tomohiro Matsushita, and Naohisa Happo

Multi-SPMD Programming Model with YML and XcalableMP 219
Miwako Tsuji, Hitoshi Murai, Taisuke Boku, Mitsuhisa Sato,
Serge G. Petiton, Nahid Emad, Thomas Dufaud, Joachim Protze,
Christian Terboven, and Matthias S. Müller

XcalableMP 2.0 and Future Directions 245
Mitsuhisa Sato, Hitoshi Murai, Masahiro Nakao, Keisuke Tsugane,
Tesuya Odajima, and Jinpil Lee

XcalableMP Programming Model and Language

Hitoshi Murai, Masahiro Nakao, and Mitsuhisa Sato

Abstract XcalableMP (XMP) is a directive-based language extension of Fortran and C for distributed-memory parallel computers, and can be classified as a partitioned global address space (PGAS) language. One of the remarkable characteristics of XMP is that it supports both global-view and local-view parallel programming. This chapter describes the programming model and language specification of XMP.

1 Introduction

Distributed-memory systems are generally used for large-scale simulations. To program such systems, Message Passing Interface (MPI) is widely adopted. However, programming with MPI is difficult because programmers must describe inter-process communications with consideration of the execution flow of their programs, which might cause deadlocks or wrong results.

To address this issue, a parallel language named High Performance Fortran (HPF) was proposed in 1991. With HPF, programmers can execute their serial programs in parallel by inserting minimal directives into them. If the programmers specify data distribution with HPF directives, the compilers do all other tasks for parallelization (e.g. communication generation and work distribution). However, HPF was not widely accepted eventually because the compilers' automatic processing prevents the programmers from performance tuning, and the performance depends heavily on the environment (e.g. compiler and hardware)

Note For more details, please refer: Ken Kennedy, Charles Koelbel and Hans Zima: The Rise and Fall of High Performance Fortran: An Historical Object Lesson, Proc. 3rd ACM SIGPLAN History of Programming Languages Conf. (HOPL-III), pp. 7-1–7-22 (2007).

H. Murai (✉) · M. Nakao · M. Sato
RIKEN Center for Computational Science, Kobe, Hyogo, Japan
e-mail: h-murai@riken.jp; masahiro.nakao@riken.jp; msato@riken.jp

In such circumstance, to develop a new parallel programming model that enables easy parallelization of existing serial programs and design a new language based on it, "the XMP Specification Working Group" was established in 2008. This group utilized the lessons from the experience of HPF to define a new parallel language *XcalableMP (XMP)*. The group was reorganized to one of the working groups of PC Cluster Consortium in 2011.

It is learned from the lessons of HPF that more automatic processing of compilers increases the gap between a program and its execution, and, as a result, decreases the usability of the language. In XMP, the programmers specify explicitly the details of parallel programs on the basis of compiler directives to make their execution easy to understand. In particular, they can specify explicitly communication, synchronization, data mapping, and work mapping to facilitate performance tuning. In addition, XMP supports features for one-sided communication on each process, which was not available in HPF. This feature might enable programmers to implement parallel algorithms more easily.

In this chapter, an overview of the programming model and language specification of XMP is shown. You can find the latest and complete language specification of XMP in: XcalableMP Specification Working Group, XcalableMP Specification Version 1.4, http://xcalablemp.org/download/spec/xmp-spec-1.4.pdf (2018).

1.1 Target Hardware

The target of XcalableMP is distributed-memory multicomputers (Fig. 1). Each compute node, which may contain several cores, has its own local memory (shared by the cores, if any), and is connected with the others via an interconnection network. Each node can access its local memory directly and remote memory (the memory of another node) indirectly (i.e. via inter-node communication). However,

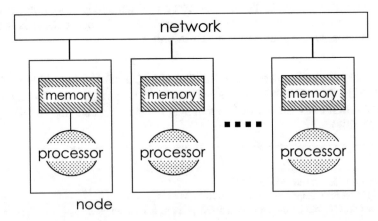

Fig. 1 Target hardware of XMP

it is assumed that accessing remote memory may be much slower than accessing local memory.

1.2 Execution Model

The execution entities in an XMP program are referred to as XMP **nodes** or, more simply, **nodes**, which has its own memory and can communicate with each other.

An XcalableMP program execution is based on the Single Program Multiple Data (SPMD) model, where each **node** starts execution from the same main routine, and continues to execute the same code independently (i.e. asynchronously) until it encounters an XcalableMP construct (Fig. 2).

A set of **nodes** that executes a procedure, statement, loop, a block, etc. is referred to as its *executing node set*, and is determined by the innermost `task`, `loop`, or `array` directive surrounding it dynamically, or at runtime. The *current executing node set* is an **executing node set** of the current context, which is managed by the XcalableMP runtime system on each **node**.

The **current executing node set** at the beginning of the program execution, or *entire node set*, is a **node set** that contains all the available **nodes**, which can be specified in an implementation-defined way (e.g. through a command-line option).

When a **node** encounters at runtime either a `loop`, `array`, or `task` construct, and is contained by the **node set** specified (explicitly or implicitly) by the on clause

Fig. 2 Execution model of XMP

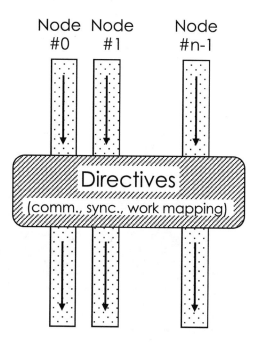

of the directive, it updates the **current executing node set** with the specified one and executes the body of the construct, after which it resumes the last **executing node set** and proceeds to execute the subsequent statements.

In particular, when a **node** in the **current executing node set** encounters a `loop` or an `array` construct, it executes the loop or the array assignment in parallel with the other **nodes**, so that each iteration of the loop or element of the assignment is independently executed by the **node** in which the specified data element resides.

When a **node** encounters a synchronization or a communication directive, synchronization or communication occurs between it and the other **nodes**. That is, such *global constructs* are performed collectively by the **current executing nodes**. Note that neither synchronization nor communication occurs unless these constructs are specified.

1.3 Data Model

There are two classes of data in XcalableMP: *global data* and *local data*. Data declared in an XcalableMP program are **local** by default.

Global data are distributed onto a **node set** by the `align` directive (see Sect. 2.4). Each fragment of distributed **global data** is allocated in the local memory of a **node** in the **node set**.

Local data comprises all data that are not **global**. They are replicated within the local memory of each of the **executing nodes**.

A **node** can access directly only local data and sections of **global data** that reside in its local memory. To access data in remote memory, explicit communication must be specified in such ways as global communication constructs and **coarray** assignments (Fig. 3).

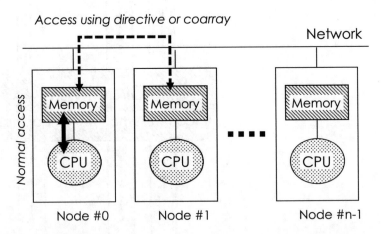

Fig. 3 Data model of XMP

1.4   Programming Models

1.4.1   Partitioned Global Address Space

XMP can be classified as a *partitioned global address space (PGAS)* language, such as Co-Array Fortran [1], Unified Parallel C [2], and Chapel [3].

In such PGAS languages, multiple executing entities (i.e. threads, processes, or **nodes** in XMP) share a part of their address space, which is, however, partitioned and a portion of which is local to each executing entity.

The two programming models, global-view and local-view, that XMP supports to achieve high performance and productivity on PGAS are explained below.

1.4.2   Global-View Programming Model

The global-view programming model is useful when, starting from a serial version of a program, the programmer parallelizes it in a data-parallel style by adding directives with minimum modification. Based on this model, the programmer specifies the distribution of data among nodes using the data distribution directives. The `loop` construct assigns each iteration of a loop to the **node** at which the computed data is located. The global-view communication directives are used to synchronize **nodes**, maintain the consistency of shadow areas of distributed data, and move sections of distributed data globally. Note that the programmer must specify explicitly communication to make all data references in their program local using appropriate directives.

In many cases, the XcalableMP program following the global-view programming model is based on a serial program, and it can produce the same result, regardless of the number of **nodes** (Fig. 4).

There are three groups of directives for this model:

- *Data mapping,* which specifies the data distribution and mapping to **nodes**
- *Work mapping (parallelization),* which specifies the work distribution and mapping to **nodes**.
- *Communication and synchronization,* which specify how a **node** communicates and synchronizes with the other **nodes**.

Because these directives are ignored as a comment by the compilers of base languages (Fortran and C), an XcalableMP program can usually be compiled by them to ensure that they run properly.

1.4.3   Local-View Programming Model

The local-view programming model is suitable for programs that implement an algorithm and a remote data reference that are to be executed by each **node** (Fig. 5).

H. Murai et al.

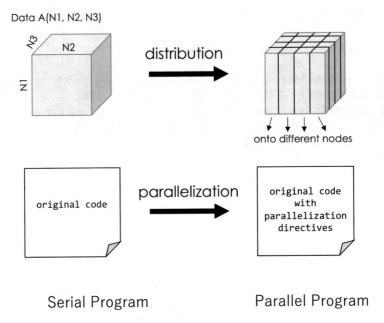

Serial Program   Parallel Program

Fig. 4 Parallelization based on the global-view programming model

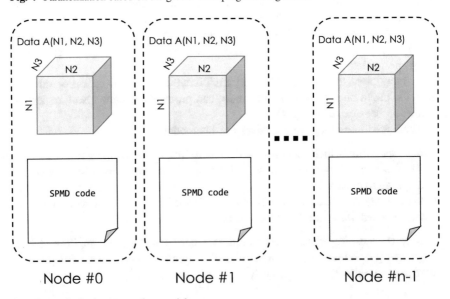

Node #0   Node #1   Node #n-1

Fig. 5 Local-view programming model

For this model, some language extensions and directives are provided. The **coarray** notation, which is imported from Fortran 2008, is one such extension, and can be used to explicitly specify data on which **node** is to be accessed. For example, the expression of A(i)[N] in XcalableMP Fortran is used to access an array element of A(i) located on the **node** N. If the access is a reference, then a one-sided communication to read the value from the remote memory (i.e. the *get* operation) is issued by the **executing node**. If the access is a definition, then a one-sided communication to write the value to the remote memory (i.e. the *put* operation) is issued by the **executing node**.

1.4.4 Mixture of Global View and Local View

In the global-view model, **nodes** are used to distribute data and works. In the local-view model, **nodes** are used to address remote data in the **coarray** notation. In application programs, the programmers should choose an appropriate data model according to the characteristics of their program. Figure 6 illustrates the global view and the local view of data.

Data can have both a global view and a local view, and can be accessed in both of the views. XcalableMP provides a directive to give the **local** name (alias) to **global data** declared in the global-view programming model to enable them to also be accessed in the local-view programming model. This feature is useful to optimize a certain part of a program by using explicit remote data access in the local-view programming model.

1.5 Base Languages

The XcalableMP language specification is defined on the basis of Fortran and C as the base languages. More specifically, the base language of XcalableMP Fortran is Fortran 90 or later, and that of XcalableMP C is ISO C90 (ANSI C89) or later with some extensions (see below).

1.5.1 Array Section in XcalableMP C

In XcalableMP C, the base language C is extended so that a part of an array, that is, an *array section* or *subarray*, can be put in an *array assignment statement*, which is described in Sect. 1.5.2, and some XcalableMP constructs. An array section is built from a subset of the elements of an array, which is specified by a sequence of square-bracketed integer expressions or *triplets*, which are in the form of:

[*base*] : [*length*] [: *step*]

When *step* is positive, the *triplet* specifies a set of subscripts that is a regularly spaced integer sequence of length *length* beginning with *base* and proceeding in increments of *step* up to the largest. The same applies to negative *step* too.

When *base* is omitted, it is assumed to be 0. When *length* is omitted, it is assumed to be the number of remainder elements of the dimension of the array. When *step* is omitted, it is assumed to be 1.

```
!$xmp nodes P(4)
!$xmp template T(100)
!$xmp distribute T(block) onto P

      real G(80, 100)        ! global variable
!$xmp align G(*,i) with T(i)

      real L(50, 40)         ! local variable (default)
```

Global address space (virtual)

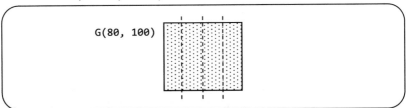

Data allocation

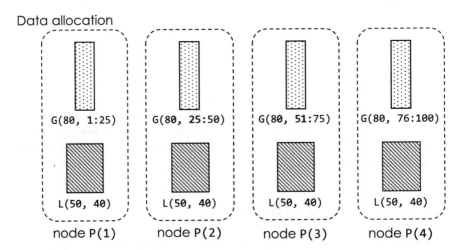

Fig. 6 Global view and local view

Assuming that an array A is declared by the following statement,

```
    int A[100];
```

some array sections can be specified as follows:

A[10:10]	array section of 10 elements from A[10] to A[19]
A[10:]	array section of 90 elements from A[10] to A[99]
A[:10]	array section of 10 elements from A[0] to A[9]
A[10:5:2]	array section of 5 elements from A[10] to A[18] by step 2
A[:]	array section of the whole of A

1.5.2   Array Assignment Statement in XcalableMP C

In XcalableMP C, the base language C is also extended so that it supports array assignment statements just as Fortran does.

With such statement, the value of each element of the result of the right-hand side expression is assigned to the corresponding element of the array section on the left-hand side. When an operator or an elemental function is applied to array sections in the right-hand side expression, it is evaluated to an array section that has the same shape as that of the operands or arguments, and each element of which is the result of the operator or function applied to the corresponding element of the operands or arguments. A scalar object is assumed to be an array section that has the same shape as that of the other array section(s) in the expression or on the left-hand side, and where each element has its value.

Note that an array assignment is a statement, and therefore cannot appear as an expression in any other statements.

In the example below, an array assignment statement in the fourth line copies the five elements from B[0] to B[4] into the elements from A[5] to A[9].

```
─────────────── XcalableMP C ───────────────
int A[10];
int B[5];
    ...
A[5:5]  =  B[0:5];
```

1.6   Interoperability

Most of the existing parallel applications are written with MPI. It is not realistic to port them over to XMP because each of them consists of millions of lines.

Because XMP is interoperable with MPI, users can develop an XMP application by modifying a part of an existing one instead of rewriting it totally. Besides, when developing a parallel application from scratch, it is possible to use XMP to write a complicated part of, for example, domain decomposition while they use MPI, which could be faster than XMP, to write a hot-spot part that need to be tuned carefully. In addition, XMP is interoperable with OpenMP and Python (see Chap. 5).

It might be difficult to develop an application with just one programming language or framework since it generally has its own strong and weak points. Thus, an XMP program is interoperable with those in other languages to provide both high productivity and performance.

2 Data Mapping

2.1 nodes Directive

The nodes directive declares a *node array*, which is an array-like arrangement of
nodes in a **node set**. A **node array** can be multi-dimensional.

———————————— XcalableMP C ————————————
```
#pragma xmp nodes p[4]
```

———————————— XcalableMP Fortran ————————————
```
!$xmp nodes p(4)
```

The nodes directive declares a one-dimensional **node array** p that includes four
nodes. In XMP/C, it is zero-based and consists of p[0], p[1], p[2], and p[3].
In XMP/Fortran, it is one-based and consists of p(1), p(2), p(3), and p(4).

———————————— XcalableMP C ————————————
```
#pragma xmp nodes p[2][3]
```

———————————— XcalableMP Fortran ————————————
```
!$xmp nodes p(3,2)
```

The nodes directive declares two-dimensional **node array** p that includes six
nodes. In XMP/C, it consists of p[0][0], p[0][1], p[0][2], p[1][0],
p[1][1], and p[1][2]. In XMP/Fortran, it consists of p(1,1), p(2,1),
p(3,1), p(1,2), p(2,2), and p(3,2).

Note The ordering of the elements in a **node array** follows that of a normal array
in the base language, C or Fortran.

———————————— XcalableMP C ————————————
```
#pragma xmp nodes p[*]
```

———————————— XcalableMP Fortran ————————————
```
!$xmp nodes p(*)
```

An asterisk can be specified as the size in the nodes directive to declare a
dynamic **node array**. In the above code, one-dimensional dynamic **node array** p
is declared with an asterisk as the size. The actual size of a dynamic **node array** is
determined at runtime to fit the size of the current executing node set. For example,
when the programmer runs the sample code with three nodes, the **node array** p
includes three nodes.

The programmer can also declare multi-dimensional dynamic **node arrays** with
an asterisk.

———————————— XcalableMP C ————————————
```
#pragma xmp nodes p[*][3]
```

```
──────────────── XcalableMP Fortran ────────────────
!$xmp nodes p(3,*)
```

When the programmer runs the sample code with 12 nodes, the **node array** p has a shape of 4 × 3, in C, or 3 × 4, in Fortran.

Note The programmer can put an asterisk only in the last dimension, in XMP/Fortran, or the first dimension, in XMP/C, of the **node array**.

Hint The dynamic **node array** may interfere with compiler optimizations. In general, programs with static ones achieve better performance.

The programmer can declare a node subarray derived from an existing node array. Node subarrays can be used, for example, to optimize inter-node communication by reducing the number of nodes participating in the communication.

```
──────────────── XcalableMP C ────────────────
#pragma xmp nodes p[16]
#pragma xmp nodes q[8]=p[0:8]
#pragma xmp nodes r[4][2]=p[8:8]
```

```
──────────────── XcalableMP Fortran ────────────────
!$xmp nodes p(16)
!$xmp nodes q(8)=p(1:8)
!$xmp nodes r(2,4)=p(9:16)
```

In line 1, a **node array** p including 16 nodes is declared. In line 2, a node subarray q corresponding to the first half of p is declared. In line 3, a two-dimensional node subarray r corresponding to the latter half of p is declared.

The programmer can declare an n-dimensional node subarray derived from an m-dimensional one (Fig. 7).

```
──────────────── XcalableMP C ────────────────
#pragma xmp nodes p[4][2]
#pragma xmp nodes row[4]=p[:][*]
#pragma xmp nodes col[2]=p[*][:]
```

```
──────────────── XcalableMP Fortran ────────────────
!$xmp nodes p(2,4)
!$xmp nodes row(4)=p(*,:)
!$xmp nodes col(2)=p(:,*)
```

In line 1, a two-dimensional **node array** p including 4 × 2 nodes is declared. In line 2, a node subarray row derived from a single row of p is declared. In line 3, a node subarray col derived from a single column of p is declared.

XMP/C

p[0][0]	p[0][1]
p[1][0]	p[1][1]
p[2][0]	p[2][1]
p[3][0]	p[3][1]

col[4]   col[4]

p[0][0]	p[0][1]	**row[2]**
p[1][0]	p[1][1]	**row[2]**
p[2][0]	p[2][1]	**row[2]**
p[3][0]	p[3][1]	**row[2]**

XMP/Fortran

p(1,1)	p(2,1)
p(1,2)	p(2,2)
p(1,3)	p(2,3)
p(1,4)	p(2,4)

col(4)   col(4)

p(1,1)	p(2,1)	**row(2)**
p(1,2)	p(2,2)	**row(2)**
p(1,3)	p(2,3)	**row(2)**
p(1,4)	p(2,4)	**row(2)**

Fig. 7 Node subarrays

A colon represents a triplet which indicates all possible indices in the dimension. An asterisk indicates the index of the current executing node in the dimension. For example, col[2] corresponds to p[0][0:2] on nodes p[0][0] and p[0][1], and to p[1][0:2] on nodes p[1][0] and p[1][1] in XMP/C. Similarly, col(2) corresponds to p(1:2,1) on nodes p(1,1) and p(2,1), and to p(1:2,2) on nodes p(1,2) p(2,2) in XMP/Fortran.

In XMP/C, row[0] corresponds to p[0][0] and p[0][1] on p[:][0] and p[:][1], respectively; col[0] corresponds to p[0][0], p[1][0], p[2][0], and p[3][0] on p[0][:], p[1][:], p[2][:], p[3][:], respectively. In XMP/Fortran, row(1) corresponds to p(1,1) and p(2,1) on p(1,:) and p(2,:), respectively; col(1) corresponds to p(1,1), p(1,2), p(1,3), and p(1,4) on p(:,1), p(:,2), p(:,3), p(:,4), respectively.

Note The semantics of an asterisk in a node reference is different from that in a declaration.

2.2 `template` Directive

The `template` directive declares a *template*, which is a virtual array that is used as a "template" of parallelization in the programs and to be distributed onto a **node array**.

```
——————————— XcalableMP C ———————————
#pragma xmp template t[10]
```

```
——————————— XcalableMP Fortran ———————————
!$xmp template t(10)
```

This `template` directive declares a one-dimensional **template** t having ten elements. **Templates** are indexed in the similar manner to arrays in the base languages. For the above examples, the **template** t is indexed from zero to nine (i.e. t[0] ⋯ t[9]), in XMP/C, or one to ten (i.e. t(1) ⋯ t(10)), in XMP/Fortran.

Hint In many cases, a template should be declared to have the same shape as your target array.

```
——————————— XcalableMP C ———————————
#pragma xmp template t[10][20]
```

```
——————————— XcalableMP Fortran ———————————
!$xmp template t(20,10)
```

The `template` directive declares a two-dimensional **template** t that has 10 × 20 elements. In XMP/C, t is indexed from t[0][0] to t[9][19], and, in XMP/Fortran, from t(1,1) to t(20,10).

```
——————————— XcalableMP C ———————————
#pragma xmp template t[:]
```

```
——————————— XcalableMP Fortran ———————————
!$xmp template t(:)
```

In the above examples, a colon instead of an integer is specified as the size to declare a one-dimensional dynamic **template** t. The colon indicates that the size of the **template** is not fixed and to be fixed at runtime by the `template_fix` construct (Sect. 2.6).

2.3 `distribute` Directive

The `distribute` directive specifies a distribution of the target **template**. Either of *block, cyclic, block-cyclic*, or *gblock* (i.e. uneven block) can be specified to distribute a dimension of a **template**.

2.3.1 Block Distribution

```
─────────────── XcalableMP C ───────────────
#pragma xmp distribute t[block] onto p
```

```
─────────────── XcalableMP Fortran ───────────────
!$xmp distribute t(block) onto p
```

The target template t is divided into contiguous blocks and distributed among nodes in the **node array** p (Fig. 8). Let's suppose that the size of the **template** is N and the number of nodes is K. If N is divisible by K, a block of size N/K is assigned to each node; otherwise, a block of size $ceil(N/K)$ is assigned to each of $N/ceil(N/K)$ nodes, a block of size $mod(N, K)$ to one node, and no block to $(K - N/ceil(N/K) - 1)$ nodes. The block distribution is useful for regular computations such as a stencil one.

Note The function $ceil(x)$ returns a minimum integer value greater than or equal to x, and $mod(x, y)$ returns x modulo y.

```
─────────────── XcalableMP C ───────────────
#pragma xmp nodes p[3]
#pragma xmp template t[22]
#pragma xmp distribute t[block] onto p
```

```
─────────────── XcalableMP Fortran ───────────────
!$xmp nodes p(3)
!$xmp template t(22)
!$xmp distribute t(block) onto p
```

Since $ceil(22/3)$ is 8, eight elements are allocated on each of p[0] and p[1], and the remaining six elements are allocated on p[2].

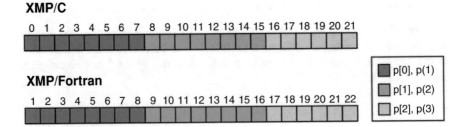

Fig. 8 Block distribution

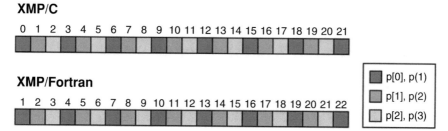

Fig. 9 Cyclic distribution

2.3.2 Cyclic Distribution

```
━━━━━━━━━━━━ XcalableMP C ━━━━━━━━
#pragma xmp distribute t[cyclic] onto p
```

```
━━━━━━━━ XcalableMP Fortran ━━━━━━
!$xmp distribute t(cyclic) onto p
```

The target **template** t is divided into chunks of size one and distributed among nodes in the **node array** p in a round-robin manner (Fig. 9). The cyclic distribution is useful for the case where the load on each element of the **template** is not balanced.

```
━━━━━━━━━━━━ XcalableMP C ━━━━━━━━
#pragma xmp nodes p[3]
#pragma xmp template t[22]
#pragma xmp distribute t[cyclic] onto p
```

```
━━━━━━━━ XcalableMP Fortran ━━━━━━
!$xmp nodes p(3)
!$xmp template t(22)
!$xmp distribute t(cyclic) onto p
```

2.3.3 Block-Cyclic Distribution

```
━━━━━━━━━━━━ XcalableMP C ━━━━━━━━
#pragma xmp distribute t[cyclic(w)] onto p
```

```
━━━━━━━━ XcalableMP Fortran ━━━━━━
!$xmp distribute t(cyclic(w)) onto p
```

The target **template** t is divided into chunks of size w and distributed among nodes in the **node array** p in a round-robin manner (Fig. 10). The block-cyclic distribution is useful for the case where the load on each element of the **template** is not balanced but the locality of the elements is required.

XMP/C

XMP/Fortran

Fig. 10 Block-cyclic distribution

```
───────────────────── XcalableMP C ─────────────────────
#pragma xmp nodes p[3]
#pragma xmp template t[22]
#pragma xmp distribute t[cyclic(3)] onto p
```

```
───────────────────── XcalableMP Fortran ─────────────────────
!$xmp nodes p(3)
!$xmp template t(22)
!$xmp distribute t(cyclic(3)) onto p
```

2.3.4 Gblock Distribution

```
───────────────────── XcalableMP C ─────────────────────
#pragma xmp distribute t[gblock(W)] onto p
```

```
───────────────────── XcalableMP Fortran ─────────────────────
!$xmp distribute t(gblock(W)) onto p
```

The target **template** t is divided into contiguous blocks of size W[0], W[1], ···, in XMP/C, or W(1), W(2), ···, in XMP/Fortran, and distributed among nodes in the **node array** p (Fig. 11). The array W is called a mapping array. The programmer can specify irregular (uneven) block distribution with the gblock format.

```
───────────────────── XcalableMP C ─────────────────────
#pragma xmp nodes p[3]
#pragma xmp template t[22]
int W[3] = {6, 11, 5};
#pragma xmp distribute t[gblock(W)] onto p
```

```
───────────────────── XcalableMP Fortran ─────────────────────
!$xmp nodes p(3)
!$xmp template t(22)
integer, parameter :: W(3) = (/6,11,5/)
!$xmp distribute t(gblock(W)) onto p
```

XMP/C

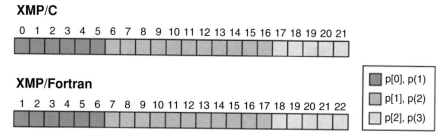

XMP/Fortran

Fig. 11 Gblock distribution

The programmer can specify an asterisk instead of a mapping array in the gblock distribution to defer fixing the actual distribution. In such a case, the actual distribution will be fixed at runtime by using the `template_fix` construct.

2.3.5 Distribution of Multi-Dimensional Templates

The programmer can distribute a multi-dimensional **template** onto a **node array**.

```
─────────────────── XcalableMP C ───────────
#pragma xmp nodes p[2][2]
#pragma xmp template t[10][10]
#pragma xmp distribute t[block][block] onto p
```

```
─────────────────── XcalableMP Fortran ───────────
!$xmp nodes p(2,2)
!$xmp template t(10,10)
!$xmp distribute t(block,block) onto p
```

The `distribute` directive declares the distribution of a two-dimensional **template** t onto a two-dimensional **node array** p. Each dimension of the **template** is divided in a block manner and each of the rectangular region is assigned to a node (Fig. 12).

The programmer can specify a different distribution format in each of the dimension of a **template** (Fig. 13).

```
─────────────────── XcalableMP C ───────────
#pragma xmp nodes p[2][2]
#pragma xmp template t[10][10]
#pragma xmp distribute t[block][cyclic] onto p
```

```
─────────────────── XcalableMP Fortran ───────────
!$xmp nodes p(2,2)
!$xmp template t(10,10)
!$xmp distribute t(cyclic,block) onto p
```

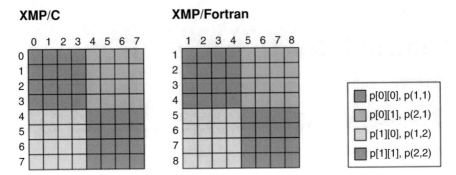

Fig. 12 Example of multi-dimensional distribution (1)

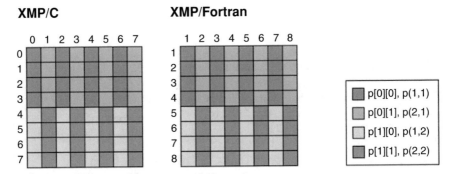

Fig. 13 Example of multi-dimensional distribution (2)

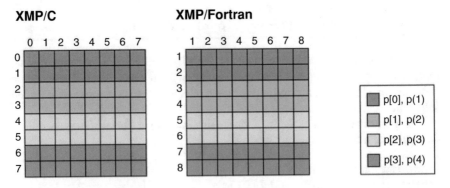

Fig. 14 Example of multi-dimensional distribution (3)

When an asterisk is specified in a `distribute` directive as a distribution format, the target dimension is "non-distributed." In the following example, the first dimension is distributed in a block manner and the second dimension is non-distributed (Fig. 14).

```
──────────────── XcalableMP C ────────────────
#pragma xmp nodes p[4]
#pragma xmp template t[10][10]
#pragma xmp distribute t[block][*] onto p
```

```
──────────────── XcalableMP Fortran ────────────────
!$xmp nodes p(4)
!$xmp template t(10,10)
!$xmp distribute t(*,block) onto p
```

2.4 align Directive

The align directive specifies that an array is to be mapped in the same way as a specified **template**. In other words, an align directive defines the correspondence of elements between an array and a **template**, and each of the array element is allocated on the node where the corresponding **template** element is assigned.

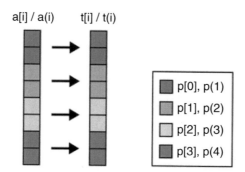

Fig. 15 Example of array alignment (1)

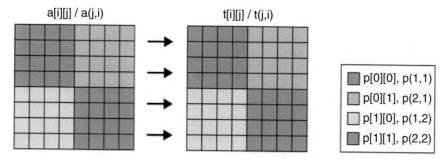

Fig. 16 Example of array alignment (2)

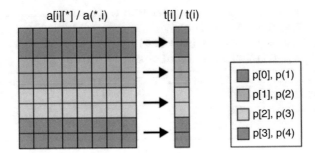

Fig. 17 Example of array alignment (3)

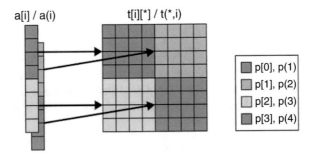

Fig. 18 Example of array alignment (4)

```
───────────────── XcalableMP C ─────────────────
#pragma xmp nodes p[4]
#pragma xmp template t[8]
#pragma xmp distribute t[block] onto p
int a[8];
#pragma xmp align a[i] with t[i]
```

```
───────────────── XcalableMP Fortran ─────────────────
!$xmp nodes p(4)
!$xmp template t(8)
!$xmp distribute t(block) onto p
integer :: a(8)
!$xmp align a(i) with t(i)
```

The array a is decomposed and laid out so that each element a(i) is colocated with the corresponding **template** element t(i) (Fig. 15).

The align directive can also be used for multi-dimensional arrays (Fig. 16).

```
───────────────── XcalableMP C ─────────────────
#pragma xmp nodes p[2][2]
#pragma xmp template t[8][8]
#pragma xmp distribute t[block][block] onto p
```

```
   int a[8][8];
 5 #pragma xmp align a[i][j] with t[i][j]
```

```
─────────────── XcalableMP Fortran ───────────────
   !$xmp nodes p(2,2)
   !$xmp template t(8,8)
   !$xmp distribute t(block,block) onto p
   integer :: a(8,8)
 5 !$xmp align a(j,i) with t(j,i)
```

The programmer can align an *n*-dimensional array with an *m*-dimensional **template** for $n > m$ (Fig. 17).

```
─────────────── XcalableMP C ───────────────
   #pragma xmp nodes p[4]
   #pragma xmp template t[8]
   #pragma xmp distribute t[block] onto p
   int a[8][8];
 5 #pragma xmp align a[i][*] with t[i]
```

```
─────────────── XcalableMP Fortran ───────────────
   !$xmp nodes p(4)
   !$xmp template t(8)
   !$xmp distribute t(block) onto p
   integer :: a(8,8)
 5 !$xmp align a(*,i) with t(i)
```

When an asterisk is specified as a subscript in a dimension of the target array in the align directive, the dimension is "collapsed" (i.e. not distributed). In the sample program above, the first dimension of the array a is distributed onto the **node array** p while the second dimension is collapsed.

In XMP/C, a[0:2][:] will be allocated on p[0] while, in XMP/Fortran, a(:,1:2) will be allocated on p(1).

The programmer also can align an *n*-dimensional array with an *m*-dimensional template for $n < m$ (Fig. 18).

```
─────────────── XcalableMP C ───────────────
   #pragma xmp nodes p[2][2]
   #pragma xmp template t[8][8]
   #pragma xmp distribute t[block][block] onto p
   int a[8];
 5 #pragma xmp align a[i] with t[i][*]
```

```
─────────────── XcalableMP Fortran ───────────────
   !$xmp nodes p(2,2)
   !$xmp template t(8,8)
   !$xmp distribute t(block,block) onto p
   integer :: a(8)
 5 !$xmp align a(i) with t(*,i)
```

When an asterisk is specified as a subscript in a dimension of the target **template** in the `align` directive, the array will be "replicated" along the axis of the dimension.

In XMP/C, `a[0:4]` will be replicated and allocated on p[0][0] and p[0][1] while, in XMP/Fortran, `a(1:4)` will be allocated on p(1,1) and p(2,1).

2.5 Dynamic Allocation of Distributed Array

This section explains how **distributed** (i.e. **global**) **arrays** are allocated at runtime. The basic procedure is common in XMP/C and XMP/Fortran with a few specific difference.

```
─────────────────────── XcalableMP C ───────────────
  #pragma xmp nodes p[4]
  #pragma xmp template t[N]
  #pragma xmp distribute t[block] onto p
  float *a;
5 #pragma xmp align a[i] with t[i]
      :
  a = xmp_malloc(xmp_desc_of(a), N);
```

In XMP/C, first, declare a pointer of the type of the target array; second, align it as if it were an array; finally, allocate memory for it with the `xmp_malloc()` function. `xmp_desc_of()` is an intrinsic/built-in function that returns the descriptor of the XMP object (i.e. **nodes, templates,** or **global arrays**) specified by the argument.

```
─────────────────── XcalableMP Fortran ───────────────
  !$xmp nodes p(4)
  !$xmp template t(N)
  !$xmp distribute t(block) onto p
  real, allocatable :: a(:)
5 !$xmp align a(i) with t(i)

  allocate(a(N))
```

In XMP/Fortran, first, declare an allocatable array; second, align it; finally, allocate memory for it with the `allocate` statement.

For multi-dimensional arrays, the procedure is the same as that for one-dimensional ones, as follows:

```
─────────────────────── XcalableMP C ───────────────
  #pragma xmp nodes p[2][2]
  #pragma xmp template t[N1][N2]
  #pragma xmp distribute t[block][block] onto p
  float (*a)[N2];
5 #pragma xmp align a[i][j] with t[i][j]
```

```
    :
a = (float (*) [N2]) xmp_malloc(xmp_desc_of(a), N1, N2);
```

```
────────────────── XcalableMP Fortran ──────────────────
!$xmp nodes p(2,2)
!$xmp template t(N2,N1)
!$xmp distribute t(block,block) onto p
real, allocatable :: a(:,:)
!$xmp align a(j,i) with t(j,i)
    :
allocate(a(N2,N1))
```

Note If the size of the **template** is not fixed until runtime, the programmer has to fix it at runtime with the `template_fix` construct.

2.6 *template_fix Construct*

The `template_fix` construct fixes the shape and/or the distribution of an unfixed **template**.

```
────────────────── XcalableMP C ──────────────────
#pragma xmp nodes p[4]
#pragma xmp template t[:]
#pragma xmp distribute t[block] onto p
double *a;
#pragma xmp align a[i] with t[i]

int n = 100;
#pragma xmp template_fix t[n]
a = xmp_malloc(xmp_desc_of(a), n);
```

```
────────────────── XcalableMP Fortran ──────────────────
!$xmp nodes p(4)
!$xmp template t(:)
!$xmp distribute t(block) onto p
real, allocatable :: a(:)
integer :: n
!$xmp align a(i) with t(i)

n = 100
!$xmp template_fix t(n)
allocate(a(n))
```

In the above sample code, first, a **template** t whose size is unfixed (":") is declared; second, a pointer a, in XMP/C, or an allocatable array a, in XMP/Fortran, is aligned with the **template**; third, the size of the **template** is fixed with a template_fix construct; finally, the pointer or the allocatable array is allocated with the xmp_malloc() built-in function in XMP/C or the allocate statement in XMP/Fortran, respectively.

Note The template_fix constructs can be applied to a **template** only once.

This construct can also be used to fix a mapping array of a **template** that is distributed in "gblock(*)" at declaration.

```
───────────────── XcalableMP C ─────────────────
#pragma xmp nodes p[4]
#pragma xmp template t[:]
#pragma xmp distribute t[gblock(*)] onto p
double *a;
#pragma xmp align a[i] with t[i]

int n = 100;
int m[] = {40,30,20,10};

#pragma xmp template_fix[gblock(m)] t[n]
a = xmp_malloc(xmp_desc_of(a), n);
```

```
───────────────── XcalableMP Fortran ─────────────────
!$xmp nodes p(4)
!$xmp template t(:)
!$xmp distribute t(gblock) onto p
real, allocatable :: a(:)
integer :: n, m(4)
!$xmp align a(i) with t(i)

n = 100
m(:) = (/40,30,20,10/)
!$xmp template_fix(gblock(m)) t(n)
allocate(a(n))
```

3   Work Mapping

3.1   *task* and *tasks* Construct

The `task` construct defines a *task* that is executed by a specified **node set**. The `tasks` construct asserts that the `task` constructs it surrounds can be executed in parallel.

3.1.1   `task` Construct

When a **node** encounters a *task* construct at runtime, it executes the associated block (called a task) if it is included by the **node set** specified by the on clause; otherwise, it skips the execution of the block (Fig. 19).

──────────────── XcalableMP C ────────────────
```
#include <stdio.h>
#pragma xmp nodes p[4]

int main(){
    int num = xmpc_node_num();
#pragma xmp task on p[1:3]
{
    printf("%d: Hello\n", num);
}

    return 0;
}
```

──────────────── XcalableMP Fortran ────────────────
```
program main
!$xmp nodes p(4)
    integer :: num

    num = xmp_node_num()
!$xmp task on p(2:4)
    write(*,*) num, ": Hello"
!$xmp end task

end program main
```

In the above example, **nodes** p[1], p[2], and p[3] invoke the printf() function, and p[1] outputs "1: Hello" in XMP/C; p(2), p(3), and p(4) execute the write statement, and p(2) outputs "2: Hello" in XMP/Fortran.

Note that a new **node set** is generated by each task construct. Let's consider inserting a bcast construct into the task.

XMP/C

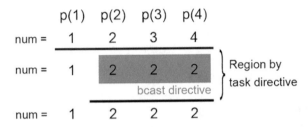

XMP/Fortran

Fig. 19 Example of task construct (1)

```
———————————— XcalableMP C ————————————
#pragma xmp task on p[1:3]
{
#pragma xmp bcast (num)
}
```
```
———————————— XcalableMP Fortran ————————————
!$xmp task on p(2:4)
!$xmp bcast (num)
!$xmp end task
```

This bcast construct is executed by the **node set** specified by the on clause of the task construct. Thus, the **node** p[1] broadcasts the value of num to p[2] and p[3] in XMP/C, and p(2) to p(3) and p(4) in XMP/Fortran.

The bcast construct in the above code is equivalent to that in the following code, where it is executed by a new **node set** q that is explicitly declared.

```
———————————— XcalableMP C ————————————
#pragma xmp nodes q[3] = p[1:3]
#pragma xmp bcast (num) on q
```
```
———————————— XcalableMP Fortran ————————————
!$xmp nodes q(3) = p(2:4)
!$xmp bcast (num) on q
```

Note that the task is executed by the **node set** specified by the on clause. Therefore, xmpc_node_num() and xmp_node_num() return the id in the **node set**.

For example, consider inserting xmpc_node_num() or xmp_node_num() into the task in the first program.

```
──────────────── XcalableMP C ────────────
#include <stdio.h>
#pragma xmp nodes p[4]

int main(){
#pragma xmp task on p[1:3]
{
  printf("%d: Hello\n", xmpc_node_num());
}

  return 0;
}
```

```
──────────────── XcalableMP Fortran ────────────
program main
!$xmp nodes p(4)

!$xmp task on p(2:4)
  write(*,*) xmp_node_num(), ": Hello"
!$xmp end task

end program main
```

The **node** p[1] outputs "0: Hello" in XMP/C, and p(2) "1: Hello" in XMP/Fortran.

Note A new **node set** should be collectively generated by all of the executing **nodes** at the point of a task construct unless it is surrounded by a tasks construct. Therefore, in the above example, p[0] in XMP/C and p(1) in XMP/Fortran must process the task construct.

3.1.2 tasks Construct

Let's consider that each of two tasks invokes a function.

```
──────────────── XcalableMP C ────────────
#pragma xmp nodes p[4]

#pragma xmp task on p[0:2]
```

```
   {
5     func_a();
   }
   #pragma xmp task on p[2:2]
   {
      func_b();
10 }
```

──────────────── XcalableMP Fortran ────────────────
```
   !$xmp nodes p(4)

   !$xmp task on p(1:2)
      call func_a()
5  !$xmp end task
   !$xmp task on p(3:4)
      call func_b()
   !$xmp end task
```

In the above example, the two tasks cannot be executed in parallel because the on clauses must be evaluated by all of the **executing nodes** (Fig. 20).

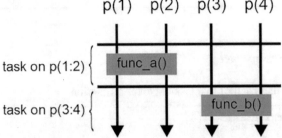

Fig. 20 Example of task construct (2)

XMP/C

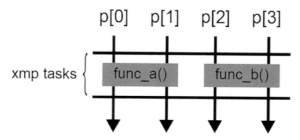

XMP/Fortran

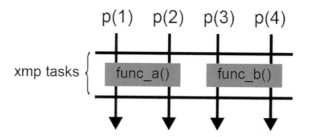

Fig. 21 Example of `tasks` construct

In such a case, the programmer must specify a `tasks` construct surrounding the tasks to execute them in parallel (Fig. 21).

```
──────────────── XcalableMP C ────────────────
#pragma xmp nodes p[4]

#pragma xmp tasks
{
#pragma xmp task on p[0:2]
{
   func_a();
}
#pragma xmp task on p[2:2]
{
   func_b();
}
}
```

```
————————————————— XcalableMP Fortran ————————
!$xmp nodes p(4)

!$xmp tasks
!$xmp task on p(1:2)
  call func_a()
!$xmp end task
!$xmp task on p(3:4)
  call func_b()
!$xmp end task
!$xmp end tasks
```

Because the **node set**s specified by the on clauses of the task constructs surrounded by a tasks construct are disjoint, they can be executed in parallel.

3.2 *loop Construct*

The loop construct is used to parallelize a loop.

```
————————————————— XcalableMP C ————————
#pragma xmp loop on t[i]
  for (int i = 0; i < 10; i++)
    a[i] = i;
```

```
————————————————— XcalableMP Fortran ————————
!$xmp loop on t(i)
  do i = 1, 10
    a(i) = i
  end do
```

The loop directive above specifies that the iteration i of the following loop is executed by the **node** that owns the **template** element t[i] or t(i), which is specified in the on clause.

Such a loop must satisfy the following two conditions:

1. There is no data/control dependence among the iterations. In other words, the iterations of the loop can be executed in any order to produce the same result.
2. Elements of **distributed arrays**, if any, are accessed only by the **node**(s) that own(s) the elements.

The programs below are examples of a right loop directive and a loop statement. Condition 1 is satisfied because i is the only one index of the **distributed array** a that is accessed within the loop, and condition 2 is also satisfied because the indices of the **template** in the on clause of the loop directive are identical to that of the **distributed array** (Fig. 22).

XMP/C   XMP/Fortran

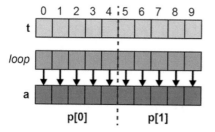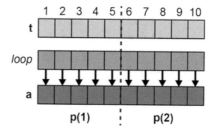

Fig. 22 Example of `loop` construct (1)

XMP/C   XMP/Fortran

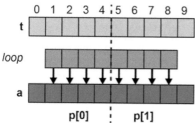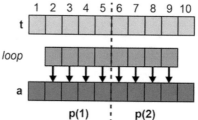

Fig. 23 Example of `loop` construct (2)

XMP/C   XMP/Fortran

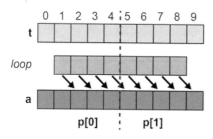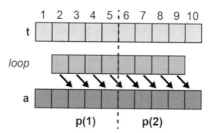

Fig. 24 Example of `loop` construct (3)

```
                              XcalableMP C
  #pragma xmp nodes p[2]
  #pragma xmp template t[10]
  #pragma xmp distribute t[block] onto p

5 int main(){
    int a[10];
  #pragma xmp align a[i] with t[i]
```

```
#pragma xmp loop on t [i]
  for(int i=0;i<10;i++)
    a[i] = i;

  return 0;
}
```

——————————— XcalableMP Fortran ———————————

```
program main
!$xmp nodes p(2)
!$xmp template t(10)
!$xmp distribute t(block) onto p
  integer a(10)
!$xmp align a(i) with t(i)

!$xmp loop on t(i)
  do i=1, 10
    a(i) = i
  enddo

end program main
```

Then, is it possible to parallelize the loops in the example below where the loop bounds are shrunk from the above?

——————————— XcalableMP C ———————————

```
#pragma xmp loop on t[i]
  for(int i=1;i<9;i++)
    a[i] = i;
```

——————————— XcalableMP Fortran ———————————

```
!$xmp loop on t(i)
  do i=2, 9
    a(i) = i
  enddo
```

In this case, conditions 1 and 2 are satisfied and therefore it is possible to parallelize them. In XMP/C, p [0] processes the indices from one to four and p [1] from five to eight. In XMP/Fortran, p (1) processes the indices from two to five and p (2) from six to nine (Fig. 23).

Next, is it possible to parallelize the below loops in which the index of the **distributed array** is different?

——————————— XcalableMP C ———————————

```
#pragma xmp loop on t[i]
  for(int i=1;i<9;i++)
    a[i+1] = i;
```

```
——————————— XcalableMP Fortran ———————————
!$xmp loop on t(i)
  do i=2, 9
    a(i+1) = i
  enddo
```

In this case, condition 1 is satisfied but 2 is not, and therefore it is not possible to parallelize them. In XMP/C, p[0] tries to access a[5] but does not own it. In XMP/Fortran, p(1) tries to access a(6) but does not own it (Fig. 24).

3.2.1 Reduction Computation

The serial programs below are examples of a reduction computation.

```
——————————————————— C ———————————————————
#include <stdio.h>

int main(){
  int a[10], sum = 0;

  for(int i=0;i<10;i++){
    a[i] = i+1;
    sum += a[i];
  }

  printf("%d\n", sum);

  return 0;
}
```

```
——————————————————— Fortran ———————————————————
program main
  integer :: a(10), sum = 0

  do i=1, 10
    a(i) = i
    sum = sum + a(i)
  enddo

  write(*,*) sum

end program main
```

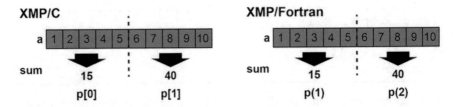

Fig. 25 Example of reduction computation (1)

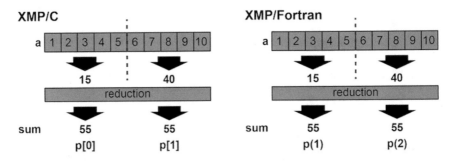

Fig. 26 Example of reduction computation (2)

If the above loops are parallelized just by adding a `loop` directive, the value of the variable `sum` varies from **node** to **node** because it is calculated separately on each **node** (Fig. 25). The value should be *reduced* to produce the right result.

```
———————————————— XcalableMP C ————————————————
#pragma xmp loop on t[i]
   for(int i=0;i<10;i++){
     a[i] = i+1;
     sum += a[i];
   }
```

```
———————————————— XcalableMP Fortran ————————————————
!$xmp loop on t(i)
  do i=1, 10
    a(i) = i
    sum = sum + a(i)
  enddo
```

Then, to correct the error in the above code, add a `reduction` clause to the `loop` directive as follows (Fig. 26).

```
———————————————— XcalableMP C ————————————————
#include <stdio.h>
#pragma xmp nodes p[2]
#pragma xmp template t[10]
#pragma xmp distribute t[block] onto p
```

```
int main(){
    int a[10], sum = 0;
#pragma xmp align a[i] with t[i]

#pragma xmp loop on t[i] reduction(+:sum)
    for(int i=0;i<10;i++){
        a[i] = i+1;
        sum += a[i];
    }

    printf("%d\n", sum);

    return 0;
}
```

———————————— XcalableMP Fortran ————————————

```
program main
!$xmp nodes p(2)
!$xmp template t(10)
!$xmp distribute t(block) onto p
    integer :: a(10), sum = 0
!$xmp align a(i) with t(i)

!$xmp loop on t(i) reduction(+:sum)
    do i=1, 10
        a(i) = i
        sum = sum + a(i)
    enddo

    write(*,*) sum

end program main
```

An operator and target variables for reduction computation are specified in a reduction clause. In the above examples, a "+" operator and a target variable sum are specified for the reduction computation to produce a total sum among **nodes**.

Operations that can be specified as an operator in a reduction clause are limited to the following associative ones.

——————————————————— C ———————————————————

```
+
*
-
&
|
```

```
^
&&
||
max
min
firstmax
firstmin
lastmax
lastmin
```

─────────────── Fortran ───────────────

```
+
*
-
.and.
.or.
.eqv.
.neqv.
max
min
iand
ior
ieor
firstmax
firstmin
lastmax
lastmin
```

Note The total result is calculated by combining the partial results on all **nodes**. The ordering of the combination is unspecified. Hence, if the target variable is a type of floating point (e.g. `float` in XMP/C or `real` in XMP/Fortran), the difference of the order can make a little bit difference in the result value from that in the original serial execution.

3.2.2 Parallelizing Nested Loop

Parallelization of nested loops can be specified similarly to a single one, as follows.

─────────────── XcalableMP C ───────────────

```
#pragma xmp nodes p[2][2]
#pragma xmp template t[10][10]
#pragma xmp distribute t[block][block] onto p
```

```
5   int main(){
       int a[10][10];
    #pragma xmp align a[i][j] with t[i][j]

    #pragma xmp loop on t[i][j]
10     for(int i=0;i<10;i++)
         for(int j=0;j<10;j++)
           a[i][j] = i*10+j;

       return 0;
15  }
```

```
─────────────── XcalableMP Fortran ───────────────
    program main
    !$xmp nodes p(2,2)
    !$xmp template t(10,10)
    !$xmp distribute t(block,block) onto p
5     integer :: a(10,10)
    !$xmp align a(j,i) with t(j,i)

    !$xmp loop on t(j,i)
      do i=1, 10
10      do j=1, 10
          a(j,i) = i*10+j
        enddo
      enddo

15  end program main
```

3.3 *array Construct*

The array construct is for work mapping of array assignment statements.

```
─────────────── XcalableMP C ───────────────
#pragma xmp align a[i] with t[i]
  :
#pragma xmp array on t[0:N]
a[0:N] = 1.0;
```

```
─────────────── XcalableMP Fortran ───────────────
!$xmp align a(i) with t(i)
  :
!$xmp array on t(1:N)
a(1:N) = 1.0
```

The above is equivalent to the below.

```
———————————————— XcalableMP C ————————————————
#pragma xmp align a[i] with t[i]
    :
#pragma xmp loop on t[i]
for(int i=0;i<N;i++)
    a[i] = 1.0;
```

```
———————————————— XcalableMP Fortran ————————————————
!$xmp align a(i) with t(i)
    :
!$xmp loop on t(i)
do i=1, N
    a(i) = 1.0
enddo
```

This construct can also be applied to multi-dimensional arrays.

```
———————————————— XcalableMP C ————————————————
#pragma xmp align a[i][j] with t[i][j]
    :
#pragma xmp array on t[:][:]
a[:][:] = 1.0;
```

```
———————————————— XcalableMP Fortran ————————————————
!$xmp align a(j,i) with t(j,i)
    :
!$xmp array on t(:,:)
a(:,:) = 1.0
```

Note The **template** appearing in the on clause must have the same shape as the arrays in the following statement. The right-hand side value in this construct must be identical among all **nodes** because the `array` construct is a **global** (i.e. collective) operation.

4 Data Communication

4.1 `shadow` Directive and `reflect` Construct

Stencil computation frequently appears in scientific simulation programs, where, to update an array element a[i], its neighboring elements a[i-1] and a[i+1] are referenced. If a[i] is on the boundary region of a block-**distributed array** on a **node**, a[i+1] may reside on another (neighboring) **node**.

Since it involves large overhead to copy a[i+1] from the neighboring **node** to update each a[i], a technique of copying collectively the elements on the neighboring **node** to the area added to the **distributed array** on each **node** is usually adopted. In XMP, such additional area is called "shadow."

4.1.1 Declaring Shadow

Shadow areas can be declared with the shadow directive. In the example below, an array a has shadow areas of width one on both the lower and upper bounds.

```
———————————— XcalableMP C ————————————
#pragma xmp nodes p[4]
#pragma xmp template t[16]
#pragma xmp distribute t[block] onto p
double a[16];
#pragma xmp align a[i] with t[i]
#pragma xmp shadow a[1]
```

```
———————————— XcalableMP Fortran ————————————
!$xmp nodes p(4)
!$xmp template t(16)
!$xmp distribute t(block) onto p
real :: a(16)
!$xmp align a(i) with t(i)
!$xmp shadow a(1)
```

In the Fig. 27, shaded elements are those that each **node** owns and white ones are shadow.

Note Arrays distributed in a cyclic manner cannot have shadow.

In some programs, it is natural that the widths of the shadow area on the lower and upper bounds are different. There is also a case where the shadow area exists

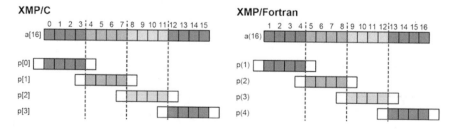

Fig. 27 Example of shadow directive (1)

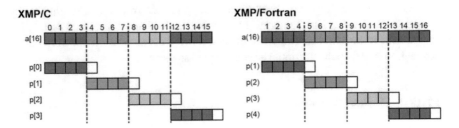

Fig. 28 Example of shadow directive (2)

only on either of the bounds. In the example below, it is declared that a **distributed array** a has a shadow area of width one only on the upper bound (Fig. 28).

```
────────────────── XcalableMP C ──────────────────
#pragma xmp nodes p[4]
#pragma xmp template t[16]
#pragma xmp distribute t(block) onto p
double a[16];
#pragma xmp align a[i] with t[i]
#pragma xmp shadow a[0:1]
```

```
────────────────── XcalableMP Fortran ──────────────────
!$xmp nodes p(4)
!$xmp template t(16)
!$xmp distribute t(block) onto p
real :: a(16)
!$xmp align a(i) with t(i)
!$xmp shadow a(0:1)
```

The values on the left- and right-hand sides of a colon designate the widths on the lower and upper bounds, respectively.

4.1.2 Updating Shadow

To copy data to shadow areas from neighboring **nodes**, use the `reflect` construct. In the example below, the shadow areas of an array a that are of width one on both the upper and lower bounds are updated (Fig. 29).

```
────────────────── XcalableMP C ──────────────────
#pragma xmp reflect (a)

#pragma xmp loop on t[i]
for(int i=1;i<15;i++)
  a[i] = (a[i-1] + a[i] + a[i+1])/3;
```

XMP/C

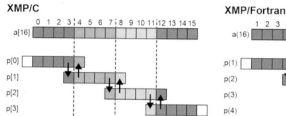

XMP/Fortran

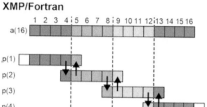

Fig. 29 Example of `reflect` construct (1)

XMP/C

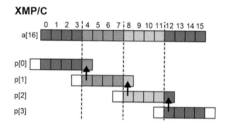

XMP/Fortran

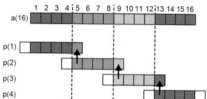

Fig. 30 Example of `reflect` construct (2)

XMP/C

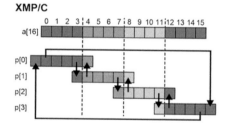

XMP/Fortran

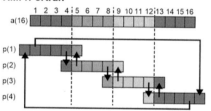

Fig. 31 Example of periodic `reflect` construct

```
———————————— XcalableMP Fortran ————
!$xmp reflect (a)

!xmp loop on t(i)
do i=2, 15
   a(i) = (a(i-1) + a(i) + a(i+1))/3
enddo
```

With this `reflect` directive, in XMP/C, **node** p[1] sends an element a[4] to the shadow area on the upper bound on **node** p[0] and a[7] to the shadow area on the lower bound on p[2]; p[0] sends an element a[3] to the shadow area on the lower bound on p[1], and p[2] sends a[8] to the shadow area on the upper bound on p[1].

Similarly, in XMP/Fortran, **node** p(2) sends an element a(5) to the shadow area on the upper bound on **node** p(1) and a(8) to the shadow area on the lower bound on p(3); p(1) sends an element a(4) to the shadow area on the lower bound on p(2), and p(3) sends a(9) to the shadow area on the upper bound on p(2).

The default behavior of a reflect directive is to update the whole of the shadow area declared by the shadow directive. However, there are some cases where a specific part of the shadow area is to be updated to reduce the communication cost at a point of the code.

To update only a specific part of the shadow area, add the width clause to the reflect directive.

The values on the left- and right-hand sides of a colon in the width clause designate the widths on the lower and upper bounds to be updated, respectively. In the example below, only the shadow area on the upper bound is updated (Fig. 30).

```
——————————————— XcalableMP C ———————————————
#pragma xmp reflect (a) width(0:1)
```

```
——————————————— XcalableMP Fortran ———————————————
!$xmp reflect (a) width(0:1)
```

Note If the widths of the shadow areas to be updated on the upper and lower bounds are equal, that is, for example, width(1:1), you can abbreviate it as width(1).

Note It is not possible to update the shadow area on a particular **node** because reflect is a collective operation.

The reflect directive does not update either the shadow area on the lower bound on the leading **node** or that on the upper bound on the last **node**. However, the values in such areas are needed for stencil computation if periodic boundary conditions are used in the computation.

To update such areas, add a periodic qualifier into the width clause. Let's look at the following example where an array a having shadow areas of width one on both the lower and upper bounds appears (Fig. 31).

```
——————————————— XcalableMP C ———————————————
#pragma xmp reflect (a) width(/periodic/1:1)
```

```
——————————————— XcalableMP Fortran ———————————————
!$xmp reflect (a) width(/periodic/1:1)
```

The periodic qualifier has the following effects, in addition to that of a normal reflect directive: in XMP/C, **node** p[0] sends an element a[0] to the shadow area on the upper bound on **node** p[3], and p[3] sends a[15] to the shadow area on the lower bound on p[0]; in XMP/Fortran, **node** p(1) sends an element a(1) to the shadow area on the upper bound on **node** p(4), and p(4) sends a(16) to the shadow area on the lower bound on p(1).

The shadow directive and reflect construct can be applied to arrays distributed in multiple dimensions. The following programs are the examples for two-dimensional **distribution**.

```
──────────── XcalableMP C ────────────
#pragma xmp nodes p[3][3]
#pragma xmp template t[9][9]
#pragma xmp distribute t[block][block] onto p
double a[9][9];
#pragma xmp align a[i][j] with t[i][j]
#pragma xmp shadow a[1][1]
    :
#pragma xmp reflect (a)
```

```
──────────── XcalableMP Fortran ────────────
!$xmp nodes p(3,3)
!$xmp template t(9,9)
!$xmp distribute t(block,block) onto p
real :: a(9,9)
!$xmp align a(j,i) with t(j,i)
!$xmp shadow a(1,1)
    :
!$xmp reflect (a)
```

The central **node** receives data from the surrounding eight **nodes** to update its shadow areas (Fig. 32). The shadow areas of the other **nodes** are also updated, which is omitted in the figure.

For some applications, data from ordinal directions are not necessary. In such a case, the data communication from/to the ordinal directions can be avoided by adding the orthogonal clause to a reflect construct (Fig. 33).

```
──────────── XcalableMP C ────────────
#pragma xmp reflect (a) orthogonal
```

```
──────────── XcalableMP Fortran ────────────
!$xmp reflect (a) orthogonal
```

Note The orthogonal clause is effective only for arrays more than one dimension of which is distributed.

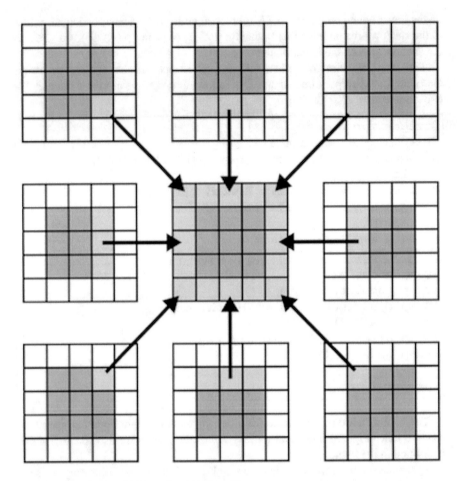

Fig. 32 Example of multi-dimensional shadow (1)

Besides, you can also add shadow areas to only specified dimension (Fig. 34).

```
───────────────────── XcalableMP C ─────────────────────
#pragma xmp nodes p[3]
#pragma xmp template t[9]
#pragma xmp distribute t[block] onto p
double a[9][9];
#pragma xmp align a[i][*] with t[i]
#pragma xmp shadow a[1][0]
   :
#pragma xmp reflect (a)
```

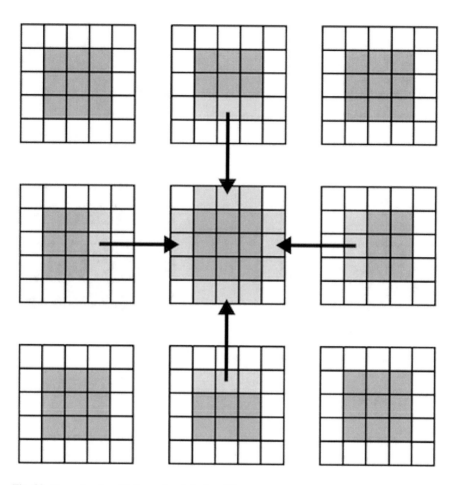

Fig. 33 Example of multi-dimensional shadow (2)

```
───────────── XcalableMP Fortran ─────────────
!$xmp nodes p[3]
!$xmp template t[9]
!$xmp distribute t[block] onto p
real :: a(9,9)
!$xmp align a(*,i) with t(i)
!$xmp shadow a(0,1)
   :
!$xmp reflect (a)
```

For the array a, 0 is specified as the shadow width in non-distributed dimensions.

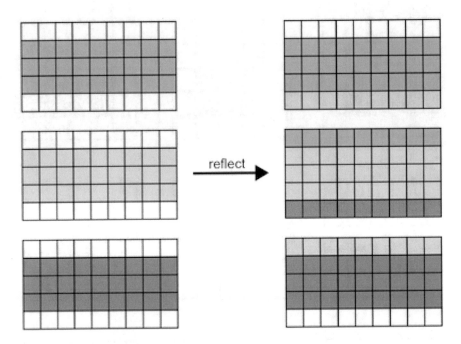

Fig. 34 Example of multi-dimensional shadow (3)

4.2 *gmove Construct*

The programmers can specify a communication of **distributed arrays** in the form of assignment statements by using the gmove construct. In other words, with the gmove construct, any array assignment between two arrays (i.e. *global data movement*) that may involve inter-node communication can be specified.

There are three modes of gmove; "collective mode," "in mode," and "out mode."

4.2.1 Collective Mode

The global data movement involved by a *collective* gmove is performed collectively, and results in implicit synchronization among the **executing nodes**.

```
――――――――――――――――――――― XcalableMP C ―――――――――
#pragma xmp nodes p[4]
#pragma xmp template t[16]
#pragma xmp distribute t[block] onto p
int a[16], b[16];
#pragma xmp align a[i] with t[i]
#pragma xmp align b[i] with t[i]
    :
```

```
#pragma xmp gmove
  a[9:5] = b[0:5];
```

```
──────── XcalableMP Fortran ────────
!$xmp nodes p(4)
!$xmp template t(16)
!$xmp distribute t(block) onto p
integer :: a(16), b(16)
!$xmp align a(i) with t(i)
!$xmp align b(i) with t(i)
      :
!$xmp gmove
  a(10:14) = b(1:5)
```

In XMP/C, p[0] sends b[0]-b[3] to p[2]-p[3], and p[1] sends b[4] to p[3]. Similarly, in XMP/Fortran, p(1) sends b(1)-b(4) to p(3)-p(4), and p(2) sends b(5) to p(4) (Fig. 35).

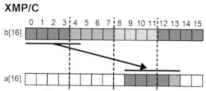

Fig. 35 Collective gmove (1)

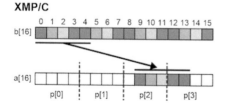

Fig. 36 Collective gmove (2)

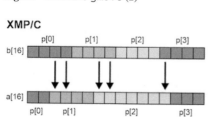

Fig. 37 Collective gmove (3)

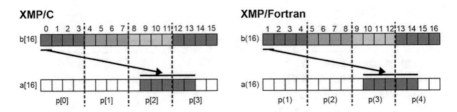

Fig. 38 Collective gmove (4)

XMP/C

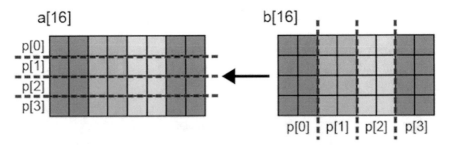

XMP/Fortran

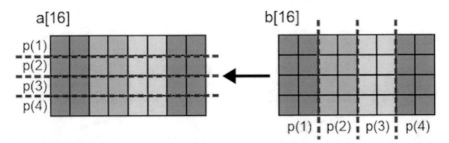

Fig. 39 Collective gmove (4)

```
                          XcalableMP C
  #pragma xmp nodes p[4]
  #pragma xmp template t1[16]
  #pragma xmp template t2[16]
  #pragma xmp distribute t1[cyclic] onto p
5 #pragma xmp distribute t2[block] onto p
  int a[16], b[16];
  #pragma xmp align a[i] with t1[i]
  #pragma xmp align b[i] with t2[i]
```

```
   :
10 #pragma xmp gmove
     a[9:5] = b[0:5];
```

```
————————————— XcalableMP Fortran —————————————
   !$xmp nodes p(4)
   !$xmp template t1(16)
   !$xmp template t2(16)
   !$xmp distribute t1(cyclic) onto p
 5 !$xmp distribute t2(block) onto p
   integer :: a(16), b(16)
   !$xmp align a(i) with t1(i)
   !$xmp align b(i) with t2(i)
      :
10 !$xmp gmove
     a(10:14) = b(1:5)
```

While array a is distributed in a cyclic manner, array b is distributed in a block manner.

In XMP/C, p[0] sends b[0] and b[4] to p[2] and p[3]. p[1] sends b[1] to p[2]. Each element of p[2] and p[3] will be copied locally. Similarly, in XMP/Fortran, p(1) sends b(1) and b(5) to p(3) and p(4). p(2) sends b(2) to p(3). Each element of p(3) and p(4) will be copied locally (Fig. 36).

By using this method, the **distribution** of an array can be "changed" during computation.

```
————————————————— XcalableMP C —————————————————
   #pragma xmp nodes p[4]
   #pragma xmp template t1[16]
   #pragma xmp template t2[16]
   int W[4] = {2,4,8,2};
 5 #pragma xmp distribute t1[gblock(W)] onto p
   #pragma xmp distribute t2[block] onto p
   int a[16], b[16];
   #pragma xmp align a[i] with t1[i]
   #pragma xmp align b[i] with t2[i]
10    :
   #pragma xmp gmove
     a[:] = b[:];
```

```
————————————— XcalableMP Fortran —————————————
   !$xmp nodes p(4)
   !$xmp template t1(16)
   !$xmp template t2(16)
   integer :: W(4) = (/2,4,7,3/)
 5 !$xmp distribute t1(gblock(W)) onto p
   !$xmp distribute t2(block) onto p
```

```
integer :: a(16), b(16)
!$xmp align a(i) with t1(i)
!$xmp align b(i) with t2(i)
      :
!$xmp gmove
  a(:) = b(:)
```

In this example (Fig. 37), the elements of an array b that is distributed in a block manner are copied to the corresponding elements of an array a that is distributed in a generalized-block manner. For the arrays a and b, communication occurs if the corresponding elements reside in different **nodes** (arrows illustrate communication between **nodes** in the figures).

In the assignment statement, if a scalar (i.e. one element of an array or a variable) is specified on the right-hand side and an array section is specified on the left-hand side, a broadcast communication occurs for it.

```
─────────────── XcalableMP C ───────────────
#pragma xmp nodes p[4]
#pragma xmp template t[16]
#pragma xmp distribute t[block] onto p
int a[16], b[16];
#pragma xmp align a[i] with t[i]
#pragma xmp align b[i] with t[i]
        :
#pragma xmp gmove
  a[9:5] = b[0];
```

```
─────────────── XcalableMP Fortran ───────────────
!$xmp nodes p(4)
!$xmp template t(16)
!$xmp distribute t(block) onto p
integer :: a(16), b(16)
!$xmp align a(i) with t(i)
!$xmp align b(i) with t(i)
        :
!$xmp gmove
  a(10:14) = b(1)
```

In this example (Fig. 38), in XMP/C, an array element b[0] of **node** p[0] will be broadcasted to the specified array section on **node** p[2] and p[3]. Similarly, in XMP/Fortran, an array element b(1) of **node** p(1) will be broadcasted to the specified array section on **node** p(3) and p(4).

Not only **distributed arrays** but also replicated arrays can be specified on the right-hand side.

```
─────────────── XcalableMP C ───────────────
#pragma xmp nodes p[4]
#pragma xmp template t[16]
```

```
   #pragma xmp distribute t[block] onto p
   int a[16], b[16], c;
 5 #pragma xmp align a[i] with t[i]
       :

 #pragma xmp gmove
    a[9:5] = b[0:5];
```

—————————— XcalableMP Fortran ——————————
```
   !$xmp nodes p(4)
   !$xmp template t(16)
   !$xmp distribute t(block) onto p
   integer :: a(16), b(16), c
 5 !$xmp align a(i) with t(i)
       :

 !$xmp gmove
    a(10:14) = b(1:5)
```

In this example, a replicated array b is locally copied to **distributed array** a without communication.

—————————— XcalableMP C ——————————
```
   #pragma xmp nodes p[4]
   #pragma xmp template t1[4]
   #pragma xmp template t2[8]
   #pragma xmp distribute t1[block] onto p
 5 #pragma xmp distribute t2[block] onto p
   int a[4][8], b[4][8];
   #pragma xmp align a[i][*] with t1[i]
   #pragma xmp align b[*][i] with t2[i]
       :
10 #pragma xmp gmove
    a[0][:] = b[0][:];
```

—————————— XcalableMP Fortran ——————————
```
   !$xmp nodes p(4)
   !$xmp template t1(4)
   !$xmp template t2(8)
   !$xmp distribute t1(block) onto p
 5 !$xmp distribute t2(block) onto p
   integer :: a(4,8), b(4,8)
   !$xmp align a(*,i) with t1(i)
   !$xmp align b(i,*) with t2(i)
       :
10 #pragma xmp gmove
    a(:,1) = b(:,1)
```

In this example (Fig. 39), in XMP/C, b[0][0:2] on p[0], b[0][2:2] of p[1], b[0][4:2] on p[2] and b[0][6:2] on p[3] are copied to a[0][:]

on p[0]. Similarly, in XMP/Fortran, b(1:2,1) on p(1), b(3:4,1) of p(2), b(5:6,1) on p(3) and b(7:8,1) on p(4) are copied to a(:,1) on p(1).

4.2.2 In Mode

The right-hand side data of the assignment, all or part of which may reside outside the **executing node set**, can be transferred from its owner **nodes** to the **executing nodes** with an *in* gmove.

```
——————————————— XcalableMP C ———————————————
#pragma xmp nodes p[4]
#pragma xmp template t[4]
#pragma xmp distribute t[block] onto p
double a[4], b[4];
#pragma xmp align a[i] with t[i]
#pragma xmp align b[i] with t[i]
    :
#pragma xmp task on p[0:2]
#pragma xmp gmove in
  a[0:2] = b[2:2]
#pragma xmp end task
```

```
——————————————— XcalableMP Fortran ———————————————
!$xmp nodes p(4)
!$xmp template t(4)
!$xmp distribute t(block) onto p
real :: a(4), b(4)
!$xmp align a(i) with t(i)
!$xmp align b(i) with t(i)
    :
!$xmp task on p(1:2)
!$xmp gmove in
  a(1:2) = b(3:4)
!$xmp end task
```

In this example, the task directive divides four **nodes** into two sets, the first-half and the second-half. A gmove construct that is in an *in* mode copies data using a *get* operation from the second-half **node** to the first-half **node** (Fig. 40).

4.2.3 Out Mode

For the left-hand side data of the assignment, all or part of which may reside outside the **executing node set**, the corresponding elements can be transferred from the **executing nodes** to its owner **nodes** with an *out* gmove construct.

Fig. 40 In gmove

XMP/C

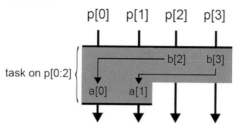

XMP/Fortran

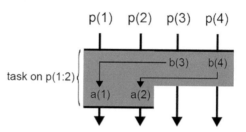

```
─────────────────── XcalableMP C ───────────────────
  #pragma xmp nodes p[4]
  #pragma xmp template t[4]
  #pragma xmp distribute t[block] onto p
  double a[4], b[4];
5 #pragma xmp align a[i] with t[i]
  #pragma xmp align b[i] with t[i]
     :
  #pragma xmp task on p[0:2]
  #pragma xmp gmove out
10   b[2:2] = a[0:2]
  #pragma xmp end task
```

```
─────────────────── XcalableMP Fortran ───────────────────
  !$xmp nodes p(4)
  !$xmp template t(4)
  !$xmp distribute t(block) onto p
  real :: a(4), b(4)
5 !$xmp align a(i) with t(i)
  !$xmp align b(i) with t(i)
     :
  !$xmp task on p(1:2)
  !$xmp gmove out
10   b(3:4) = a(1:2)
  !$xmp end task
```

Fig. 41 Out gmove

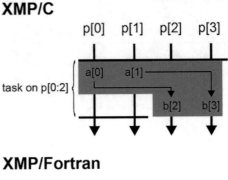

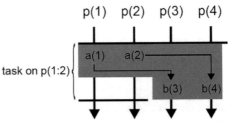

A gmove construct that is in *out* mode copies data using a *put* communication from the first-half **nodes** to the second-half **nodes** (Fig. 41).

4.3 *barrier* Construct

The barrier construct executes a barrier synchronization.

XcalableMP C
```
#pragma xmp barrier
```

XcalableMP Fortran
```
!$xmp barrier
```

You can specify a **node set** on which the barrier synchronization is to be performed by using the on clause. In the example below, a barrier synchronization is performed among the first two **nodes** of p.

XcalableMP C
```
#pragma xmp barrier on p[0:2]
```

XcalableMP Fortran
```
!$xmp barrier on p(1:2)
```

4.4 `reduction` *Construct*

This construct performs a `reduction` operation. It has the same meaning as the `reduction` clause of the `loop` construct, but this construct can be specified anywhere *executable* constructs can be located (Fig. 42).

```
──────────────── XcalableMP C ────────────
#pragma xmp nodes p[4]
  :
sum = xmpc_node_num() + 1;
#pragma xmp reduction (+:sum)
```

```
──────────────── XcalableMP Fortran ────────────
!$xmp nodes p(4)
  :
sum = xmp_node_num()
!$xmp reduction (+:sum)
```

You can specify the **executing node set** by using the on clause. In the example below, only the values on the last two of the four **nodes** are targeted by the `reduction` construct (Fig. 43).

```
──────────────── XcalableMP C ────────────
#pragma xmp nodes p[4]
  :
sum = xmpc_node_num() + 1;
#pragma xmp reduction (+:sum) on p[2:2]
```

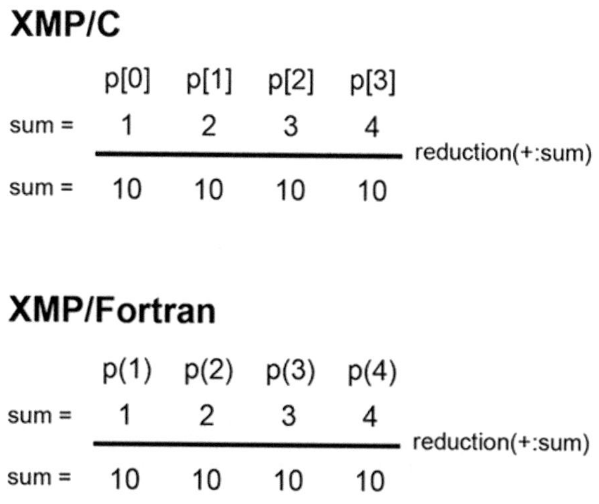

XMP/C

	p[0]	p[1]	p[2]	p[3]
sum =	1	2	3	4
sum =	10	10	10	10

reduction(+:sum)

XMP/Fortran

	p(1)	p(2)	p(3)	p(4)
sum =	1	2	3	4
sum =	10	10	10	10

reduction(+:sum)

Fig. 42 `reduction` construct (1)

XMP/C

	p[0]	p[1]	p[2]	p[3]
sum =	1	2	3	4
sum =	1	2	7	7

reduction (+:sum) on p[2:2]

XMP/Fortran

	p(1)	p(2)	p(3)	p(4)
sum =	1	2	3	4
sum =	1	2	7	7

reduction (+:sum) on p(3:4)

Fig. 43 reduction construct (2)

```
─────────── XcalableMP Fortran ───────────
!$xmp nodes p(4)
  :
sum = xmp_node_num()
!$xmp reduction (+:sum) on p(3:4)
```

The operators you can use in the reduction construct are as follows:

```
─────────── XcalableMP C ───────────
+
*
-
&
|
^
&&
||
max
min
```

```
─────────── XcalableMP Fortran ───────────
+
*
-
.and.
.or.
.eqv.
.neqv.
max
min
```

```
10  iand
    ior
    ieor
```

Note In contrast to the reduction clause of the loop construct, which precedes loops, the reduction construct does not accept operators of firstmax, firstmin, lastmax, and lastmin.

Note Similar to the reduction clause, the reduction construct may generate slightly different results in a parallel execution from those in a sequential execution, because the results depend on the order of combining the value.

4.5 *bcast Construct*

The bcast construct broadcasts the values of the variables on the **node** specified by the from clause, that is, the *root node*, to the **node set** specified by the on clause. If there is no from clause, the first **node** of the **executing node set** is selected as the root **node**. If there is no on clause, the current **executing node set** of the construct is selected as the **executing node set**.

In the example below, the first **node** of the **node set** p, that is, p[0] or p(1), is the root **node** (Fig. 44).

```
——————————————— XcalableMP C ———————
#pragma xmp nodes p[4]

  :
num = xmpc_node_num() + 1;
#pragma xmp bcast (num)
```

```
——————————————— XcalableMP Fortran ———————
!$xmp nodes p(4)

  :
num = xmp_node_num()
!$xmp bcast (num)
```

In the example below, the last **node**, that is, p[3] or p(4), is the root **node** (Fig. 45).

```
——————————————— XcalableMP C ———————
#pragma xmp nodes p[4]

  :
```

Fig. 44 bcast construct (1)

XMP/C

	p[0]	p[1]	p[2]	p[3]
num =	1	2	3	4
num =	1	1	1	1

bcast (num)

XMP/Fortran

	p(1)	p(2)	p(3)	p(4)
num =	1	2	3	4
num =	1	1	1	1

bcast (num)

Fig. 45 bcast construct (2)

XMP/C

	p[0]	p[1]	p[2]	p[3]
num =	1	2	3	4
num =	4	4	4	4

bcast (num) from p[3]

XMP/Fortran

	p(1)	p(2)	p(3)	p(4)
num =	1	2	3	4
num =	4	4	4	4

bcast (num) from p(4)

```
num = xmpc_node_num() + 1;
#pragma xmp bcast (num) from p[3]
```

```
——————————— XcalableMP Fortran ———————————
!$xmp nodes p(4)
    :
num = xmp_node_num()
!$xmp bcast (num) from p(4)
```

In the example below, only the last three of four **nodes** are included by the **executing node set** of the bcast construct (Fig. 46).

```
——————————— XcalableMP C ———————————
#pragma xmp nodes p[4]
    :
sum = xmpc_node_num() + 1;
#pragma xmp bcast (num) from p[3] on p[1:3]
```

XMP/C

```
          p[0]   p[1]   p[2]   p[3]
num =      1      2      3      4
          ─────────────────────────   bcast (num) from p[3] on p[1:3]
num =      1      4      4      4
```

XMP/Fortran

```
          p(1)   p(2)   p(3)   p(4)
num =      1      2      3      4
          ─────────────────────────   bcast (num) from p(4) on p(2:4)
num =      1      4      4      4
```

Fig. 46 bcast construct (3)

```
──────────────────── XcalableMP Fortran ────────────────────
!$xmp nodes p(4)
   :
sum = xmp_node_num()
!$xmp bcast (num) from p(4) on p(2:4)
```

4.6 *wait_async Construct*

Communication directives (i.e. reflect, gmove, reduction, bcast, and reduce_shadow) can perform asynchronous communication if the async clause is added. The wait_async construct is used to guarantee the completion of such an asynchronous communication.

```
──────────────────── XcalableMP C ────────────────────
#pragma xmp bcast (num) async(1)
   :
#pragma xmp wait_async (1)
```

```
──────────────────── XcalableMP Fortran ────────────────────
!$xmp bcast (num) async(1)
   :
!$xmp wait_async (1)
```

Since the bcast directive has an async clause, communication may not be completed immediately after the bcast directive. The completion of that communication is guaranteed with the wait_async construct having the same value as that of the async clause. Therefore, between the bcast construct and the wait_async constructs, you may not reference the target variable of the bcast directive.

Hint Asynchronous communication can be overlapped with the following computation to hide its overhead.

Note Expressions that can be specified as *tags* in the `async` clause are of type int,
in XMP/C, or integer, in XMP/Fortran.

4.7 `reduce_shadow` Construct

The `reduce_shadow` directive adds the value of a shadow object to the corresponding data object of the array.

```
———————————————— XcalableMP C ————————————————
#pragma xmp nodes p[2]
#pragma xmp template t[8]
#pragma xmp distribute t[block] onto p
int a[8];
#pragma xmp align a[i] with t[i]
#pragma xmp shadow a[1]
  :
#pragma xmp loop on t[i]
  for(int i=0;i<8;i++)
    a[i] = i+1;

#pragma xmp reflect (a)
#pragma xmp reduce_shadow (a)
```

```
———————————————— XcalableMP Fortran ————————————————
!$xmp nodes p(2)
!$xmp template t(8)
!$xmp distribute t(block) onto p
  integer a(8)
!$xmp align a(i) with t(i)
!$xmp shadow a(1)

!$xmp loop on t(i)
  do i=1, 8
    a(i) = i
  enddo

!$xmp reflect (a)
!$xmp reduce_shadow (a)
```

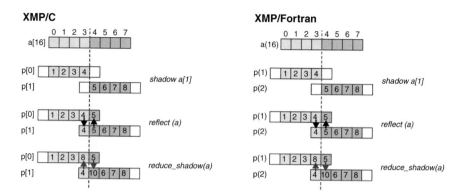

Fig. 47 `reduce_shadow` construct (1)

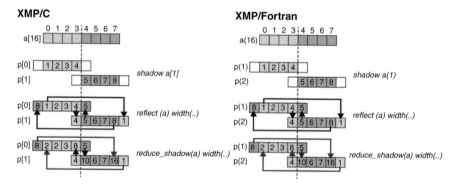

Fig. 48 `reduce_shadow` construct (2)

For the above example, in XMP/C, a[3] on p[0] has a value of eight, and a[4] on p[1] has a value of ten. Similarly, in XMP/Fortran, a(4) of p(1) has a value of eight, and a(5) on p(2) has a value of ten (Fig. 47).

The programmers can add the `periodic` modifier to the `width` clause to reduce shadow objects to the corresponding data object periodically.

```
──────────────── XcalableMP C ────────────────
#pragma xmp reflect (a) width(/periodic/1)
#pragma xmp reduce_shadow (a) width(/periodic/1)
```

```
──────────────── XcalableMP Fortran ────────────────
!$xmp reflect (a) width(/periodic/1)
!$xmp reduce_shadow (a) width(/periodic/1)
```

In addition to the first example, in XMP/C, a[0] on p[0] has a value of two, and a[7] on p[1] has a value of 16. Similarly, in XMP/Fortran, a(1) in p(1) has a value of two, and a(8) in p(2) has a value of 16 (Fig. 48).

5   Local-View Programming

5.1   Introduction

The programmer can use **coarrays** to specify one-sided communication in the local-view model.

Depending on the environment, such one-sided communication might achieve better performance than global communication in the global-view model. However, it is more difficult and complicated to write parallel programs in the local-view model because the programmer must specify every detail of parallelization, such as data mapping, work mapping, and communication.

The **coarray** feature in XMP/Fortran is upward-compatible with that in Fortran 2008; that in XMP/C is defined as an extension to the base language.

An execution entity in local-view XMP programs is referred to as an "image" while a **node** in global-view ones. These two words have almost the same meaning in XMP.

5.2   Coarray Declaration

```
─────────────── XcalableMP C ───────────────
int a[10]:[*];
```

```
─────────────── XcalableMP Fortran ───────────────
integer a(10)[*]
```

In XMP/C, the programmer declares a **coarray** by adding "`:[*]`" after the array declaration. In XMP/Fortran, the programmer declares a **coarray** by adding "`[*]`" after the array declaration.

Note Based on Fortran 2008, **coarrays** should have the same size among all images.

Coarrays can be accessed in expressions by remote images as well as the local images.

5.3   Put Communication

When a **coarray** appears in the left-hand side of an assignment statement, it involves *put* communication.

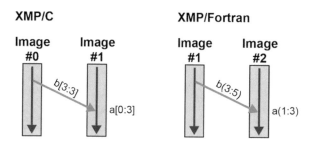

Fig. 49 Remote write to a coarray

```
───────────────── XcalableMP C ─────────────────
int a[10]:[*], b[10];

if (xmpc_this_image() == 0)
  a[0:3]:[1] = b[3:3];
```

```
───────────────── XcalableMP Fortran ─────────────────
integer a(10)[*]
integer b(10)

if (this_image() == 1) then
  a(1:3)[2] = b(3:5)
end if
```

The integer in the square bracket specifies the target image index. The image index is zero-based, in XMP/C, or one-based, in XMP/Fortran. xmpc_this_image() in XMP/C and this_image() in XMP/Fortran return the current image index.

In the above example, in XMP/C, an image zero puts b[3:3] to a[0:3] on image one; in XMP/Fortran, an image one puts b(3:5) to a(1:3) on image two. Figure 49 illustrates the put communication performed in the example.

5.4 Get Communication

When a **coarray** appears in the right-hand side of an assignment statement, it involves *get* communication.

```
───────────────── XcalableMP C ─────────────────
int a[10]:[*], b[10];

if (xmpc_this_image() == 0)
  b[3:3] = a[0:3]:[1];
```

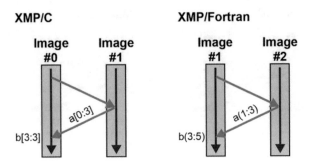

Fig. 50 Remote read from a coarray

```
_____ XcalableMP Fortran _____
  integer a(10)[*]
  integer b(10)

  if (this_image() == 1) then
5    b(3:5) = a(1:3)[2]
  end if
```

In the above example, in XMP/C, an image 0 gets a[0:3] from an image 1 and copies it to b[3:3]; in XMP/Fortran, an image 1 gets a(1:3) from an image 2 and copies it to b(3:5) of an image 1. Figure 50 illustrates the get communication performed in the example.

Hint As illustrated above, get communication involves an extra step to send a request to the target **node**. Put communication achieves better performance than get because there is no such extra step.

5.5 Synchronization

5.5.1 Sync All

```
_____ XcalableMP C _____
  void xmp_sync_all(int *status)
```
```
_____ XcalableMP Fortran _____
  sync all
```

At "sync all," each image waits until all issued one-sided communication is complete and then performs barrier synchronization among the all images.

Fig. 51 sync all

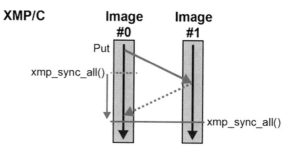

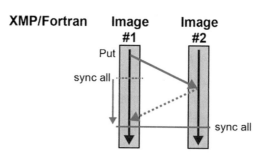

In the above example, the left image puts data to the right image and both **nodes** invoke sync all. When both **nodes** return from it, the execution continues to the following statements (Fig. 51).

5.5.2 Sync Images

```
─────────────────── XcalableMP C ───────────────────
void xmp_sync_images(int num, int *image-set, int *status)
```
```
─────────────────── XcalableMP Fortran ───────────────────
sync images (image-set)
```

Each image in the specified image set waits until all one-sided communication issued is complete, and performs barrier synchronization among the images.

```
─────────────────── XcalableMP C ───────────────────
int image_set[3] = {0,1,2};
xmp_sync_images(3, image_set, NULL);
```
```
─────────────────── XcalableMP Fortran ───────────────────
integer :: image_set(3) = (/ 1, 2, 3/)
sync images (image_set)
```

5.5.3 Sync Memory

```
———————————— XcalableMP C ————————————
void xmp_sync_memory(int *status)
```

```
———————————— XcalableMP Fortran ————————————
sync memory
```

Each image waits until all one-sided communication is complete. This function/statement does not imply barrier synchronization, unlike `sync all` and `sync images`, and therefore can be locally executed.

6 Procedure Interface

Procedure calls in XMP are almost the same as those in the base language. Procedure calls between other languages or to external libraries are also allowed if the base language supports them.

In the example below, a function/subroutine `sub1()` calls another function/subroutine `sub2()` with a **distributed array** x as an argument.

```
———————————— XcalableMP C ————————————
void sub1(){
#pragma xmp nodes p[2]
#pragma xmp template t[10]
#pragma xmp distribute t[block] onto p
5    double x[10];
#pragma xmp align x[i] with t[i]
     sub2(x);
}

10 void sub2(double a[10]){
#pragma xmp nodes p[2]
#pragma xmp template t[10]
#pragma xmp distribute t[block] onto p
     double a[10];
15 #pragma xmp align a[i] with t[i]
     :
}
```

```
———————————— XcalableMP Fortran ————————————
subroutine sub1()
!$xmp nodes p(2)
!$xmp template t(10)
!$xmp distribute t(block) onto p
5    real x(10)
!$xmp align x(i) with t(i)
```

```
     call sub2(x)
   end subroutine

10 subroutine sub2(a)
   !$xmp nodes p(2)
   !$xmp template t(10)
   !$xmp distribute t(block) onto p
     real a(10)
15 !$xmp align a(i) with t(i)
     :
   end subroutine
```

To handle a parameter or dummy argument as a **global data** in the callee procedure, the programmer need to explicitly distribute it with an `align` directive (Fig. 52).

If no `align` directive is specified in the callee procedure for a parameter or dummy argument that is declared as a **global data** in the caller procedure, it is handled as if it were declared in the callee procedure as a **local data** on each **node**, as follows (Fig. 53).

Fig. 52 Passing a global argument to a global parameter

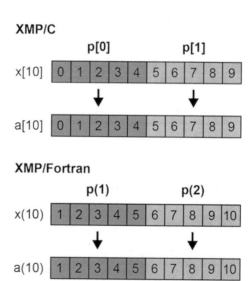

```
_____ XcalableMP C _____
void sub1(){
#pragma xmp nodes p[2]
#pragma xmp template t[10]
#pragma xmp distribute t[block] onto p
5   double x[10];
#pragma xmp align x[i] with t[i]
   sub2(x);
}

10 void sub2(double a[5]){
   :
}
```

```
_____ XcalableMP Fortran _____
subroutine sub1()
!$xmp nodes p(2)
!$xmp template t(10)
!$xmp distribute t(block) onto p
5   real x(10)
!$xmp align x(i) with t(i)
   call sub2(x)
end subroutine

10 subroutine sub2(a)
   real a(5)
   :
end subroutine
```

7 XMPT Tool Interface

7.1 Overview

XMPT is the tool interface of XMP and inspired by OMPT, which is the tool interface of OpenMP [4]. Hence, XMPT is designed as event-based and callback-based as OMPT; that is, for each event at runtime, the corresponding callback is invoked. One or more XMPT events are defined corresponding to each of XMP constructs and coarray-related actions (e.g. remote write/read and synchronization).

XMPT is preliminarily implemented in the Omni XMP compiler chapter "Implementation and Performance Evaluation of Omni Compiler", and used in MUST [5] and experimentally in Extrae [6]. More details of the application of XMPT in MUST are described in [7].

XMP/C

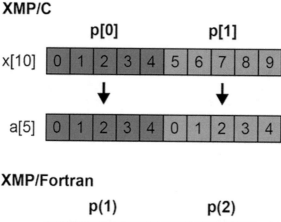

XMP/Fortran

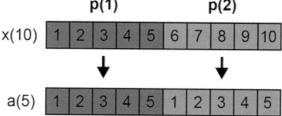

Fig. 53 Passing a global argument to a local parameter

7.2 Specification

7.2.1 Initialization

Tool developers can provide the `xmpt_initialize` function in which they register a callback for each of the XMPT events of interest, as follows.

```c
void xmpt_initialize(...){
  xmpt_set_callback(xmpt_event_bcast_begin, callback_bcast_begin);
  xmpt_set_callback(xmpt_event_bcast_end, callback_bcast_end);
  ...
}
```

In the above example, the tool developer implements callbacks `callback_bcast_begin` and `callback_bcast_end` that interact with his/her tool.

When an XMP program starts execution, the XMP runtime implicitly invokes `xmpt_initialize`, if provided, to set up the callbacks.

7.2.2 Events

XMPT defines XMPT events each of which corresponds to an XMP construct or a coarray-related action. Below is the list of XMPT events. For each of the events, the function signature of the corresponding callback is specifically defined. Note that the ones from `xmpt_event_coarray_remote_write` to `xmpt_event_sync_images_end` are coarray-related.

```
xmpt_event_task_begin
xmpt_event_task_end
xmpt_event_tasks_begin
xmpt_event_tasks_end
xmpt_event_loop_begin
xmpt_event_loop_end
xmpt_event_array_begin
xmpt_event_array_end
xmpt_event_reflect_begin
xmpt_event_reflect_begin_async
xmpt_event_reflect_end
xmpt_event_gmove_begin
xmpt_event_gmove_begin_async
xmpt_event_gmove_end
xmpt_event_barrier_begin
xmpt_event_barrier_end
xmpt_event_reduction_begin
xmpt_event_reduction_begin_async
xmpt_event_reduction_end
xmpt_event_bcast_begin
xmpt_event_bcast_begin_async
xmpt_event_bcast_end
xmpt_event_wait_async_begin
xmpt_event_wait_async_end
xmpt_event_coarray_remote_write
xmpt_event_coarray_remote_read
xmpt_event_coarray_local_write
xmpt_event_coarray_local_read
xmpt_event_sync_memory_begin
xmpt_event_sync_memory_end
xmpt_event_sync_all_begin
xmpt_event_sync_all_end
xmpt_event_sync_image_begin
xmpt_event_sync_image_end
xmpt_event_sync_images_all_begin
```

```
xmpt_event_sync_images_all_end
xmpt_event_sync_images_begin
xmpt_event_sync_images_end
```

When one of the XMPT events for which callbacks are registered occurs at runtime, the corresponding callback is invoked by the XMP runtime. For example, if callbacks are registered for events `xmpt_event_bcast_begin` and `xmpt_event_bcast_end` as in the example in the previous section, the callbacks `callback_bcast_begin` and `callback_bcast_end` are invoked immediately before and after each of `bcast` constructs, respectively.

The XMP runtime passes therein all the information about the construct, including the mapping of the target global arrays, to the callback as its parameters. Thus, the tool is able to extract necessary information from the arguments.

References

1. R.W. Numrich, J. Reid, Co-array Fortran for parallel programming, in *ACM SIGPLAN Fortran Forum*, vol. 17, No. 2 (ACM, New York, 1998)
2. UPC Consortium, UPC Specifications, v1.2. Lawrence Berkeley National Lab (LBNL-59208) (2005)
3. D. Callahan, B.L. Chamberlain, H.P. Zima, The cascade high productivity language, in *Proceedings of the 9th Int'l. Workshop on High-Level Parallel Programming Models and Supportive Environments (HIPS 2004)* (2004), pp. 52–60
4. OpenMP Architecture Review Board, OpenMP Application Programming Interface Version 5.0 (2018)
5. The MUST Project, https://www.itc.rwth-aachen.de/must
6. The Extrae Project, https://tools.bsc.es/extrae
7. J. Protze, C. Terboven, M.S. Müller, S. Petiton, N. Emad, H. Murai, T. Boku. Runtime correctness checking for emerging programming paradigms, in *Proceedings of the First International Workshop on Software Correctness for HPC Applications (Correctness'17)*. Association for Computing Machinery (New York, NY, USA, 2017), pp. 21–27. https://doi.org/10.1145/3145344.3145490

Implementation and Performance Evaluation of Omni Compiler

Masahiro Nakao and Hitoshi Murai

Abstract This chapter describes the implementation and performance evaluation of Omni compiler, which is a reference implementation of the compiler for XcalableMP. For performance evaluation, this chapter also presents how to implement the HPC Challenge benchmarks, which is a benchmark suite for an HPC parallel language. The results show that the performance of XMP is comparable to that of MPI in many cases.

1 Overview

Omni compiler is a source-to-source compiler that translates a sequential code in C and Fortran with XcalableMP (XMP), XcalableACC (XACC), and OpenACC directives into a parallel code (https://omni-compiler.org). The translated parallel code is compiled with a native compiler linked with Omni compiler runtime library. Omni compiler has been developed by Programming Environment Research Team of RIKEN Center for Computational Science [1] and HPCS laboratory [2] of University of Tsukuba in Japan.

2 Implementation

2.1 Operation Flow

In Omni compiler, XcodeML [3] is used to analyze a code in an intermediate code format of XML expression. Figure 1 shows an operation flow of Omni compiler. Firstly, Omni compiler translates directives in a user code into the runtime functions.

M. Nakao (✉) · H. Murai
RIKEN Center for Computational Science, Kobe, Hyogo, Japan
e-mail: masahiro.nakao@riken.jp; h-murai@riken.jp

© The Author(s) 2021
M. Sato (ed.), *XcalableMP PGAS Programming Language*,
https://doi.org/10.1007/978-981-15-7683-6_2

73

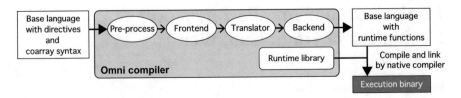

Fig. 1 Operation flow of Omni compiler (https://omni-compiler.org)

If necessary, a code besides the directives is also modified. Secondly, a native compiler (e.g., gcc or Intel) compiles the translated code and creates an execution binary with linking to Omni compiler runtime library. The runtime library uses MPI in XMP, and CUDA in OpenACC, and both MPI and CUDA in XACC. As for XMP, Omni compiler may create better runtime libraries by adding a one-sided communication library to MPI, which is described in Chap. 3.

2.2   Example of Code Translation

This section describes how Omni compiler translates a user code for the global-view memory model. A code translation for the local-view memory model is described in Chap. 3.

2.2.1   Distributed Array

Figure 2 shows an XMP example code using an **align** directive to declare a distributed array *a[][]*.

```
double a[10][10];
#pragma xmp align a[i][j] with t[i][j]
```

```
void *_XMP_DESC_a;
double *_XMP_ADDR_a;
unsigned long long _XMP_ACC_a_0;
_XMP_init_array_desc(&_XMP_DESC_a, .., sizeof(double), 10, 10);
      :
_XMP_alloc_array(&_XMP_ADDR_a, &_XMP_ACC_a_0, ..., _XMP_DESC_a);
```

Fig. 2 Code translation of align directive

Firstly, Omni compiler deletes a declaration of a local array *a[][]* and the **align** directive. Next, Omni compiler creates a descriptor *_XMP_DESC_a* by a function `_XMP_init_array_desc()` to set information of the distributed array. Omni compiler also adds a function `_XMP_alloc_array()` to allocate memory for the distributed array, and it sets values in an address *_XMP_ADDR_a* and a leading dimension *_XMP_ACC_a_0*. Note that a multidimensional distributed array is expressed as a one-dimensional array in the translated code since the size of each dimension of the array may be determined dynamically.

2.2.2 Loop Statement

Figure 3 shows an XMP example code using a **loop** directive to parallelize the following nested loop statement depending on the template *t*. Each dimension of *t* is distributed onto two nodes, which is omitted there.

In the translated code above, a pointer *_XMP_MULTI_ADDR_a* is used which has the size of each dimension as a head pointer of the distributed array *a[][]*. To improve performance, operations in a loop statement are performed using the pointer [4]. Note that this pointer can be used when the number of elements in each dimension of a distributed array is divisible by the number of nodes. If the condition is not met, a one dimensional pointer *_XMP_ADDR_a* and an offset *_XMP_ACC_a_0* are used as shown in the translated code below.

Moreover, because values in ending conditions of the loop statement ($i < 10$, $j < 10$) are constants in a pre-translated code and are divisible by the number of nodes,

---

```
#pragma xmp loop on t[i][j]
for(int i=0;i<10;i++)
  for(int j=0;j<10;j++)
    a[i][j] = ...
```

⬇

```
double (*_XMP_MULTI_ADDR_a)[5] = (double (*)[5])(_XMP_ADDR_a);
for(int i=0;i<5;i++)
  for(int j=0;j<5;j++)
    _XMP_MULTI_ADDR_a[i][j] = ...
```

---

or

```
for(int i=0;i<5;i++)
  for(int j=0;j<5;j++)
    *(_XMP_ADDR_a + i * _XMP_ACC_a_0 + j) = ...
```

Fig. 3 Code translation of loop directive

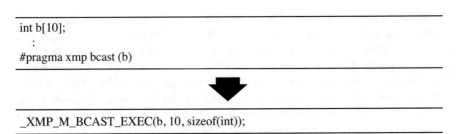

```
int b[10];
   :
#pragma xmp bcast (b)
```

```
_XMP_M_BCAST_EXEC(b, 10, sizeof(int));
```

Fig. 4 Code translation of bcast directive

the values are translated to constants ($i < 5$, $j < 5$) automatically. If the values are variables in the pre-translated code or not divisible by the number of nodes, the runtime function is inserted just before the loop statement to calculate values for ending conditions. The calculated values are set in newly created variables.

2.2.3 Communication

Figure 4 shows an XMP example code using a **bcast** directive to broadcast a local array b. Basically translations of communication directives are simple. The runtime functions call MPI functions directly.

3 Installation

This section describes how to install the latest Omni compiler version 1.3.2. Omni compiler is installed by a general installation method on UNIX (./configure; make; make install). When executing ./configure without options, only XMP is installed. When installing OpenACC and/or XACC, it is required for some options to "./configure", which is described in Sect. 3.5.

3.1 Overview

We provide two versions of Omni compiler, the one is "stable version" and the other is "nightly build version." While the stable version is a so-called official version that has a version number, the nightly build version is a trial version that is released at midnight on our website (https://omni-compiler.org). Omni compiler is developed in GitHub repository (https://github.com/omni-compiler/omni-compiler). Our web server gets the source code from the GitHub repository and generates the nightly build version every day.

3.2 Get Source Code

3.2.1 From GitHub

Please visit the GitHub repository (https://github.com/omni-compiler/omni-compiler) which provides only nightly build version. Otherwise, please execute the following `git` command.

```
$ git clone --recursive https://github.com/omni-compiler/omni-compiler.git
```

Note that the source code of Omni compiler does not contain that of XcodeML, so the `--recursive` option is required. As a supplement, XcodeML is also developed in the GitHub repository (https://github.com/omni-compiler/xcodeml-tools).

3.2.2 From Our Website

Please visit our website (https://omni-compiler.org) which provides packages of stable version and nightly build version. The package of nightly build version is generated every midnight around 12:00 a.m. (JST) if the latest GitHub repository was updated yesterday. These packages contain XcodeML.

3.3 Software Dependency

Before installation of Omni compiler, the following software must be installed.

```
yacc, lex, C Compiler (C99 or over), Fortran Compiler (Fortran 2008 or over),
Java Compiler, MPI (version 2 or over), libxml2, make
```

3.4 General Installation

This section explains how to install Omni compiler in a general Unix environment.

3.4.1 Build and Install

```
$ ./configure --prefix=(INSTALL PATH)
$ make
$ make install
```

3.4.2 Set PATH

- bash and zsh

```
$ export PATH=(INSTALL PATH)/bin:$PATH
```

- csh and tcsh

```
% setenv PATH (INSTALL PATH)/bin:$PATH
```

3.5 Optional Installation

3.5.1 OpenACC

Please add "`--enable-openacc`" and "`--with-cuda=(CUDA PATH)`" options to "`./configure`".

```
$ ./configure --enable-openacc --with-cuda=(CUDA PATH)
$ make
$ make install
```

It may be possible to generate a more suitable runtime library by adding options to "nvcc" command, which is used to generate the runtime library for OpenACC and XACC. In that case, please also add the "`--with-gpu-cflags=(NVCC CFLAGS)`" option.

```
$ ./configure --enable-openacc --with-cuda=(CUDA PATH) --with-gpu-
cflags=(NVCC CFLAGS)
$ make
$ make install
```

3.5.2 XcalableACC

Please add "`--enable-openacc --enable-xacc`" to "`./configure`".

```
$ ./configure --enable-openacc --enable-xacc
$ make
$ make install
```

As with OpenACC, if necessary, please add the "`--with-cuda=(CUDA PATH)`" and "`--with-gpu-cflags=(NVCC CFLAGS)`" options to "`./configure`".

3.5.3 One-Sided Library

Omni compiler may generate a better runtime library by a one-sided library for XMP. Omni compiler supports the following one-sided libraries.

- Fujitsu MPI Extended RDMA (FJRDMA)
  It is low-level communication layer for Fujitsu machines (e.g., the K computer, FX100, and FX10). When using it, please specify a target machine to ./configure. (e.g., "`$ ./configure --target=FX100-linux-gnu`")
- GASNet (https://gasnet.lbl.gov)
  It is a one-sided communication library developed by U.C. Berkeley. When using it, please specify "install path of GASNet" and "its conduit" to ./configure. (e.g., `$ ./configure --with-gasnet=/usr --with-gasnet-conduit=ibv`)
- MPI version 3
  Omni compiler automatically selects MPI version 3 under the following conditions.

  - MPI implementation supports MPI version 3
  - Specifying neither FJRDMA nor GASNet.

4 Creation of Execution Binary

This section describes how to create an execution binary from a code with XMP, XACC, and OpenACC directives, and how to execute it. Note that Omni compiler supports only C language for OpenACC.

4.1 Compile

- XMP in C language

```
$ xmpcc a.c
```

- XMP in Fortran

```
$ xmpf90 a.f90
```

- XACC in C language

```
$ xmpcc -xacc a.c
```

- XACC in Fortran

```
$ xmpf90 -xacc a.f90
```

- OpenACC in C language

```
$ ompcc -acc a.c
```

A native compiler finally compiles the code translated by Omni compiler. Thus, all compile options of XMP are passed to the native compiler. For example, when using the optimization option "-O2", it is passed to the native compiler.

```
$ xmpcc -O2 a.c
```

4.2 Execution

4.2.1 XcalableMP and XcalableACC

Because the runtime libraries of XMP and XACC use MPI, a program is executed via an MPI execution command (e.g., "mpiexec"). However, when using GASNet, a program is executed via a GASNet execution command (e.g., "gasnetrun_ibv").

```
$ mpiexec -n 2 ./a.out
```

```
$ gasnetrun_ibv -n 2 ./a.out
```

4.2.2 OpenACC

```
$ ./a.out
```

4.3 Cooperation with Profiler

In order to improve the performance of an application, it is useful to take a profile. Omni compiler has a function to cooperate with Scalasca (https://www.scalasca.org) and tlog which are profiling tools. The function can profile the execution of XMP directives. Note that the function supports only the XMP in C language now.

4.3.1 Scalasca

Scalasca is an opensource software that measures and analyzes the runtime behaviors.

When profiling all XMP directives that exist in code, please add the "`--profile scalasca`" option to a compile command.

```
$ xmpcc --profile scalasca a.c
```

When profiling selected XMP directives there, please add the "`profile`" clause to the directives and the "`--selective-profile scalasca`" option to a compile command.

```
#pragma xmp bcast (a) profile
```

```
$ xmpcc --selective-profile scalasca a.c
```

Figure 5 shows an example of profiling by Scalasca.

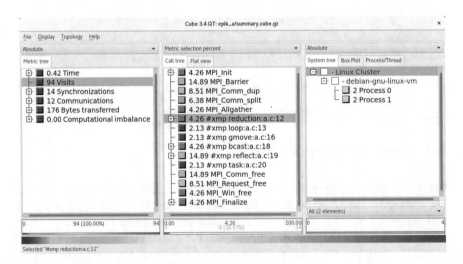

Fig. 5 Profile by Scalasca (https://omni-compiler.org)

4.3.2 tlog

Omni compiler package contains tlog that measures executing time of the XMP directives.

When profiling all XMP directives that exist in code, please add the "--profile tlog" option to a compile command.

```
$ xmpcc --profile tlog a.c
```

When profiling selected XMP directives there, please add the "profile" clause to the directives as in Sect. 4.3.1 and the "--selective-profile tlog" option to a compile command.

```
$ xmpcc --selective-profile tlog a.c
```

After executing a program, tlog generates a file "trace.log" which stores profiling results. To open the result, please use the "tlogview" command. Figure 6 shows an example of profiling by tlog.

```
$ tlogview trace.log
```

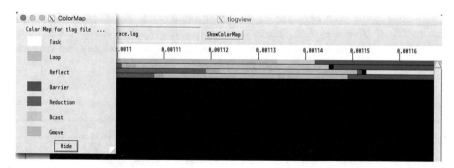

Fig. 6 Profile by tlog (https://omni-compiler.org)

5 Performance Evaluation

In order to evaluate the performance of XMP, we implemented the HPC Challenge (HPCC) benchmark (https://icl.utk.edu/hpcc/), namely, EP STREAM Triad (STREAM), High-Performance Linpack (HPL), Global fast Fourier transform (FFT), and RandomAccess [5]. While the HPCC benchmark is used to evaluate multiple attributes of HPC systems, the benchmark is also useful to evaluate the properties of a parallel language. The HPCC benchmark was used at the HPCC Award Competition (https://www.hpcchallenge.org). The HPCC Award Competition consists of two classes. While the purpose of class 1 is to evaluate the performance of a machine, the purpose of class 2 is to evaluate both the productivity and performance of a parallel programming language. XMP won the class 2 prizes in 2013 and 2014.

5.1 Experimental Environment

For performance evaluation, this section uses 16,384 compute nodes on the K computer and 128 compute nodes on a Cray CS300 system named "the COMA system." Tables 1 and 2 show the hardware specifications and software environments.

For comparison purposes, this section also evaluates the HPCC benchmark in C language and MPI library. We execute STREAM, HPL, and FFT with eight threads per process on each CPU of the K computer, and with ten threads per process on each CPU of the COMA system. Since RandomAccess is not parallelized with threads and can be executed by the power of only two processes, we execute it with eight processes on each CPU of both systems.

The specification of HPCC Award Competition class 2 defines the minimum problem size for each benchmark. While the main array of HPL should occupy at least half of the system memory, the main arrays of STREAM, FFT, and RandomAccess should occupy at least a quarter of the system memory. We set each

Table 1 Experimental environment for the K computer

CPU	SPARC64 VIIIfx 2.0 GHz, 8 Cores
Memory	DDR3 SDRAM 16 GB, 64 GB/s
Network	Torus fusion six-dimensional mesh/torus network, 5 GB/s × 10
Library	Fujitsu Compiler K-1.2.0-19, Fujitsu MPI K-1.2.0-19, Fujitsu SSLII K-1.2.0-19

Table 2 Experimental environment for the COMA system

CPU	Xeon E5-2670v2, 2.5 GHz (Turbo Boost 3.3 GHz), 10 Cores × 2CPUs
Memory	DDR3 SDRAM 64 GB, 119.4 GB/s (= 59.7 GB/s × 2 CPUs)
Network	InfiniBand FDR, fat-tree, 7 GB/s
Library	Intel Compiler 15.0.5, Intel MPI 5.1.1, GASNet 1.26.0, Intel MKL 11.2.4

problem size to be equal to the minimum size. As for coarray syntax, Omni compiler uses FJRDMA on the K computer and uses GASNet on the COMA system.

5.2   EP STREAM Triad

5.2.1   Design

STREAM measures the memory bandwidth to use simple vector kernel ($a \leftarrow b + \alpha c$). STREAM is so straightforward that its kernel does not require communication.

5.2.2   Implementation

Figure 7 shows a part of the STREAM code. In line 1, the **node** directive declares a node array p to parallelize the program. In line 2, normal arrays *a[ ]*, *b[ ]*, and *c[ ]*, and a scalar value *scalar* are declared. In lines 5 and 14, the **barrier** directive is inserted before xmp_wtime() to measure time. The directives of lines 8–9 are optimization directives for the Fujitsu compiler. While the **#pragma loop xfill** ensures one cache line to store write-only data, the **#pragma loop noalias** indicates that different pointer variables cannot possibly indicate the same storage area. These optimization directives are used on only the K computer. In lines 10–12, STREAM kernel is parallelized by the OpenMP **parallel** directive. In line 17, **local_performance()**

```
1   #pragma xmp nodes p[*]
2   double a[N], b[N], c[N], scalar;
3   ...
4   for(k=0;k<TIMES;k++){
5   #pragma xmp barrier
6       times[k] = −xmp_wtime();
7
8   #pragma loop xfill
9   #pragma loop noalias
10  #pragma omp parallel for
11      for (i=0; i<N; i++)
12          a[i] = b[i] + scalar * c[i];
13
14  #pragma xmp barrier
15      times[k] += xmp_wtime();
16  }
17  double performance = local_performance(time, TIMES, N);
18  #pragma xmp reduction(+:performance)
```

Fig. 7   Part of the STREAM code [5]

calculates the performance on each node locally. In line 18, the **reduction** directive performs a reduction operation among nodes to calculate the total performance.

5.2.3 Evaluation

First of all, in order to consider the effectiveness of **#pragma loop xfill** and **#pragma loop noalias**, we evaluate STREAM with and without these directives on a single node of the K computer. We also insert these directives into the MPI implementation for evaluation. Figure 8 shows that the performance results with these directives are about 1.46 times better than those without the directives. Therefore, we use the directives in next evaluations.

Figure 9 shows the performance results and a comparative performance evaluation of both implementations. The comparative performance evaluation is called the "performance ratio." When the performance ratio is greater than 1, the performance result of the XMP implementation is better than that of the MPI implementation. XMP's best performance results are 706.38 TB/s for 16,384 compute nodes on the

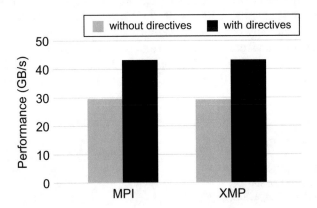

Fig. 8 Preliminary evaluation of STREAM [5]

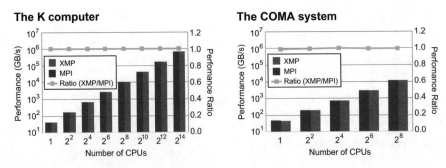

Fig. 9 Performance results for STREAM [5]

K computer, and 11.55 TB/s for 128 compute nodes on the COMA system. The values of the performance ratio are between 0.99 and 1.00 on both systems.

5.3 High-Performance Linpack

5.3.1 Design

HPL evaluates the floating point rate of execution for solving a linear system of equations. The performance result has been used in the TOP500 list (https://www. top500.org). To achieve a good load balance on HPL, we distribute the main array in a *block-cyclic* manner. Moreover, in order to achieve high performance with portability, our implementation calls BLAS [6] to perform the matrix operations. These techniques are inherited from the MPI implementation.

5.3.2 Implementation

Figure 10 shows that each dimension of the coefficient matrix *A[][]* is distributed in the *block-cyclic* manner. The **template** and the **nodes** directives declare a two-dimensional template *t* and node array *p*. The **distribute** directive distributes *t* onto $Q \times P$ nodes with the same block size *NB*. The **align** directive aligns *A[][]* with *t*.

HPL has an operation in which a part of the coefficient matrix is broadcast to the other process columns asynchronously. This operation, called "panel broadcast," is one of the most important operations for overlapping panel factorizations and data transfer. Figure 11 shows the implementation that uses the **gmove** directive with the **async** clause. The second dimension of array *L[][]* is also distributed in a *block-cyclic* manner and *L[][]* is replicated. Thus, the **gmove** directive broadcasts elements *A[j:NB][j+NB:len]* to *L[0:NB][j+NB:len]* asynchronously.

Figure 12 shows that **cblas_dgemm()**, which is a BLAS function for a matrix multiplication, applies the distributed arrays *L[][]* and *A[][]*. Note that **cblas_dgemm()** is executed by multiple threads locally. In lines 2–3, **xmp_desc_of()** gets descriptors of *L[][]* and *A[][]*, and **xmp_array_lda()** gets the leading dimensions *L_ld* and *A_ld*. In line 5, the *L_ld* and *A_ld* are used in

Fig. 10 Block-cyclic
distribution in HPL [5]

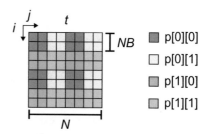

```
1   double L[NB][N];
2   #pragma xmp align L[*][i] with t[*][i]
3   ...
4   int len = N – j – NB;
5   #pragma xmp gmove async (tag)
6   L[0:NB][j+NB:len] = A[j:NB][j+NB:len];
```

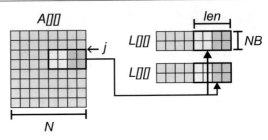

Fig. 11 Panel broadcast in HPL [5]

```
1   int L_ld, A_ld;
2   xmp_array_lda(xmp_desc_of(L), &L_ld);
3   xmp_array_lda(xmp_desc_of(A), &A_ld);
4   ...
5   cblas_dgemm(..., &L[0][j], L_ld, ..., &A[i][j], A_ld, ...);
```

Fig. 12 Calling the function **cblas_dgemm**() in HPL [5]

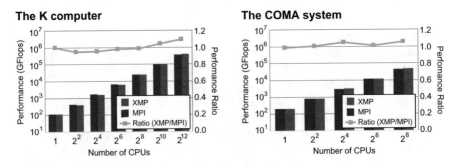

Fig. 13 Performance results for HPL [5]

cblas_dgemm(). Note that L_ld and A_ld remain unchanged from the beginning of the program, and so each **xmp_array_lda**() is called only once.

5.3.3 Evaluation

Figure 13 shows the performance results and performance ratios. XMP's best performance results are 402.01 TFlops (76.68% of the peak performance) for

4096 compute nodes on the K computer, and 47.32 TFlops (70.02% of the peak performance) for 128 compute nodes on the COMA system. The values of the performance ratio are between 0.95 and 1.09 on the K computer, and between 0.99 and 1.06 on the COMA system.

5.4 Global Fast Fourier Transform

5.4.1 Design

FFT evaluates the performance for a double-precision complex one-dimensional discrete Fourier transform. We implement a six-step FFT algorithm [7, 8] using FFTE library [9]. The six-step FFT algorithm is also used in the MPI implementation. In the six-step FFT algorithm, both the computing performance and the all-to-all communication performance for a matrix transpose are important. The six-step FFT algorithm reduces the cache-miss ratio by expression of a two-dimensional array. In order to develop the XMP implementation, we use XMP in Fortran because FFTE library is written in Fortran and therefore it is easy to call it. In addition, we use the XMP intrinsic subroutine **xmp_transpose**() to transpose a distributed array in the global-view memory model. Figure 14 shows an example of **xmp_transpose**(). The first argument is an output array, and the second argument is the input array. The third argument is an option to save memory, and is "0" or "1." If it is "0," an input array must not be changed. If it is "1," an input

```
1   complex*16 a(4,12), b(12,4)
2   !$xmp template ty(12)
3   !$xmp template tx(4)
4   !$xmp nodes p(4)
5   !$xmp distribute ty(block) onto p
6   !$xmp distribute tx(block) onto p
7   !$xmp align a(*,i) with ty(i)
8   !$xmp align b(*,i) with tx(i)
9   call xmp_transpose(a, b, 1)
```

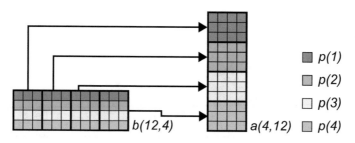

Fig. 14 Action of subroutine **xmp_transpose**() [5]

array may be changed but less memory may be used. Thus, we use "1" in the XMP implementation. In Fig. 14, the second dimensions of arrays $a()$ and $b()$ are distributed in the *block* manner, and array $b()$ is transposed to array $a()$. For example, elements $b(1:3,2)$ on $p(2)$ are transferred to elements $a(2,1:3)$ on $p(1)$.

5.4.2   Implementation

Figure 15 shows a part of the XMP implementation. In lines 1–9, arrays $a()$, $b()$, and $w()$ are distributed in a *block* manner. The $a()$ is aligned with template ty, and the $b()$ and $w()$ arrays are aligned with template tx. In lines 16–20, each thread on all nodes calls the FFTE subroutine *zfft1d()*, which applies the distributed array $b()$. Note that the subroutine *zfft1d()* executes with a single thread locally. In lines 22–23, the XMP **loop** directive and the OpenMP **parallel** directive parallelize the loop statement. In line 30, **xmp_transpose()** is used to transpose the distributed two-dimensional array.

```
 1   complex*16 a(nx,ny), b(ny,nx), w(ny,nx)
 2   !$xmp template ty(ny)
 3   !$xmp template tx(nx)
 4   !$xmp nodes p(*)
 5   !$xmp distribute ty(block) onto p
 6   !$xmp distribute tx(block) onto p
 7   !$xmp align a(*,i) with ty(i)
 8   !$xmp align b(*,i) with tx(i)
 9   !$xmp align w(*,i) with tx(i)
10
11   integer, save :: ithread
12   !$omp threadprivate (ithread)
13   !$omp parallel
14      ithread = omp_get_thread_num()
15   !$omp end parallel
16   !$xmp loop on tx(i)
17   !$omp parallel do
18   do i=1,nx
19      call zfft1d(b(1,i),ny,−1,cy(1,ithread))
20   end do
21
22   !$xmp loop on tx(i)
23   !$omp parallel do
24   do i=1,nx
25      do j=1,ny
26         b(j,i)=b(j,i)*w(j,i)
27      end do
28   end do
29
30   call xmp_transpose(a,b,1)
```

Fig. 15 Part of the FFT code [5]

5.4.3 Evaluation

Figure 16 shows the performance results and performance ratios. XMP's best performance results are 39.01 TFlops for 16,384 compute nodes on the K computer, and 0.94 TFlops for 128 compute nodes on the COMA system. The values of the performance ratio are between 0.94 and 1.13 on the K computer, and between 0.94 and 1.12 on the COMA system.

5.5 RandomAccess

5.5.1 Design

RandomAccess evaluates the performance of random updates of a single table of 64-bit integers which may be distributed among processes. The random update for a distributed table requires an all-to-all communication. We implement a recursive exchange algorithm [10], as with the MPI implementation. The recursive exchange algorithm consists of multiple steps. A process sends a data chunk to another process in each step. Because RandomAccess requires a random communication pattern, as its name suggests, the pattern is not supported by the global-view memory model. Thus, we use the local-view memory model to implement RandomAccess. Note that the MPI implementation uses functions **MPI_Isend()** and **MPI_Irecv()**.

5.5.2 Implementation

A source node transfers a data chunk to a destination node, and then the destination node updates own table using the received data. The MPI implementation repeatedly executes the recursive exchange algorithm by 1024 elements in the table. The HPCC Award Competition class 2 specification defines the constant value 1024. The recursive exchange algorithm sends about half of the 1024 elements in each

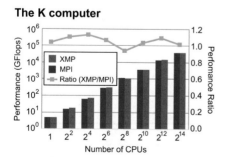
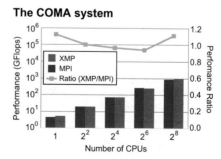

Fig. 16 Performance results for FFT [5]

step. Therefore, the chunk size is about 4096 Bytes ($= 1024/2 \times 64$ bits$/8$). Note that the destination node cannot know how many elements are sent by the source node. Thus, the MPI implementation gets the number of elements using the function **MPI_Get_count()**. We implement the algorithm using a coarray and the **post/wait** directives for the recursive exchange algorithm, and the number of elements is added to the first element of the coarray.

Figure 17 shows a part of the XMP implementation. In line 2, the coarrays *recv[][][]* and *send[][]* are declared. In line 6, the data chunk size is set at the first element of the coarray, and it is put in line 7. In line 8, the node sends notification of the completion of the coarray operation of line 7 to the node *p[ipartner]*. In line 10, the node receives the notification from the node *p[jpartner]*, which ensures that the node *p[jpartner]* receives the data. In line 11, the node gets the number of elements in the received data. In line 12, the node updates own table by using the received data.

5.5.3 Evaluation

Figure 18 shows the performance results and performance ratios. The Giga-updates per second (GUPS) on the vertical axis is the measurement value, which is the number of update tables per second divided by 10^9. XMP's best performance results are 259.73 GUPS for 16,384 compute nodes on the K computer, and 6.23 GUPS for 128 compute nodes on the COMA system. The values of the performance ratio are between 1.01 and 1.11 on the K computer, and between 0.57 and 1.03 on the COMA system. On the K computer, the performance results for the XMP implementation are always slightly better than those for the MPI implementation. However, on the COMA system, the performance results for the XMP implementation are worse than those for the MPI implementation using multiple CPUs.

```
1   #pragma xmp nodes p[*]
2   unsigned long long recv[ITER][LOGPROCS][CHUNK]:[*], send[2][CHUNKBIG]:[*];
3   ...
4   for(j=0;j<logNumProcs;j++){
5     ...
6     send[i][0] = nsend;
7     recv[iter_mod][j][0:nsend+1]:[ipartner] = send[i][0:nsend+1];
8   #pragma xmp post(p[ipartner], tag)
9     ...
10  #pragma xmp wait(p[jpartner], tag)
11    nrecv = recv[iter_mod][j−1][0];
12    update_table(&recv[iter_mod][j−1][1], ..., nrecv, ...);
13    ...
14  }
```

Fig. 17 Part of the RandomAccess code [5]

The K computer

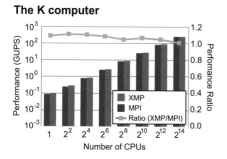

The COMA system

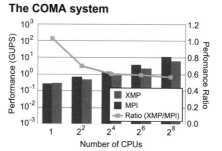

Fig. 18 Performance results for RandomAccess [5]

5.6 Discussion

We implement STREAM, HPL, and FFT using the global-view memory model, which enables programmers to develop the parallel codes from the sequential codes using the XMP directives and functions easily. Specifically, in order to implement the parallel STREAM code, a programmer only adds the XMP directives into the sequential STREAM code. The XMP directives and existing directives, such as OpenMP directives and Fujitsu directives, can coexist. Moreover, existing high-performance libraries, such as BLAS and FFTE, can be used with an XMP distributed array. These features improve the portability and performance of XMP applications.

We also implement RandomAccess using the local-view memory model, where the coarray syntax enables a programmer to transfer data intuitively. In the evaluation, the performance of the XMP implementation is better than that of the MPI implementation on the K computer, but is worse than that of the MPI implementation on the COMA system.

To clarify the reason why XMP performance is dropped on the COMA system, we develop a simple ping-pong benchmark using the local-view memory model. The benchmark measures the latency for transferring data repeatedly between two nodes. For comparison purposes, we also implement one using **MPI_Isend()** and **MPI_Irecv()** that are used in the MPI version RandomAccess.

Figure 19 shows parts of the codes. In XMP of Fig. 19, in line 5, *p[0]* puts a part of *src_buf[]* into *dst_buf[]* in *p[1]*. In line 6, the **post** directive ensures the completion of the coarray operation of line 5 and sends a notification to *p[1]*. In line 10, *p[1]* waits until receiving the notification from *p[0]*. In line 11, *p[1]* puts a part of *src_buf[]* into *dst_buf[]* in *p[0]*. In line 12, the **post** directive ensures the completion of the coarray operation of line 11 and sends a notification to *p[0]*. In line 7, *p[0]* waits until receiving the notification from *p[1]*. Figure 19 also shows the ping-pong benchmark that uses MPI functions.

Figure 20 shows the latency for transferring data. The results on the K computer show that the latency for the XMP implementation is better than that for the

```
1   int me = xmpc_node_num();
2   int target = (me == 0)? 1 : 0;
3   ...
4   if(me == 0){
5      dst_buf[0:size]:[target] = src_buf[0:size];
6   #pragma xmp post(p[target], tag)
7   #pragma xmp wait(p[target], tag)
8   }
9   else if(me == 1){
10  #pragma xmp wait(p[target], tag)
11     dst_buf[0:size]:[target] = src_buf[0:size];
12  #pragma xmp post(p[target], tag)
13  }
```

```
1   int me;
2   MPI_Comm_rank(..., &me);
3   int target = (me == 0)? 1 : 0;
4   ...
5   if(me == 0){
6      MPI_Isend(src_buf, ..., target, ...);
7      MPI_Wait(...);
8      MPI_Irecv(dst_buf, ..., target, ...);
9      MPI_Wait(...);
10  }
11  else if(me == 1){
12     MPI_Irecv(dst_buf, ..., target, ...);
13     MPI_Wait(...);
14     MPI_Isend(src_buf, ..., target, ...);
15     MPI_Wait(...);
16  }
```

Fig. 19 Part of the ping-pong benchmark code in XMP and MPI [5]

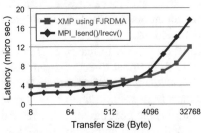

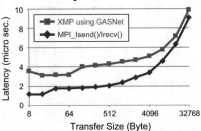

Fig. 20 Performance results for ping-pong benchmark [5]

MPI implementation for 2048 Bytes or greater transfer size on the K computer. In contrast, the results on the COMA system show that the latency of the XMP implementation is always worse than that of the MPI implementation on the COMA system. The latency of XMP with FJRDMA at 4096 Bytes, which is the average data chunk size, is 5.83 μs and the latency of MPI is 6.89 μs on the K computer. The latency of XMP with GASNet is 5.05 μs and that of MPI is 3.37 μs on the COMA system. Thus, we consider the reason for the performance difference of RandomAccess is the communication performance. The performance difference is also due to the differences in the synchronization mechanism of the one-sided XMP coarray and the two-sided MPI functions. Note that a real application would not synchronize after every one-sided communication. It is expected that a single synchronization should occur after multiple one-sided communications to achieve higher performance.

In addition, the performance results for HPL and FFT are slightly different from those for the MPI implementations. We consider that these differences are caused by small differences in the implementations. In HPL, for the panel-broadcast operation, the XMP implementation uses the **gmove** directive with the **async** clause, which calls **MPI_Ibcast()** internally. In contrast, the MPI implementation uses **MPI_Send()** and **MPI_Recv()** to perform the operation by the "modified increasing ring" [11]. In FFT, the XMP implementation uses XMP in Fortran, but the MPI implementation uses C language. Both implementations call the same FFTE library. In addition, the MPI implementation uses **MPI_Alltoall()** to transpose a matrix. Since **xmp_transpose()** calls **MPI_Alltoall()** internally, the performance levels for both **xmp_transpose()** and **MPI_Alltoall()** must be the same. Therefore, the language differences and refactoring may have caused the performance difference.

6   Conclusion

The chapter describes the implementation and performance evaluation of Omni compiler. We evaluate the performance of the HPCC benchmark in XMP on the K computer up to 16,384 compute nodes and a generic cluster system up to 128 compute nodes. The performance results for the XMP implementations are almost the same as those for the MPI implementations in many cases. Moreover, it demonstrates that the global-view and the local-view memory models are useful to develop the HPCC benchmark.

References

1. Programming Environment Research Team, https://pro-env.riken.jp
2. High Performance Computing System laboratory, University of Tsukuba, Japan, https://www.hpcs.cs.tsukuba.ac.jp

3. M. Sato et al., Omni compiler and XcodeML: an infrastructure for source-to-source transformation, in *Platform for Advanced Scientific Computing Conference (PASC16)*, Lausanne (2016)
4. M. Nakao et al., Performance evaluation for Omni XcalableMP compiler on many-core cluster system based on knights landing, in *IXPUG Workshop Asia 2018*, Tokyo (2018), pp. 52–58
5. M. Nakao et al., Implementation and evaluation of the HPC challenge benchmark in the XcalableMP PGAS language. Int. J. High Perform. Comput. Appl. **33**(1), 110–123 (2017)
6. BLAS: Basic Linear Algebra Subprograms, http://www.netlib.org/blas/ (2016)
7. D.H. Bailey, FFTs in external or hierarchical memory. J. Supercomput. **4**, 23–35 (1990)
8. C. Van Loan, *Computational Frameworks for the Fast Fourier Transform* (Society for Industrial and Applied Mathematics, Philadelphia, 1992)
9. D. Takahashi, *A Fast Fourier Transform Package*, http://www.ffte.jp (2014)
10. R. Ponnusamy et al., Communication overhead on the CM5: an experimental performance evaluation, in *Fourth Symposium on the Frontiers of Massively Parallel Computation* (1992), pp.108–115
11. HPL Algorithm Panel Broadcast, http://www.netlib.org/benchmark/hpl/algorithm.html (2016)

Coarrays in the Context of XcalableMP

Hidetoshi Iwashita and Masahiro Nakao

Abstract Coarray features have been implemented on the Omni XcalableMP compiler with a source-to-source translator and layered runtime libraries. Three memory allocation methods for coarrays were implemented for the GASNet and MPI-3 communication libraries and the native interface of Fujitsu. For the coarray PUT/GET communication, algorithms using DMA (zero-copy) and buffering were introduced. Important techniques for achieving high performance were the non-blocking PUT communication implemented in the runtime library and the optimization for the GET communication in the translator. Using the ping-pong benchmark and the modified version, the fundamental performance was evaluated and analyzed. The MPI version of the Himeno benchmark was ported to the coarray version and modified for fully using the non-blocking PUT. As a result of the evaluation, the non-blocking coarray version clearly outperformed the original and non-blocking MPI versions.

1 Introduction

XcalableMP (XMP) [1] has complementary global-view and local-view programming models. The former is a directive-based language extension to the base languages Fortran and C, and the latter adopts the coarray features defined in Fortran 2008 [2] and a part of the coarray features defined in Fortran 2018 [3]. The purpose of the coarray features as the local-view part of XMP is (1) writing applications that are not suitable for global-view programming and (2) writing important parts of programs that are critical to performance with an easier programming model than MPI message passing. Therefore, the coarray features in XMP must be naturally

H. Iwashita (✉)
Fujitsu Limited, Numazu-shi, Shizuoka, Japan
e-mail: iwashita.hideto@fujitsu.com

M. Nakao
RIKEN Center for Computational Science, Kobe, Hyogo, Japan
e-mail: masahiro.nakao@riken.jp

© The Author(s) 2021
M. Sato (ed.), *XcalableMP PGAS Programming Language*,
https://doi.org/10.1007/978-981-15-7683-6_3

merged into the global-view XMP language and must exhibit high performance, comparable to that of MPI.

The Omni XMP compiler is an open-source implementation developed at RIKEN and the University of Tsukuba [4]. The kernel of the Omni XMP compiler is a source-to-source compiler that converts an XMP program into a Fortran program by calling a runtime library. The coarray translator has been implemented on the Omni XMP compiler. Since the images are mapped one-to-one to XMP nodes, each image was implemented as a process, and the definition and reference to coarrays were implemented as inter-node one-sided communications.

This chapter describes the techniques used in the coarray compiler and the runtime library, and a comparison to MPI message passing. The remainder of this chapter is organized as follows. Section 2 introduces the requirements of the coarray features. Section 3 describes the implementation used to solve the requirements, and Sect. 4 evaluates the performance and productivity of coarray programs. Related research is described in Sect. 5, and Sect. 6 concludes this chapter.

2 Requirements from Language Specifications

The XMP Fortran language specification [1] supports many of the coarray features defined in the Fortran 2008 standard [2], and intrinsic procedures CO_SUM, CO_MAX, CO_MIN, and CO_BROADCAST defined in the Fortran 2018 standard [3] are supported. In addition, the XMP C language specification was extended to support coarray features.

This section introduces the coarray features and what is required of the compiler in order to implement the coarray features.

2.1 Images Mapped to XMP Nodes

In the Fortran standard, an **image** is defined as an instance of a program. Each image executes the same program and has its own individual data. Each image has a different image index k. While the Fortran standard itself does not specify where each image is executed, XMP specifies that images are mapped to executing nodes on a one-to-one basis. Therefore, image k is always executed on executing node k, where $1 \leq k \leq n$, and n is the number of images as well as the number of executing nodes. Since each MPI rank number of MPI_COMM_WORLD (0-origin) is always mapped to an XMP node number in order, image k corresponds to rank $(k - 1)$.

Note that the executing nodes can be a subset of the entire (initial) node set. For example, two distinct node sets can execute two coarray subprograms concurrently. The first executing images at the start of the program are entire images. Coarray features are compatible with those of the Fortran standard, unless the TASK and END TASK directives are used. If the execution encounters a TASK directive specified with a subset of nodes, then the corresponding subset of images will be the executing images for the task region. The current number of images and my image number, which are given by inquire functions `num_images` and `this_image` also match the executing images, and the `SYNC_IMAGES` statement synchronizes the executing images. When the execution encounters the `END TASK` directive corresponding to the `TASK` directive, the set of executing images is reinstated.

Requirement for the Implementation The runtime library should manage the executing image set and the current image index in a stack in order to reinstate them at the exit point of the task.

2.2 Allocation of Coarrays

A **coarray** or a coarray variable is a variable that can be referred from the other images. A coarray with the `ALLOCATABLE` attribute is called an **allocatable coarray**, and is otherwise called a non-allocatable coarray. A non-allocatable coarray may not be a pointer and must have an explicit shape and the `SAVE` attribute. In order to help intuitive understanding, we refer to a non-allocatable coarray a **static coarray**. The lifetime of a static coarray is throughout execution of the program on all images, even if the coarray is declared in a procedure called with a subset of images.

On the other hand, an allocatable coarray is allocated with the `ALLOCATE` statement and freed either explicitly with the `DEALLOCATE` statement or implicitly at the end of the scope in which the `ALLOCATE` statement is executed (**automatic deallocation**).

Static coarrays can be declared as scalar or array variables as follows:

```
real(8), save :: a(100,100)[*]
type(user_defined_type), save :: s[2,2,*]
```

The square brackets in the declaration distinguish coarray variables from other (non-coarray) variables. The declaration declares the virtual shape of the images, and the last dimension must be deferred (as '`*`').

Allocatable coarrays can be declared as follows:

```
real(8), allocatable :: b(:,:)[:]
type(user_defined_type), allocatable :: t[:,:,:]
```

A notable constraint is that at any synchronization point in program execution, coarrays must have the same dimensions (sizes of all axes) for all images (**symmetric memory allocation**). Therefore, a static coarray must have the same shape for all images during program execution, and an allocatable coarray must be allocated and deallocated collectively at the same time with the same dimensions for the executing images. Thanks to the symmetric memory allocation rule, all executing images can have the same symmetrical memory layout, which makes it possible to calculate the address of the remote coarray with no prior inter-image communication.

Requirement for the Implementation Static coarrays must be allocated and made accessible remotely before execution of the user program and made inaccessible remotely and be freed after execution of the user program. In contrast, allocatable coarrays must be allocated and made accessible remotely when the ALLOCATE statement is encountered and made inaccessible remotely and freed when the DEALLOCATE statement is encountered or the exit point of the scope to which the corresponding ALLOCATE statement is encountered.

2.3 Communication

Coarray features in XMP include three types of communications between images, i.e., reference and definition to remote coarrays, collective communications (intrinsic subroutines CO_SUM, CO_MAX, CO_MIN, and CO_BROADCAST), and atomic operations (ATOMIC_DEFINE and ATOMIC_REF). Collective communications and atomic operations are similar to those in MPI library. Communications for reference and definition to remote coarrays are characteristic for coarray features.

PUT communication is caused by an assignment statement with a **coindexed variable** as the left-hand side expression, e.g.,

```
a(i,j)[k] = alpha * b(i,j) + c(i,j)
```

This statement causes the PUT communication to the array element a(i,j) on image k with the value of the left-hand side. Using the Fortran array assignment statement, array-to-array PUT communication can be written easily, e.g., the following statement causes M×N-element PUT communication:

```
a(1:M,1:N)[k] = alpha * b(1:M,1:N) + c(1:M,1:N)
```

GET communication is caused by referencing the **coindexed object**, which is represented by a coarray variable with cosubscripts enclosed by square brackets, e.g., s[1,2] and a(i,j)[k], where s and a are scalar and two-dimensional array coarrays, respectively. A coindexed object can appear in almost any expression, including array expressions.

Requirement for the Implementation In order to implement definition/reference to a coindexed variable/object, PUT/GET one-sided communication is suitable for use. In order to avoid costly processing, such as a remote procedure call, remote direct memory access-based (RDMA-based) implementation is desirable. In PUT/GET communication for large data, redundant multiple memory copies should carefully be avoided for all software layers, the communication library, the runtime, the Fortran library, and the object.

2.4   Synchronization

The access order of coarrays between images is explicitly controlled by the programmer using the **image control statement**, such as SYNC ALL and SYNC IMAGES statements. The statement allows the compiler system to make PUT/GET communication asynchronous. The sequence of execution between the image control statements is called as a **segment**. An asynchronous communication must be completed by the end of the segment.

Inside each image, the compiler must maintain data dependency as before, even if the program contains coarray communications. The compiler must suppress the **non-blocking communication**, which postpones waiting for communication completion. In order to keep data dependency among the definitions and references to the same coarray in the same segment, non-blocking communication should be restricted. The example below in which the same remote coarray is accessed a number of times inside the same segment.

```
1        if (this_image()==1) then
2            a[2]=
3            =a[2]
4            a[2]=
5            a[2]=
6        endif
```

Between lines 2 and 3, the completion wait for PUT communication is necessary in order to avoid referencing data that is not defined completely. Similarly, between lines 3 and 4, the completion wait for GET communication is necessary in order to avoid referencing data that is being updated. However, between lines 4 and 5, the completion wait is not necessary. The issue of race condition on image 2 cannot be avoided by the completion wait on image 1 in general, and avoiding this issue is up to the programmer.

Requirement for the Implementation   Unless the same remote data is accessed from the same segment, non-blocking completion can be delayed until the end of the segment. Since the data received by the GET communication is usually referenced soon, non-blocking GET communication is hard to use. Therefore, if GET communication is always on blocking, then only the flow dependency (between lines 2 and 3) should be considered.

2.5   Subarrays and Data Contiguity

Except for a dummy argument, an array is fully **contiguous** across the dimensions. A subarray of the array can be fully or partially contiguous or non-contiguous. For example, if an array is declared with the shape a(1:M,1:N), then the whole array (referenced as a or a(:,:) or a(1:M,1:N)) is fully contiguous and a subarray a(2:5,3) is partially contiguous. We defined a term **contiguous length** as the length for which the data is partially contiguous. For example, the contiguous lengths of a(2,3) and a(2:5,3) are 1 and 4, respectively. a(1:M,1:3) is two-dimensionally contiguous and has contiguous length $2 \times M$. a(1:M-1,1:3) is one-dimensionally contiguous and has a contiguous length (M − 1).

Requirement for the Implementation For high-performance communication, it is important to find the contiguous length across the dimensions, because thousands of bytes of contiguous data is needed in order to be comparable to the communication latency in general, and only the first dimension of the array is not always long enough.

2.6 Coarray C Language Specifications

The XMP language specification extends the C language to support coarray features. Array notations, such as subarray and array assignment statements, are adopted in the C language. In XMP/C, a coarray is a data object but is not a pointer. A coarray is either (1) of basic type, (2) a structure in which no component is a pointer or (3) an array of 1, 2, or 3.

XMP/C also has static and allocatable coarrays. Coarray variables declared directly in the file and declared with the static attribute are static. Coarray variables can be allocated with intrinsic functions.

3 Implementation

3.1 Omni XMP Compiler Framework

The coarray translator was added to the Omni XMP compiler [4], as shown in Fig. 1. The Omni XMP compiler is a source-to-source translator that converts XMP programs into the base language (Fortran or C). The component "coarray translator" (CAF translator) is located in front of the XMP translator to solve coarray features previously. The output of the decompiler is a standard Fortran/C program, which may include calls to the XMP runtime library.

The following procedures are generated in advance or in the coarray translator to initialize static coarray variables prior to the execution of the user program:

- The built-in main program calls subroutine xmpf_traverse_init, the entry procedure of initialization subroutines, before executing the user main program.
- Subroutine xmpf_traverse_init is generated by the coarray translator to call initialization subroutines corresponding to all user-defined procedures.

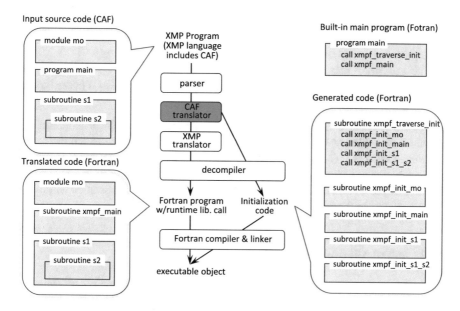

Fig. 1 XMP compiler and an example of coarray program compilation

- Each initialization subroutine `xmpf_init_foo` is generated from user-defined procedure *foo* by the coarray translator, which initializes all static coarrays declared in *foo*.

3.2 Allocation and Registration

In order to be accessed using the underlying communication library, the allocated coarray data must be registered to the library. The registration contains all actions to allow the data to be accessed from the other nodes, including pin-down memory, acquirement of the global address, and sharing information among all nodes.

3.2.1 Three Methods of Memory Management

The coarray translator and the runtime library implements three methods of memory management.

- The **runtime sharing (RS) method** allocates and registers a large memory for all static and dynamic coarrays at the initialization phase. The registered memory is shared by all static and allocatable coarrays.

- The **runtime allocation (RA) method** allocates and registers a large memory for all static coarrays at the initialization phase. The RA method also allocates and registers each allocatable coarray at runtime.
- The **compiler allocation (CA) method** allocates all coarray objects by the Fortran system (at compile time or at runtime), and the address is passed to the runtime library to be registered.

For the RS and RA methods, since the allocated memory address is determined in the runtime library, the object code must accept the address allocated inside the runtime system as an address of a regal Fortran variable. To make this connection, it was necessary to use the Cray pointer, which is not in the Fortran standard. In the case of the CA method, the runtime library accepts the address allocated in the Fortran system and registers to the communication library.

3.2.2 Initial Allocation for Static Coarrays

Static coarrays are allocated and registered in the initialization subroutines `xmpf_init_foo`.

In the RS and RA methods, static coarrays are initialized before execution of the user program, as follows.

- In the first pass, all sizes of static (non-allocatable) coarrays are summed. The size of each static coarray is evaluated form the lower and upper bounds specified in the dimension declaration statement of each coarray. The lower and upper bound expressions, possibly including binary and unary operations, references to names of constants, and basic intrinsic functions, such as min/max and sum, are evaluated by constant folding. Since the size of the structure that contains allocatable or pointer components differs depending on the target compiler, the coarray translator obtains the necessary parameters to calculate the size of structures at build time.
- Then, the total size of static coarrays is allocated and the address and size are registered to the underlying communication library.
- In the second pass, the addresses of all of the coarrays are calculated to share the registered data. Due to the language specification, the sizes of the same coarray are the same among all images (nodes). Therefore, the offset from the base address of the registered data for each coarray can be the same among all images.

In the RS method, allocatable coarrays also share the registered memory. The total size of the memory to be registered should be specified with an environment variable by the user. In the RA method, the total size is fully calculated by the runtime library, and no information is required of the user because allocatable coarrays will be dynamically allocated on the other memories.

In the CA method, the Fortran processor allocates each coarray, and the runtime library then registers the address. Each static coarray is converted into a common (external) variable to share between the user-defined procedure (say *foo*) and its initialization procedure (`xmpf_init_foo`). The data is statically allocated by the Fortran system in a manner similar to the usual common variable. The address is registered in the initialization procedure via the runtime library.

3.2.3 Runtime Allocation for Allocatable Coarrays

For the RS method, the runtime library has a memory management system for cutting out and retrieving memory for each allocation and deallocation of coarrays.

Figure 2 illustrates the memory allocation and registration for allocatable coarrays in the RA and CA methods.

These methods are properly used by the underlying communication library. For GASNet, only the RS method is adopted because its allocation function can be used only once in the program. For MPI-3, the CA method is not suitable because frequent allocation and deallocation of coarrays cause expensive creation

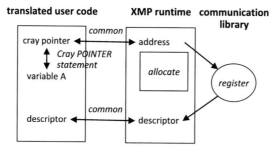

The runtime allocates and registers coarrays and passes the address to the user code.

(a)

The user code allocates coarrays and causes the runtime to register with the address.

(b)

Fig. 2 Memory allocation for coarrays in RA and CA methods. (**a**) RA method. (**b**) CA method

and freeing of MPI windows. In the case of FJ-RDMA, the RS method has no advantage over the other methods. Since the allocated address is used for registration to FJ-RDMA, no advantage was found for managing memory outside of the Fortran system. The unusual connection through the Cray pointer causes degradation of the Fortran compiler optimization.

3.3   PUT/GET Communication

In order to avoid disturbing the execution on the remote image, PUT and GET communications are always implemented using remote direct memory access (RDMA) provided by the communication library (except coarrays with pointer/allocatable structure components). In contrast, local data access is selective between using direct memory access (DMA) or using a local buffer. For the buffer scheme, one of the four algorithms will be chosen.

3.3.1   Determining the Possibility of DMA

Coarray variables must be registered when allocated to be the target of RDMA communication. In contrast, since the local data, which is the source of PUT or the destination of GET, was not registered or linked to registered information, the data could not be the target of DMA communication and had to be communicated via the registered buffer.

When the local data is an entire coarray or a part of coarray, the coarray must be registered, and efficient DMA-RDMA communication can be made. Since the analysis at compile time is limited, we implemented the detector in the runtime library using binary-tree search, as follows.

1. When a chunk of coarray data is registered to the communication library, the runtime library adds the set of the local address and the size to a sorted table called `SortedChunkTable`. The sort key is the local base address of the data.
2. When a chunk of coarray data is deregistered from the communication library, the runtime library deletes the record in `SortedChunkTable`.
3. When a PUT or GET runtime library is called corresponding to a reference/definition to a coindexed object/variable, the local address is searched in `SortedChunkTable` with binary search. The local data is already registered if $addr_i \leq addr < addr_i + size_i$ for any i, where $addr$ is the said local address and add_i and $size_i$ are the i-th address and size, respectively, in `SortedChunkTable`.

If the communication data is large, then the cost of procedure 3 is relatively small and is worth using. If the data is small, then the buffering algorithm, as shown in Sect. 3.3.2, may be better.

3.3.2 Buffering Communication Methods

For the buffer scheme, one of the four algorithms will be chosen depending on three parameters: the size of the local buffer B and the local and remote contiguous lengths N_L and N_R, respectively. Here, B should be large enough to ignore communication latency overhead and we use approximately 400 kilo-bytes by default. Unlike the case of MPI message passing, coarray PUT/GET communication requires only one local buffer for any number of other images. Both N_L and N_R can be evaluated at runtime. The Fortran syntax guarantees that N_L is a multiple of N_R or N_R is a multiple of N_L. An algorithm to obtain the contiguous length is shown in a previous paper [5].

Table 1 summarizes our algorithm for PUT/GET communication for five cases. The unit size is the chunk length of the PUT/GET communication. Case 0 shows the algorithm using RDMA-DMA PUT/GET communication, and Cases 1 through 4 show the algorithms using RDMA and local-buffering. Due to its strict condition, the DMA scheme is rarely used. In addition, this scheme is not always faster than the buffering scheme for Cases 2 and 3 because of the difference in the unit sizes. The advantage of Cases 2 and 3 is that the unit size is extended to a multiple of N_L by gathering a number of short contiguous data in the buffer, or by scattering from the buffer into a number of short contiguous data.

3.3.3 Non-blocking PUT Communication

For higher performance, the PUT communication should be non-blocking, and the completion wait should be delayed until the end of the segment. Writing and reading the same remote data from the same image in the same segment appears to be a very rare case, as described in Sect. 2.4. However, this is difficult to detect with

Table 1 Summary of the PUT/GET algorithm related to N_L, N_R, and B

Scheme	Case	Condition	Unit size
DMA		Local data is registered	$\min(N_L, N_R)$
Buffering	1	$N_R \leq B,\ N_R \leq N_L$	N_R
	2	$N_L < N_R \leq B$	N_R
	3	$N_L < B < N_R$	Multiple of N_L ($\leq B$)
	4	$B < N_R,\ B \leq N_L$	B (or less than B at last)

Scheme	Case	PUT action for each unit	GET action for each unit
DMA		Put once	Get once
Buffering	1	Buffer once, and put once	Get once, and unbuffer once
	2	Buffer for each N_L, and put once	Get once, and unbuffer for each N_L
	3	Buffer for each N_L, and put once	Get once, and unbuffer for each N_L
	4	Buffer once, and put once	Get once, and unbuffer once

low cost. Since the subscripts and image indices are often variable expressions, the compiler rarely selects non-blocking communication and usually generates safe but slow code. We do not have a reasonable solution for this issue.

In the current implementation, the user selects blocking or non-blocking for PUT communication at runtime with the environment variable.

3.3.4   Optimization of GET Communication

A reference to an array-coindexed object is converted to a call of a runtime library function that returns a Fortran array value. For example, array assignment statement:

```
b(j1:j2) = a(i1:i2)[k]
```

is converted to

```
b(j1:j2) = xmpf_coarray_get_generic(dp_a,k,a(i1:i2))
```

by the coarray translator, where dp_a is the descriptor of coarray a. The issue is that the result of the library function is an array value, which causes several memory copies. As a countermeasure, we optimized a specific but common case by the translator. If a coindexed object is only the right-hand side of an array assignment statement, then the entire assignment statement can be converted into a single library call. The above example satisfies this condition and so can be converted again as follows:

```
call xmpf_coarray_getsub_generic(dp_a,k,a(i1:i2),b(j1:j2))
```

In this runtime library subroutine, the variable b(j1:j2) is expected to be the local target of GET communication, instead of the local buffer that would be generated by the Fortran runtime.

3.4   Runtime Libraries

The layer of the runtime libraries is shown in Fig. 3. One of the three communication libraries is selected at the build time of the Omni compiler. The coarray runtime consists of three layered libraries. The **Fortran wrapper** mediates the arguments and the result value of the translated user program (written in Fortran) and the upper-layer runtime (ULR) (written in C). The **(ULR) library** performs the algorithms described above in this section. The **lower-layer runtime (LLR) library** abstracts the difference between the communication libraries, except for the memory management of coarray data.

Fig. 3 Software stack for coarray features

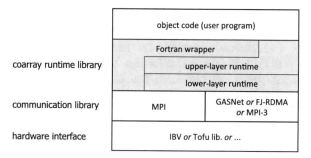

object code (user program)		
Fortran wrapper		
upper-layer runtime		
lower-layer runtime		
MPI	GASNet *or* FJ-RDMA *or* MPI-3	
IBV *or* Tofu lib. *or* ...		

coarray runtime library

communication library

hardware interface

3.4.1 Fortran Wrapper

Each set of Fortran wrapper procedures has a generic name and dozens of corresponding specific names. For example, the object code contains a call to a function with the generic name xmpf_coarray_get_generic. If the data is a two-dimensional array of the 16-byte complex type, the Fortran compiler selects the corresponding specific name xmpf_coarray_get2d_z16 at compile time and generates the object code by calling a ULR function by the specific name.

The Fortran wrapper accepts Fortran array notations as the arguments and the result variable and converts these notations into structures that can be handled in a runtime library written in C. The Fortran wrapper also converts a C pointer to a Fortran pointer with the shape using the Cray pointer.

The Fortran wrapper calls ULR procedures basically and calls MPI library functions directly for collective communications.

3.4.2 Upper-layer Runtime (ULR) Library

The major role of ULR is performing the algorithms for coarray data allocation/registration (Sect. 3.2) and PUT/GET communications (Sect. 3.3). Additionally, for atomic communications caused by intrinsic subroutines ATOMIC_DEFINE and ATOMIC_REF, ULR calls the corresponding function of LLR after address calculation.

3.4.3 Lower-layer Runtime (LLR) Library

The LLR basically abstracts the difference between the communication libraries. The only exception is the allocation and registration of coarray data. Major functions are shown below.

- Functions to allocate and register coarray variables, and functions to register coarray variables that are already allocated. They are alternatively used in the

RS and RA methods and in the CA method. Correspondingly, a set of functions to deregister and deallocate and a set of functions to deregister are provided.

- Fundamental functions for RDMA-DMA GET communication and DMA-RDMA PUT communication. It is assumed that both remote and local data are previously registered. Blocking and non-blocking can be switched.
- Functions corresponding to image control statements, atomic subroutines, and inquire functions.

The LLR also has the features for multi-dimensional data developed for the C implementation, which are not used in the Fortran implementation because this implementation is solved in ULR.

3.4.4   Communication Libraries

MPI-3 can be selected for all platforms on which it is implemented. Coarrays are registered and deregistered at the start and end point of the MPI window. Coarrays perform one-sided communication by MPI_Put and MPI_Get and are synchronized by MPI_Win_fence. Implementation on MPI incurs certain costs for dynamic allocation of coarrays and waiting for communication completion.

GASNet can be selected for more advanced implementation over InfiniBand. Since allocation and registration of are inseparable and can be performed only once on GASNet, the implementation allocates and registers a pool of memory, the size of which should be large enough to contain all static and allocatable coarrays. The XMP runtime should allocate and deallocate coarrays without using the Fortran library but using the memory manager constructed for the pool.

FJ-RDMA can be selected for the implementation over the Tofu interconnection of the K computer and Fujitsu PRIMEHPC FX series supercomputers. Basically, each coarray is allocated by the Fortran library and the address is registered with the FJ-RDMA interface FJMPI_Rdma_reg_mem. The address is deregistered with FJMPI_Rdma_dereg_mem before being deallocated (freed) by the Fortran library. One-sided communication is performed with FJMPI_Rdma_put and FJMPI_Rdma_get.

4   Evaluation

We evaluated the Omni XMP coarray compiler in the environments shown in Table 2.

Table 2 Specifications of the computers and evaluation environment

	RIKEN RCCS The K computer	RIKEN RCCS HOKUSAI GreatWare Fujitsu PRIMEHPC FX100	CCS, University of Tsukuba HA-PACS/TCA
CPU	SPARK64™VIIIfx, 2 GHz, 128 Gflop/s, 8-core, 1 CPU/node	SPARK64™XIfx, 1.975 GHz, 1 CPU/node, 4-SIMD × 32-core	E5-2680 v2 (Ivy Bridge), 10-core, 224 Gflop/s, 2 CPU/node
Memory	16 GB/node,	32 GB/node,	128 GB/node,
	Bandwidth 64 GB/s	Bandwidth 480 GB/s	119.4 GB/s
Interconnect	Tofu	Tofu2, 12.5 GB/s × 2	InfiniBand FDR, 7 GB/s
Coarray	Omni XcalableMP 1.3.1	Omni XcalableMP 1.3.1	Omni XcalableMP 1.3.1
Fortran	Fujitsu Fortran 2.0.0	Fujitsu Fortran 2.0.0	Intel Fortran 16.0.4
MPI	Fujitu MPI 2.0.0	Fujitu MPI 2.0.0	Intel MPI 5.1.3
Comm. layer	Tofu library	Tofu library	GASNet 1.24.2 (IBV-conduit, built with Intel compilers)

Table 3 Ping-pong codes

	PUT version	GET version	MPI version

Ping
phase
	if (me == 1) then
	  x(1:n)[2] = x(1:n)
	  sync images(2)
	else if (me == 2) then
	  sync images(1)
	end if
		if (me == 1) then
		  sync images(1)
		else if (me == 2) then
		  x(1:n) = x(1:n)[1]
		  sync images(1)
		end if
			if (id == 0) then
			  call MPI_Send(x, n, … 1, …)
			else if (id == 1) then
			  call MPI_Recv(x, n, … 0, …)
			end if

Pong
phase
	if (me == 1) then
	  sync images(2)
	else if (me == 2) then
	  x(1:n)[1] = x(1:n)
	  sync images(1)
	end if
		if (me == 1) then
		  x(1:n) = x(1:n)[2]
		  sync images(2)
		else if (me == 2) then
		  sync images(1)
		end if
			if (id == 0) then
			  call MPI_Recv(x, n, … 1, …)
			else if (id == 1) then
			  call MPI_Send(x, n, … 0, …)
			end if

me is the image index, id is the MPI rank number

4.1 Fundamental Performance

Using the EPCC Fortran Coarray micro-benchmark [6], we evaluated the ping-pong performance of PUT and GET communications compared with MPI_Send/Recv. The codes are briefly shown in Table 3.

Corresponding to the codes in Table 3, Fig. 4 shows how data and messages are exchanged between two images or processes. In coarray PUT (a) and GET (b), inter-image synchronization is necessary for each end of the phases to make the passive image active and to make the active image passive. Whereas in MPI message passing (c) and (d), such synchronization is not necessary because both processes are always active. On the other hand, MPI message passing has its own overhead that coarray PUT/GET does not have. Since the eager protocol (c) does not use RDMA, the

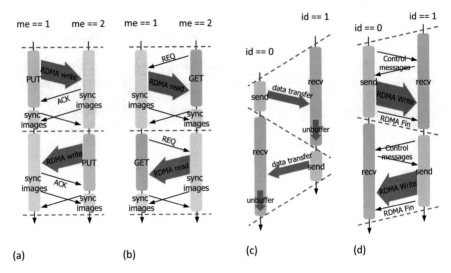

Fig. 4 Diagrams for ping-pong codes. (**a**) Coarray PUT. (**b**) Coarray GET. (**c**) MPI send/recv eager protocol. (**d**) MPI send/recv Rendezvous protocol

receiver must copy the received data in the local buffer to the target. The larger the data, the greater the overhead cost. In the rendezvous protocol (d), negotiations, including remote address notification, are required prior to communication. The overhead cost is not negligible when the data is small.

The result of the comparison between coarray PUT/GET and MPI message passing is shown in Fig. 5. As the underlying communication libraries, FJ-RDMA and MPI-3 are used on FX100 and GASNet. And MPI-3 is used on HA-PACS. GET (a) and GET (b) use the code without and with the optimization described in Sect. 3.3.4, respectively. Bandwidth is the communication data size per elapsed time, and latency is half of the ping-pong elapsed time. The difference between GET (a) and GET (b) is the compile time optimization level of the coarray translator described in Sect. 3.3.4.

The following was found regarding coarray PUT/GET communication.

Bandwidth　Coarray PUT and GET slightly outperforms MPI rendezvous communication for large data on FJ-RDMA and MPI-3. On FJ-RDMA/FX100 (a), the bandwidths of PUT and GET (b) are, respectively, +0.1% to +18% and -0.4% to +9.3% higher than MPI rendezvous in the rendezvous range of 32k through 32M bytes. In addition, on MPI-3 and/or HA-PACS, the bandwidths of PUT and GET are, respectively, +0.3% to +0.8% and +0.1% to +1.3% higher in the rendezvous range of 512k through 32M bytes. Based on the runtime log, zero-copy communication was confirmed to have been performed both in PUT and GET (b) by selecting the DMA scheme described in Sect. 3.3.1.

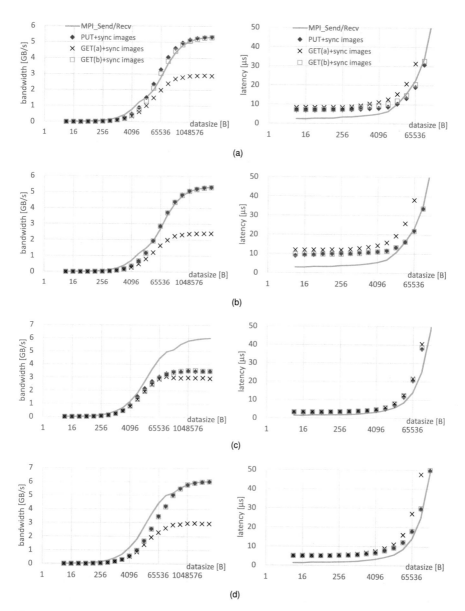

Fig. 5 Ping-pong performance on Fujitsu PRIMEHPC FX100 and HA-PACS/TCA. (**a**) FJ-RDMA/FX100 (CA-method). (**b**) MPI-3/FX100 (RA-method). (**c**) GASNet/HA-PACS (RS-method). (**d**) MPI-3/HA-PACS (RS-method)

However, on GASNet/HA-PACS (c), PUT and GET (b) were only approximately 60% of the bandwidth of MPI rendezvous for a large amount of data. It is presumed that data copy was caused internally.

Latency On FJ-RDMA (a) and MPI-3 (b) and (d), PUT and GET (b) have larger (worse) latency than MPI eager communication in the range of $\leq$16kB on FX100 and $\leq$256kB on HA-PACS.

Coarray on GASNet (c) behaves differently than other cases on (a), (b), and (d). Although the latency is larger than that for MPI for all data sizes, the difference is smaller than in the other cases. At a data size of 8B, the latency of PUT is 2.93 μs and 2.1 times larger than the one of MPI while 5.73μs and 3.7 times larger for the case of MPI-3 (d).

Effect of GET optimization For all ranges in all cases, GET (a) has a smaller bandwidth and a larger latency than GET (b). On FJ-RDMA (a), the bandwidth is 1.41 to 1.85 times improved in the range of 32kB to 32MB by changing the object code of GET (a) to GET (b). We found GET (a) caused two extra memory copies. One copy performs the array assignment by the Fortran library, and the other copy is from the communication buffer to the result variable of the array function `xmpf_coarray_get_generic`. The optimization described in Sect. 3.3.4 eliminated these two data copies.

The large latency of coarray PUT/GET communication is problematic. In the next subsection, we discuss how this problem should be solved by the compiler and the programming.

4.2 Non-blocking Communication

For latency hiding, asynchronous and non-blocking features can be expected in coarray PUT communication. The principle is shown in Fig. 6.

Figure 6a shows the half pattern of the ping-pong PUT communication. Coarray one-sided communication is basically asynchronous, unless synchronization is explicitly specified. Therefore, multiple communications without synchronization, as shown in (b), are closer to actual applications. In addition, coarray one-sided communication can be optimized using non-blocking communication, as shown in (c). Blocking and non-blocking communications can be switched with the runtime environment variable in the current implementation of the Omni compiler. In MPI message passing, non-blocking communication can be written with `MPI_Isend`, `MPI_Irecv`, and `MPI_Wait`.

Figure 7 compares blocking/non-blocking coarray PUT and MPI message passing communications. The two original graphs are the same as those of Fig. 5a. Four other graphs display the results of the eight-variable ping-pong program, which repeats the ping phase, sending eight individual variables from one to the other in order, and, similarly, the pong phase in the opposite direction. Each block size indicates the size of variables, and latency includes the time for eight variables.

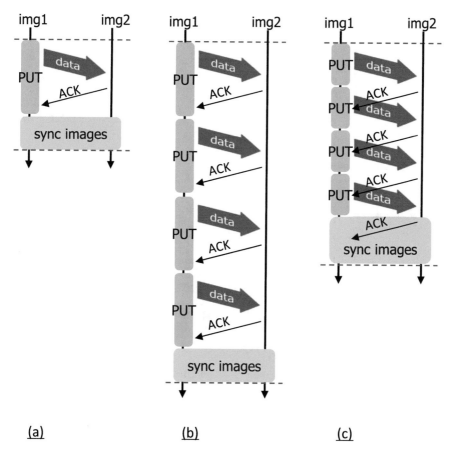

Fig. 6 Blocking and non-blocking PUT communications. (**a**) 1-variable/blocking. (**b**) *n*-variable/blocking. (**c**) *n*-variable/non-blocking

The following was found from the results:

- Non-blocking PUT significantly improves the latency of PUT communication. From 8 B to 8 kB, the latency of non-blocking PUT communication is 4.63 times faster on average than blocking PUT. Compared to the original PUT, from 8 B to 8 kB, it performs communication eight times for a period of time 2.11 times longer, on average. Hiding completion wait behind communication (Fig. 6c) greatly improves the performance.
- Reduction of synchronization (Fig. 6b) itself does not improve the performance. Compared to the original blocking PUT, eight-variable blocking PUT has 9.5–10.1 times larger latency for a data set that is eight times larger.

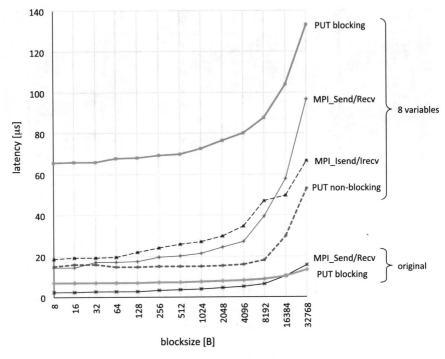

Fig. 7 Eight-variable ping-pong latency on PRIMEHPC FX100

- Unless data size exceeds approximately 8 kB, the latency of non-blocking PUT does not depend on the amount of data. The graph of non-blocking PUT is very flat, within ±4%, over the range from 8 B to 4 kB.
- MPI eager communication has no effect on non-blocking for latency hiding. The eager protocol, including the unbuffering process of the receiver, appears not to be suitable for non-buffering.
- Non-blocking coarray PUT outperforms MPI eager message passing, except for very fine grain data. The latency of eight-variable non-blocking PUT is −9% to 54% and 18% to 61%, as compared to eight-variable blocking and non-blocking MPI eager, respectively. At only two plots for 8 B and 16 B, the non-blocking PUT is 4% and 9% slower than the values for blocking MPI. Otherwise, non-blocking PUT is faster than MPI eager, and the more block size, the larger difference in the latency.

4.3   Application Program

The Himeno benchmark is a part of the 2D Poisson equation solver using the Jacobi iteration method [7]. The MPI version of the Himeno benchmark is a strong scaling program distributing up to three-dimensional nodes. The K computer shown in Table 2 was used in this evaluation.

4.3.1   Coarray Version of the Himeno Benchmark

For comparison, we prepared the following three versions of Himeno programs.

MPI/original   The original MPI version of Himeno benchmark was used as a two-dimensionally distributed in the y and z axes. The x axis was automatically SIMD-vectorized by the Fortran compiler. The program executes the computation and communication parts repetitively. The communication part consists of two steps: z-axis direction communication and y-axis direction communication, as shown in Fig. 8a. Each communication is written with non-blocking MPI message passing and completion wait at the end of each step.

MPI/non-blocking   The two-step communication was replaced by non-blocking scrambled communication, as shown in Fig. 8b. With this replacement, the

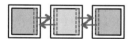

Step 1: exchange data with nodes on
both sides in the z direction

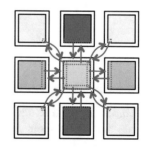

Exchange data with all 8 adjacent
nodes at once

Step2: exchange data with nodes on
both sides in the y direction

(a)   (b)

Fig. 8 Two algorithms of stencil communication in the Himeno benchmark. (**a**) Original MPI version. (**b**) Non-blocking MPI and coarray versions

number of communications increases from four to eight per node, but all communications become independent and can be non-blocking.

Coarray PUT/non-blocking   The communication pattern is the same as that of MPI/non-blocking. The data was declared as a coarray, and each communication was written with a coarray PUT, i.e., an assignment statement with coindexed variable as the left-hand side. Since the right-hand side of the statement is a reference to the same variable as the left-hand side coarray, the PUT communication was converted to zero-copy DMA-RDMA communication.

4.3.2   Measurement Result

Figure 9 shows the measurement results for Himeno sizes M, L, and XL, executed on 1×1, 2×2, 4×4, $\cdots$, 32×32 nodes on the K computer. The following results were obtained:

- PUT non-blocking was the fastest at 76% of the measurement points of the graph. On 1024 nodes, PUT non-blocking is 1.2%, 27%, and 42% faster than MPI original for sizes M, L, and XL, respectively.
- As a result of analyzing the contents of elapsed time, it was confirmed that the difference in the performance is caused by the difference in communication time. As shown in (b) and (c), the communication times of PUT non-blocking are 56% and 51% of those of MPI blocking on 256 nodes on L and XL Himeno sizes, respectively.
- MPI non-blocking is not always faster than the MPI original. The effect of non-blocking seems to be limited in MPI.

4.3.3   Productivity

Table 4 compares the scale of the source codes. The following features can be found.

- PUT blocking requires fewer characters for programming, especially in subroutines `initcomm` and `initmax`. The MPI programmer must describe the Cartesian coordinates to represent neighboring nodes in `initcomm`, and must declare MPI vector types to describe the communication pattern in `initmax`. In contrast, the coarray programmer easily represents neighboring images with coindex notation, e.g., `[i,j-1,k]`, and communication patterns with subarray notations, e.g., `p(1:imax, 1:jmax, 1)`.
- The Fortran statement of the MPI program tends to be longer than that of coarray. Since, comparing PUT non-blocking to MPI non-blocking, the number of characters is one third while the number of statements is almost the same. This means that the coarray program is more compact than the MPI program for each statement. MPI library functions often require long sequences of arguments.

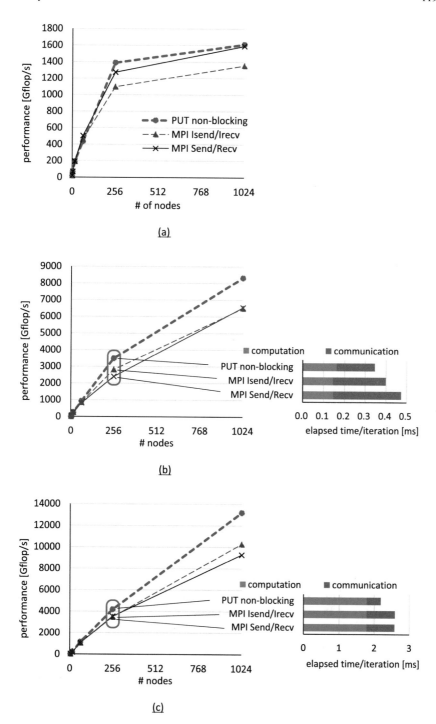

Fig. 9 Results for Himeno benchmarks. (**a**) Himeno size-M ($256 \times 128 \times 128$). (**b**) Himeno size-L ($512 \times 256 \times 256$). (**c**) Himeno size-XL ($1024 \times 512 \times 512$)

Table 4 Source code scales for the Himeno benchmark

Subroutine	MPI original			MPI non-blocking			PUT non-blocking		
	LOC	SOC	Chars	LOC	SOC	chars	LOC	SOC	Chars
Jacobi	50	33	1546	50	32	1546	43	31	1314
Initcomm	65	39	1724	80	54	2380	19	19	421
Initmax	95	77	2336	115	85	2939	71	71	1584
Sendp	152	59	3724	299	91	7617	96	96	2435
Others	248	225	5872	250	227	5923	232	231	5276
Total	610	433	15,202	794	489	29,495	461	448	11,030

LOC: Number of lines of codes excluding comment and empty lines
SOC: Number of Fortran statements, which may span multiple lines
chars: Number of characters excluding those in comment lines

5 Related Work

The University of Rice has implemented coarray features with their own extension called CAF2.0 [8]. CAF2.0 is a source-to-source compiler based on the ROSE compiler. GASNet is used as its communication layer. Similarly to our RS and RA methods, the Cray pointer is used to pass the data allocated in C to Fortran. Houston University developed UH-CAF on the Open64-base OpenUH compiler [9]. UH-CAF supports the coarray features defined in the Fortran 2008 standard. As the communication layer, GASNet and ARMCI can be used selectively. OpenCoarrays is an open-source software project [10]. OpenCoarrays is a library that can be used with GNU Fortran (gfortran) V5.1 or later and supports the coarray features specified in Fortran 2008 and a part of Fortran 2018. As the communication layer, MPICH and GASNet can be used selectively. In the vendors, Cray and Intel fully support and Fujitsu partially supports the coarray features specified in Fortran 2008.

In the latest Fortran standard, Fortran 2018, a subset of coarrays is referred to as a team. It is similar to the executing images in the term of XMP, but does not affect the parallel execution among images.

While non-blocking PUT communication is effective, non-blocking GET communication is difficult to put into practical use because the acquired data is used immediately. Cray has the directive extension for prefetching a remote coarray corresponding to the GET communication.

Coarray C++ is a coarray implementation in C++. The coarray features are implemented with the template library, unlike XMP/C, which is based on the C language.

6 Conclusion

This chapter described the coarray features in the context of XMP and the characteristic implementation of the coarray translator.

For memory allocation and registration, the RS, RA, and CA methods were implemented corresponding to the communication library GASNet, FJ-RDMA, and MPI-3.

For the coarray PUT and GET communications, DMA and four buffering methods were described. The effect of the non-blocking PUT communication was analyzed, and the knowledge is used to make the coarray version of the Himeno benchmark from the original MPI version. The measurement results on 1024 nodes of the K computer, the coarray version is 27% and 42% faster than the original MPI version for Himeno sizes L and XL, respectively. The effect of the optimization of GET communication was also obvious on the ping-pong benchmark on HA-PACS/TCA and Fujitsu PRIMEHPC FX100.

As an evaluation of productivity, the coarray program uses fewer than half as many characters as the MPI message passing program to write the same algorithm as the Himeno benchmark.

Acknowledgments The present research used the computational resources of HA-PACS provided by the Interdisciplinary Computational Science Program at the Center for Computational Sciences at the University of Tsukuba.

The results were obtained in part using the K computer at the RIKEN Advanced Institute for Computational Science.

References

1. XcalableMP Language Specification, http://xcalablemp.org/specification.html
2. J. Reid, JKR Associates, UK. Coarrays in the next Fortran Standard. ISO/IEC JTC1/SC22/WG5 N1824, April 21, 2010
3. ISO/IEC TS 18508:2015, Information technology – Additional Parallel Features in Fortran, Technical Specification, December 1, 2015
4. Omni Compiler Project, http://omni-compiler.org
5. H. Iwashita, M. Nakao, M. Sato, Preliminary implementation of coarray Fortran translator based on Omni XcalableMP, in *PGAS2015, Proceedings of 9th International Conference on PGAS Programming Models*, Washington, DC (2015), pp.70–75
6. EPCC Fortran Coarray micro-benchmark suite, https://www.epcc.ed.ac.uk/research/computing/performance-characterisation-and-benchmarking/epcc-co-array-fortran-micro
7. Himeno Benchmark, http://accc.riken.jp/en/supercom/himenobmt/
8. J. Mellor-Crummey, L. Adhianto, W.N. Scherer III, G. Jin, *PGAS'09, 3rd Conference on Partitioned Global Address Space Programming Models*, Ashburn, VA (2009)

9. D. Eachempati, H.J. Jun, B. Chapman, An open-source compiler and runtime implementation for coarray Fortran, in *PGAS'10, 4th Conference on Partitioned Global Address Space Programming Models, No.13* (2010)
10. A. Fanfarillo, T. Burnus, V. Cardellini, S. Filippone, D. Nagle, D. Rouson, OpenCoarrays: open-source transport layers supporting coarray Fortran compilers, in *PGAS'14, Proc. of 8th International Conference on Partitioned Global Address Space Programming Models, No. 4* (2014)

XcalableACC: An Integration of XcalableMP and OpenACC

Akihiro Tabuchi, Hitoshi Murai, Masahiro Nakao, Tetsuya Odajima, and Taisuke Boku

Abstract XcalableACC (XACC) is an extension of XcalableMP for accelerated clusters. It is defined as a diagonal integration of XcalableMP and OpenACC, which is another directive-based language designed to program heterogeneous CPU/accelerator systems. XACC has features for handling distributed-memory parallelism, inherited from XMP, offloading tasks to accelerators, inherited from OpenACC, and two additional functions: data/work mapping among multiple accelerators and direct communication between accelerators.

1 Introduction

This chapter describes the specification of XACC (XACC) which is an extension of XMP version 1.3 [2] and OpenACC version 2.5 [3]. XACC provides a parallel programming model for accelerated clusters which are distributed memory systems equipped with accelerators.

In this chapter, terminologies of XMP and OpenACC are indicated by **bold font**. For details, refer to each specification [2, 3].

The work on XACC and the Omni XcalableACC compiler was supported by the Japan Science and Technology Agency, Core Research for Evolutional Science and Technology program entitled "Research and Development on Unified Environment of Accelerated Computing and Interconnection for Post-Petascale Era" in the

A. Tabuchi
Fujitsu Laboratories Ltd., Kawasaki, Kanagawa, Japan

H. Murai · M. Nakao (✉) · T. Odajima
RIKEN Center for Computational Science, Kobe, Hyogo, Japan
e-mail: h-murai@riken.jp; masahiro.nakao@riken.jp; tetsuya.odajima@riken.jp

T. Boku
Center for Computationl Sciences, University of Tsukuba, Tsukuba, Ibaraki, Japan
e-mail: taisuke@ccs.tsukuba.ac.jp

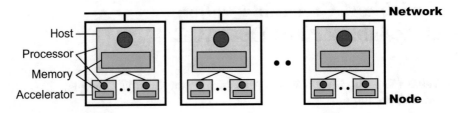

Fig. 1 Hardware model

research area of "Development of System Software Technologies for Post-Peta Scale High Performance Computing."

1.1 Hardware Model

The target of XACC is an accelerated cluster, a hardware model of which is shown in Fig. 1.

An execution unit is called **node** as with XMP. Each **node** consists of a single host and multiple accelerators (such as GPUs and Intel MICs). Each host has a processor, which may have several cores, and own local memory. Each accelerator also has them. Each **node** is connected with each other via network. Each **node** can access its local memories directly and remote memories, that is, the memories of another **node** indirectly. In a host, the accelerator memory may be physically and/or virtually separate from the host memory as with the memory model of OpenACC. Thus, a host may not be able to read or write the accelerator memory directly.

1.2 Programming Model

XACC is a directive-based language extension based on Fortran 90 and ISO C90 (ANSI C90). To develop applications on accelerated clusters with ease, XACC extends XMP and OpenACC independently as follows: (1) XMP extensions are to facilitate cooperation between XMP and OpenACC directives. (2) OpenACC extensions are to deal with multiple accelerators.

1.2.1 XMP Extensions

In a program using the XMP extensions, XMP, OpenACC, and XACC directives are used. Figure 2 shows a concept of the XMP extensions.

XMP directives define a **template** and a **node set**. The **template** represents a global index space, which is distributed onto the **node set**. Moreover, XMP

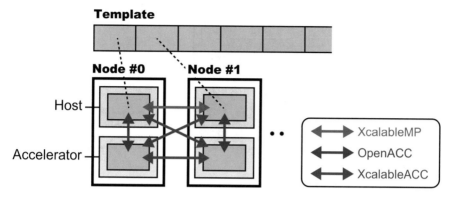

Fig. 2 Concept of XMP extensions

directives declare **distributed arrays,** parallelize loop statements, and transfer data among host memories according to the distributed **template**. OpenACC directives transfer the **distributed arrays** between host memory and accelerator memory on the same **node** and execute the loop statements parallelized by XMP on accelerators in parallel. XACC directives, which are XMP communication directives with an acc clause, transfer data among accelerator memories and between accelerator memory and host memory on different **nodes**. Moreover, **coarray** features also transfer data on different nodes.

Note that the XMP extensions are not a simple combination of XMP and OpenACC. For example, if you represent communication of **distributed array** among accelerators shown in Fig. 2 by the combination of XMP and OpenACC, you need to specify explicitly communication between host and accelerator by OpenACC and that between hosts by XMP. Moreover, you need to calculate manually indices of the **distributed array** owned by each **node**. By contrast, XACC directives can represent such communication among accelerators directly using global indices.

1.2.2   OpenACC Extensions

The OpenACC extension can represent offloading works and data to multiple-accelerators on a **node**. Figure 3 shows a concept of the OpenACC extension.

OpenACC extension directive defines a **device set**. The **device set** represents a set of devices on a **node**. Futher, OpenACC extension directives declare **distributed arrays** on the **device set** while maintaining the arrays on the host memory, and the directives distribute offloading loop statement and memory copy between host and device memories for the **distributed-arrays**. Moreover, OpenACC extension directives synchronize devices among the **device set**. XACC directives also transfer data between device memories on the **node**.

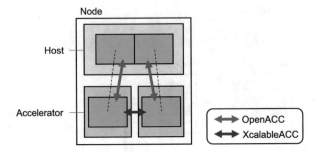

Fig. 3 Concept of OpenACC extension

1.3 Execution Model

The execution model of XACC is a combination of those of XMP and OpenACC. While the execution model of a host CPU programming is based on that of XMP, that of an accelerator programming is based on that of OpenACC. Unless otherwise specified, each **node** behaves exactly as specified in the XMP specification[2] or the OpenACC specification[3].

An XACC program execution is based on the SPMD model, where each **node** starts execution from the same main routine and keeps executing the same code independently (i.e. asynchronously), which is referred to as the replicated execution until it encounters an XMP construct or an XMP-extension construct. In particular, the XMP-extension construct may allocate, deallocate, or transfer data on accelerators. An OpenACC construct or an OpenACC-extension construct may define **parallel regions**, such as work-sharing loops, and offloads it to accelerators under control of the host.

When a **node** encounters a loop construct targeted by a combination of XMP `loop` and OpenACC `loop` directives, it executes the loop construct in parallel with other **accelerators**, so that each iteration of the loop construct is independently executed by the **accelerator** where a specified data element resides.

When a **node** encounters a XACC synchronization or a XACC communication directive, synchronization or communication occurs between it and other accelerators. That is, such **global constructs** are performed collectively by the **current executing nodes**. Note that neither synchronizations nor communications occur without these constructs specified.

1.4 Data Model

There are two classes of data in XACC: **global data** and **local data** as with XMP. Data declared in an XACC program are local by default. Both **global data** and **local**

data can exist on host memory and accelerator memory. About the data models of host memory and accelerator memory, refer to the OpenACC specification[3].

Global data are ones that are distributed onto the **executing node set** by the `align` directive. Each fragment of a **global data** is allocated in host memory of a **node** in the **executing node set**. OpenACC directives can transfer the fragment from host memory to accelerator memory.

Local data are all of the ones that are not global. They are replicated in the local memory of each of the **executing nodes**.

A **node** can access directly only **local data** and sections of **global data** that are allocated in its local memory. To access data in remote memory, explicit communication must be specified in such ways as the global communication constructs and the **coarray** assignments.

Particularly in XcalableACC Fortran, for common blocks that include any global variables, the ways how the storage sequence of them is defined and how the storage association of them is resolved are implementation-dependent.

2 XcalableACC Language

XACC is roughly defined as a diagonal integration of XMP and OpenACC with some additional XACC extensions, where XMP directives are for specifying distributed-memory parallelism, OpenACC for offloading, and the extensions for other XACC-specific features.

The syntax and semantics of XMP and OpenACC directives appearing in XACC codes follow those in XMP and OpenACC, respectively, unless specified below.

2.1 Data Mapping

Global arrays distributed with XMP directives can be globally-indexed in OpenACC constructs. **Global arrays** may appear in the `update`, `enter data`, `exit data`, `host_data`, `cache`, and `declare` directives; and the data clauses such as `deviceptr`, `present`, `copy`, `copyin`, `copyout`, `create`, and `delete`. When data transfer of a **global array** between host and accelerator memory is specified by an OpenACC directive, it is performed locally for the local section of the array within each node.

Example

In lines 2–6 of Fig. 4, the directives declare **global arrays** a and b. In line 8, the `enter data` directive transfers a section of a from host memory to accelerator

```
 _____ XcalableACC Fortran _____          _____ XcalableACC C _____
 integer :: a(N), b(N)                       int a[N], b[N];
 !$xmp template t(N)                          #pragma xmp template t[N]
 !$xmp nodes p(*)                             #pragma xmp nodes p[*]
 !$xmp distribute t(block) onto p             #pragma xmp distribute t[block] onto p
5 !$xmp align a(i) with t(i)                  #pragma xmp align a[i] with t[i]      5
 !$xmp align b(i) with t(i)                   #pragma xmp align b[i] with t[i]
 ...                                          ...
 !$acc enter data copyin(a(1:K))              #pragma acc enter data copyin(a[0:K])
 !$acc data copy(b)                           #pragma acc data copy(b)
10 ...                                         { ...                                10
```

Fig. 4 XACC code with `enter_data` directive

memory. Note that a is globally-indexed. In line 9, the `data` directive transfers the whole of b from host memory to accelerator memory.

2.2 Work Mapping

In order to parallelize a loop statement among nodes and on accelerators, the XMP `loop` directive and OpenACC `loop` directive are used. While an XMP `loop` directive parallelizes a loop statement among nodes, an OpenACC `loop` directive further parallelizes the loop statement on accelerators within each node. For ease of writing, the nesting order of XMP `loop` directive and OpenACC `loop` directive does not matter.

When an `acc` clause appears in an XMP loop directive with a `reduction` clause, the directive performs a reduction operation for the variable specified in the `reduction` clause on accelerator memory.

Restriction

- In an OpenACC **compute region**, no XMP directives except for `loop` directive without `reduction` clauses is allowed.
- In an OpenACC **compute region**, the parameter (i.e., the lower bound, upper bound, and step) of the target loop must remain unchanged.
- An `acc` clause can be specified in an XMP loop directive only when a `reduction` clause is also specified.

Example 1

In lines 2–6 of Fig. 5, the directives declare **global arrays** a and b. In line 8, the `copy` clause on the `parallel` directive transfers a and b from host memory

```
  _____ XcalableACC Fortran _____       _____ XcalableACC C _____
  integer :: a(N), b(N)                       int a[N], b[N];
  !$xmp template t(N)                          #pragma xmp template t[N]
  !$xmp nodes p(*)                             #pragma xmp nodes p[*]
  !$xmp distribute t(block) onto p            #pragma xmp distribute t[block] onto p
5 !$xmp align a(i) with t(i)                   #pragma xmp align a[i] with t[i]       5
  !$xmp align b(i) with t(i)                   #pragma xmp align b[i] with t[i]
  ...                                          ...
  !$acc parallel loop copy(a, b)              #pragma acc parallel loop copy(a, b)
  !$xmp loop on t(i)                           #pragma xmp loop on t[i]
10 do i=0, N                                   for(int i=0;i<N;i++){              10
     b(i) = a(i)                                 b[i] = a[i];
  end do                                       }
  !$acc end parallel
```

Fig. 5 XACC code with OpenACC `loop` construct

to accelerator memory. In lines 8–9, the `parallel` directive and XMP `loop` directive parallelize the following loop on an accelerator within a node and among nodes, respectively.

Example 2

In lines 2–5 of Fig. 6, the directives declare a **global array** a. In line 7, the `copy` clause on the `parallel` directive transfers a and a variable `sum` from host memory to accelerator memory. In lines 7–8, the `parallel` directive and XMP `loop` directive parallelize the following loop on an accelerator within a **node** and in among nodes, respectively. After finishing the calculation of the loop, the OpenACC `reduction` clause and the XMP `reduction` clause with `acc` in lines 7–8 perform a reduction operation for `sum` first on the accelerator within a node and then among all **nodes**.

2.3 Data Communication and Synchronization

When an `acc` clause is specified in an XMP's communication and synchronization directive, the directive works for the data on accelerator memory to transfer it.

The `acc` clause can be specified on the following XMP's communication and synchronization directives:

- `reflect`
- `gmove`
- `barrier`
- `reduction`
- `bcast`
- `wait_async`

```
─────────────────────── XcalableACC Fortran ───────────────────
   integer :: a(N), sum = 10
   !$xmp template t(N)
   !$xmp nodes p(*)
   !$xmp distribute t(block) onto p
 5 !$xmp align a(i) with t(i)
   ...
   !$acc parallel loop copy(a, sum) reduction(+:sum)
   !$xmp loop on t(i) reduction(+:sum) acc
   do i=0, N
10   sum = sum + a(i)
   end do
   !$acc end parallel loop
─────────────────────────── XcalableACC C ─────────────────────
   int a[N], sum = 10;
   #pragma xmp template t[N]
   #pragma xmp nodes p[*]
   #pragma xmp distribute t[block] onto p
 5 #pragma xmp align a[i] with t[i]
   ...
   #pragma acc parallel loop copy(a, sum) reduction(+:sum)
   #pragma xmp loop on t[i] reduction(+:sum) acc
   for(int i=0;i<N;i++){
10   sum += a[i];
   }
```

Fig. 6 XACC code with OpenACC `loop` construct with `reduction` clause

Note that while a `gmove` directive with `acc` and **coarray** features can perform communication both between accelerators and between accelerator and host memory that may be on different **nodes**, other directives with `acc` can perform communication only between accelerators.

Example

In lines 2–5 of Fig. 7, the directives declare a **global array** a. In line 6, the `shadow` directive allocates the shadow areas of a. In line 8, the `enter data` directive transfers a with the shadow areas from host memory to accelerator memory. In line 9, the `reflect` directive updates the shadow areas of the **distributed array** a on accelerator memory on all nodes.

2.4 Coarrays

In XACC, programmers can specify one-sided communication (i.e., put and get operation) for data on accelerator memory using **coarray** features. A combination of

```
─────── XcalableACC Fortran ───────      ────── XcalableACC C ──────
  integer :: a(N)                         int a[N];
  !$xmp template t(N)                      #pragma xmp template t[N]
  !$xmp nodes p(*)                         #pragma xmp nodes p[*]
  !$xmp distribute t(block) onto p         #pragma xmp distribute t[block] onto p
5 !$xmp align a(i) with t(i)               #pragma xmp align a[i] with t[i]      5
  !$xmp shadow a(1)                        #pragma xmp shadow a[1]
  ...                                      ...
  !$acc enter data copyin(a)               #pragma acc enter data copyin(a)
  !$xmp reflect (a) acc                    #pragma xmp reflect (a) acc
```

Fig. 7 Code example in `reflect` construct

coarray and the `host_data` construct enables one-sided communication between accelerators.

If **coarrays** appear in a `use_device` clause of an enclosing `host_data` construct, data on accelerator memory is selected as the target of the communication. The synchronization for **Coarray** operations on accelerators is similar to that in XMP.

Restriction

- **Coarrays** on accelerator memory can be declared only with the `declare` directive.
- No **coarray** syntax is allowed in the OpenACC **compute region**.

Example

In line 3 of Fig. 8, the `declare` directive declares a **coarray** a and an array b on accelerator memory. In lines 6–7, **node** 1 performs a put operation, where the whole of b on the accelerator memory of **node** 1 is transferred to a on the accelerator memory of **node** 2. In lines 9–10, **node** 1 performs a get operation, where the whole of a on the accelerator memory of **node** 3 is transferred to b on the host memory of **node** 1. In line 13, the `sync all` statement in XACC/F or the `xmp_sync_all` function in XACC/C performs a barrier synchronization among all **nodes** and guarantees the completion of ongoing coarray accesses.

2.5 Handling Multiple Accelerators

XACC also has a feature for handling multiple accelerators. This section provides a brief overveiw of this feature. Please refer to [4] for more detail.

```
────── XcalableACC Fortran ──────        ────── XcalableACC C ──────
integer :: a(N)[*]                       int a[N]:[*];
integer :: b(N)                          int b[N];
!$acc declare create(a, b)               #pragma acc declare create(a, b)
...                                      ...
if(this_image() == 1) then               if(xmp_node_num() == 1){          5
!$acc host_data use_device(a, b)         #pragma acc host_data use_device(a, b)
  a(:)[2] = b(:)                           a[:]:[2] = b[:];

!$acc host_data use_device(a)            #pragma acc host_data use_device(a)
  b(:) = a(:)[3]                           b[:] = a[:]:[3];               10
end if                                   }
...                                      ...
sync all                                 xmp_sync_all(NULL);
```

Fig. 8 XACC code with coarray

```
────── XcalableACC Fortran ──────        ────── XcalableACC C ──────
!$acc devices d(*)                       #pragma acc devices d[*]
!$acc devices e(2) = nvidia(3:4)         #pragma acc devices e[2] = nvidia[2:2]
```

Fig. 9 XACC code with devices directive

2.5.1 devices Directive

The devices directive declares a **device array** that corresponds to a device set. This directive is analogous to the nodes directive for nodes in XMP.

Example

Figure 9 is an example of declaring devices. The device array d corresponds to a set of entire default devices, and e is a subset of the predefined device array nvidia. The program must be executed by a node which is equipped with four or more NVIDIA accelerator devices.

2.5.2 on_device Clause

The on_device clause in a directive specifies a device set that the directive targets.

The on_device clause may appear on parallel, parallel loop, kernels, kernels loop, data, enter data, exit data, declare, update, wait, and barrier_device directives.

The directive is applied to each device in the device set in parallel. If there is no layout clause, the all devices process the directive for same data or work redundantly.

2.5.3 `layout` Clause

The `layout` clause specifies data or work mapping on devices.

The `layout` clause may appear on `declare` directives and on `loop`, `parallel loop`, and `kernels loop` constructs. If the `layout` clause appears on a `declare` directive, it specifies the data mapping to the device set for arrays which are appeared in data clauses on the directive. "`*`" represents that the dimension is not distributed, and `block` represents that the dimension is divided into contiguous blocks, which are distributed onto the device array.

Example

Figure 10 is an example of the `layout` clause. In line 2, the `devices` directive defines a device set d. In lines 3–4, the `declare` directive declares that an array a is distributed and allocated on d. In lines 6–9, the `kernels loop` directive distributes and offloads the following loops to d.

2.5.4 `shadow` Clause

The `shadow` clause in the `declare` directive specifies the width of the shadow area of arrays, which is used to communicate the neighbor element of the block of the arrays.

Example

Figure 11 is an example of the `shadow` clause. In line 2, the `devices` directive defines a device set d. In lines 3–5, the `declare` directive declares that an array a is distributed and allocated with shadow areas on the device set d. In lines 7–10, the `kernels loop` construct divides and offloads the loop to the device set d. In

```
———— XcalableACC Fortran ————
integer :: a(N)
!$acc devices d(*)
!$acc declare create(a)
!$acc+layout((block)) on_device(d)
...
!$acc kernels loop layout(a(i))
do i = 1, N
  a(i) = i * 2
end do
```

```
———— XcalableACC C ————
int a[N];
#pragma acc devices d[*]
#pragma acc declare create(a) \
        layout([block]) on_device(d)
...
#pragma acc kernels loop layout(a[i])
for(int i = 0; i < N; i++){
  a[i] = i * 2;
}
```

Fig. 10 Xacc Code example with `layout` clause

```
 ┌──────── XcalableACC Fortran ────────┐  ┌──────── XcalableACC C ────────┐
 │ integer :: a(N)                     │  │ int a[N];                      │
 │ !$acc devices d(*)                  │  │ #pragma acc devices d[*]       │
 │ !$acc declare create(a)             │  │ #pragma acc declare create(a) \│
 │ !$acc+layout((block))               │  │         layout([block]) \      │
5│ !$acc+shadow((1:1)) on_device(d)    │  │         shadow([1:1]) on_device(d) │5
 │ ...                                 │  │ ...                            │
 │ !$acc kernels loop layout(a(i))     │  │ #pragma acc kernels loop layout(a[i]) │
 │ do i = 1, N                         │  │ for(int i = 0; i < N; i++){    │
 │   a(i) = i * 3                      │  │   a[i] = i * 3;                │
10│ end do                             │  │ }                              │10
 │ !$acc reflect(a)                    │  │ #pragma acc reflect(a)         │
 └─────────────────────────────────────┘  └────────────────────────────────┘
```

Fig. 11 XACC code with shadow clause

```
 ┌──────── XcalableACC Fortran ────────┐  ┌──────── XcalableACC C ────────┐
 │ !$acc devices d(*)                  │  │ #pragma acc devices d[*]       │
 │ !$acc devices e(2) = d(1:2)         │  │ #pragma acc devices e[2] = d[0:2] │
 │ ...                                 │  │ ...                            │
 │ !$acc barrier_device               │  │ #pragma acc barrier_device     │
5│ !$acc barrier_device on_device(e)   │  │ #pragma acc barrier_device on_device(e) │5
 └─────────────────────────────────────┘  └────────────────────────────────┘
```

Fig. 12 XACC Code with barrier_device construct

line 11, the reflect directive updates the shadow areas of the distributed array a on the device memory.

2.5.5 barrier_device Construct

The barrier_device construct specifies an explicit barrier among devices at the point which the construct appears.

The barrier_device construct blocks accelerator devices until all ongoing asynchronous operations on them are completed regardless of the host operations.

Example

Figure 12 is an example of the barrier_devices construct. In lines 1–2, the devices directives define device sets d and e. In lines 4–5, the first barrier_device construct performs a barrier operation for all devices, and the second one performs a barrier operation for devices in the device set e.

3 Omni XcalableACC Compiler

We have developed the Omni XACC compiler as the reference implementation of XACC compilers.

Figure 13 shows the compile flow of Omni XACC. First, Omni XACC accepts XACC source codes and translates them into those in the base languages with runtime calls. Next, the translated code is compiled by a native compiler, which supports OpenACC, to generate an object file. Finally, the object files and the runtime library are linked by the native compiler to generate an execution file.

In particular, for the data transfer between NVIDIA GPUs across nodes, we have implemented the following three methods in Omni XACC:

(a) TCA/IB hybrid communication
(b) GPUDirect RDMA with CUDA-Aware MPI
(c) MPI and CUDA

Item (a) performs communication with the smallest latency, but it requires a computing environment equipped with the Tightly Coupled Accelerator (TCA) feature[1, 7]. Item (b) is superior in performance to Item (c), but also requires specific software and hardware (e.g., MVAPICH2-GDR and Mellanox InfiniBand). Whereas (a) and (b) can realize direct communication between GPUs without the intervention of CPU, Item (c) cannot. It copies the data from accelerator memory to host memory using CUDA and then transfers the data to other compute nodes using MPI. Therefore, although its performacnce is the lowest, it requires neither specific software nor hardware.

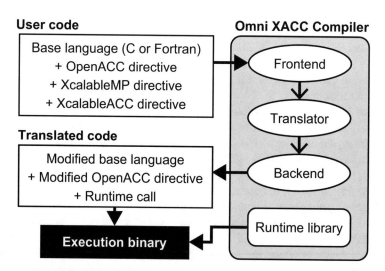

Fig. 13 Compile flow of Omni XcalableACC compiler

4   Performance of Lattice QCD Application

This section describes the evaluations of XACC performance and productivity for a lattice quantum chromodynamics (Lattice QCD) application.

4.1   Overview of Lattice QCD

The Lattice QCD is a discrete formulation of QCD that describes the strong interaction among "quarks" and "gluons." While the quark is a species of elementary particles, the gluon is a particle that mediates the strong interaction. The Lattice QCD is formulated on a four-dimensional lattice (time: T and space:ZYX axes). We impose a periodic boundary condition in all the directions. The quark degree of freedom is represented as a field that has four components of "spin" and three components of "color," namely a complex vector of $12 \times N_{site}$ components, where N_{site} is the number of lattice sites. The gluon is defined as a 3×3 complex matrix field on links (bonds between neighboring lattice sites). During a Lattice QCD simulation, one needs to solve many times a linear equation for the matrix that represents the interaction between the quark and gluon fields. This linear equation is the target of present work. The matrix acts on the quark vector and has nonzero components only for the neighboring sites, and thus sparse.

4.2   Implementation

We implemented a Lattice QCD code based on the existing Lattice QCD application Bridge++[5]. Since our code was implemented by extracting the main kernel of the Bridge++, it can be used as a mini-application to investigate its productivity and performance more easily than use of the original Bridge++.

Figure 14 shows a pseudo code of the implementation, where the CG method is used to solve quark propagators. In Fig. 14, *WD()* is the Wilson-Dirac operator[6], *U* is a gluon, the other uppercase characters are quarks. The Wilson-Dirac operator is a main kernel in the Lattice QCD, which calculates how the quarks interact with each other under the influence of the gluon.

Figure 15 shows how to declare distributed arrays of the quark and gluon. In lines 1–8, the quark and gluon structure arrays are declared. The last dimension "[2]" of both structures represents real and imaginary parts for a complex number. *NT*, *NZ*, *NY*, and *NX* are the numbers of TZYX axis elements. In lines 10–18, distributed arrays are declared where the macro constant values *NODES_T* and *NODES_Z* indicate the number of nodes on the T and Z axes. Thus, the program is parallelized on T and Z axes. Note that an "*" in the **align** directive means that the dimension is not divided. In the **shadow** directive, halo regions are added to the arrays because

1	S = B	10	T = WD(U,P)
2	R = B	11	V = WD(U,T)
3	X = B	12	pap = dot(V,P)
4	sr = norm(S)	13	cr = rr/pap
5	T = WD(U,X)	14	X = cr $*$ P + X
6	S = WD(U,T)	15	R = $-$cr $*$ V + R
7	R = R $-$ S	16	rr = norm(R)
8	P = R	17	bk = rr/rrp
9	rr = norm(R)	18	P = bk $*$ P + R
10	rrp = rr	19	rrp = rr
11	**do**{	20	}**while**(rr/sr > 1.E$-$16)

Fig. 14 Lattice QCD pseudo code

```
1   typedef struct Quark {
2     double v[4][3][2];
3   } Quark_t;
4   typedef struct Gluon {
5     double v[3][3][2];
6   } Gluon_t;
7   Quark_t v[NT][NZ][NY][NX], tmp_v[NT][NZ][NY][NX];
8   Gluon_t u[4][NT][NZ][NY][NX];
9
10  #pragma xmp template t[NT][NZ]
11  #pragma xmp nodes n[NODES_T][NODES_Z]
12  #pragma xmp distribute t[block][block] onto n
13  #pragma xmp align v[i][j][*][*] with t[i][j]
14  #pragma xmp align tmp_v[i][j][*][*] with t[i][j]
15  #pragma xmp align u[*][i][j][*][*] with t[i][j]
16  #pragma xmp shadow v[1:1][1:1][0][0]
17  #pragma xmp shadow tmp_v[1:1][1:1][0][0]
18  #pragma xmp shadow u[0][1:1][1:1][0][0]
19  ...
20  int main(){
21  ...
22  #pragma acc enter data copyin(v, tmp_v, u)
```

Fig. 15 Declaration of distributed arrays for Lattice QCD

each quark and gluon element is affected by its neighboring orthogonal elements. Note that "0" in the **shadow** directive means that no halo region exists. In line 22, the **enter data** directive transfers the distributed arrays from host memory to accelerator memory.

Figure 16 shows how to call *WD()*. The **reflect** directives are inserted before *WD()* in order to update own halo region. In line 2, "1:0" in **width** clause means only the lower halo region is updated because only it is needed in *WD()*. The *u* is not updated before the second *WD()* function because values of *u* are not updated

```
1  #pragma xmp reflect(v) width(/periodic/1:1,/periodic/1:1,0,0) orthogonal acc
2  #pragma xmp reflect(u) width(0,/periodic/1:0,/periodic/1:0,0,0) orthogonal acc
3  WD(tmp_v, u, v);
4  #pragma xmp reflect(tmp_v) width(/periodic/1:1,/periodic/1:1,0,0) orthogonal acc
5  WD(v, u, tmp_v);
```

Fig. 16   Calling Wilson-Dirac operator

```
1  void WD(Quark_t v_out[NT][NZ][NY][NX], const Gluon_t u[4][NT][NZ][NY][NX],
           const Quark_t v[NT][NZ][NY][NX])
2  {
3  #pragma xmp align v_out[i][j][*][*] with t[i][j]
4  #pragma xmp align u[*][i][j][*][*] with t[i][j]
5  #pragma xmp align v[i][j][*][*] with t[i][j]
6  #pragma xmp shadow v_out[1:1][1:1][0][0]
7  #pragma xmp shadow u[0][1:1][1:1][0][0]
8  #pragma xmp shadow v[1:1][1:1][0][0]
9    ...
10 #pragma xmp loop (t,z) on t[t][z]
11 #pragma acc parallel loop collapse(4) present(v_out, u, v)
12   for(int t=0;t<NT;t++)
13    for(int z=0;z<NZ;z++)
14     for(int y=0;y<NY;y++)
15      for(int x=0;x<NX;x++){
```

Fig. 17   A portion of Wilson-Dirac operator

in *WD()*. Moreover, the **orthogonal** clause is added because diagonal updates of the arrays are not required in *WD()*.

Figure 17 shows a part of the Wilson-Dirac operator code. All arguments in *WD()* are distributed arrays. In XMP and XACC, distributed arrays which are used as arguments must be redeclared in function to pass their information to a compiler. Thus, the **align** and **shadow** directives are used in *WD()*. In line 10, the **loop** directive parallelizes the outer two loop statements. In line 11, the **parallel loop** directive parallelizes all loop statements. In the loop statements, a calculation needs neighboring and orthogonal elements. Note that while the *WD()* updates only the *v_out*, it only refers the *u* and *v*.

Figure 18 shows L2 norm calculation code in the CG method. In line 8, the **reduction** clause performs a reduction operation for the variable *a* in each accelerator when finishing the next loop statement. The calculated variable *a* is located in both host memory and accelerator memory. However, at this point, all nodes have individual values of *a*. To obtain the total value of the variable *a*, the XMP **reduction** directive in line 18 also performs a reduction operation among nodes. Since the total value is used on only host after this function, the XMP **reduction** directive does not have **acc** clause.

```
1   double norm(const Quark_t v[NT][NZ][NY][NX])
2   {
3   #pragma xmp align v[i][j][*][*] with t[i][j]
4   #pragma xmp shadow v[1:1][1:1][0][0]
5     double a = 0.0;
6
7   #pragma xmp loop (t,z) on t[t][z]
8   #pragma acc parallel loop collapse(7) present(v) reduction(+:a)
9     for(int t=0;t<NT;t++)
10     for(int z=0;z<NZ;z++)
11      for(int y=0;y<NY;y++)
12       for(int x=0;x<NX;x++)
13        for(int i=0;i<4;i++)
14         for(int j=0;j<3;j++)
15          for(int k=0;k<2;k++)
16           a += v[t][z][y][x].v[i][j][k]*v[t][z][y][x].v[i][j][k];
17
18   #pragma xmp reduction (+:a)
19     return a;
20   }
```

Fig. 18 L2 norm calculation code

5   Performance Evaluation

5.1   *Result*

This section evaluates the performance level of XACC on the Lattice QCD code. For comparison purposes, those of MPI+CUDA and MPI+OpenACC are also evaluated. For performance evaluation, we use the HA-PACS/TCA system[7], the hardware specifications and software environments of which are shown in Table 1. Since each compute node has four GPUs, we assign four `nodes` per compute node and direct each `node` to deal with a single GPU. We use the Omni OpenACC compiler[8] as a backend compiler in the Omni XACC compiler. We execute the Lattice QCD codes with strong scaling in regions (32,32,32,32) as (*NT,NZ,NY,NX*). The Omni XACC compiler provides various types of data communication among accelerators[9]. We

Table 1 Evaluation environment

CPU	Intel Xeon-E5 2680v2 2.8 GHz × 2 Sockets
Memory	DDR3 1866 MHz 59.7 GB/s 128 GB
GPU	NVIDIA Tesla K20X (GDDR5 250 GB/s 6 GB) × 4 GPUs
Network	InfiniBand Mellanox Connect-X3 Dual-port QDR 8 GB/s
Software	Intel 16.0.2, CUDA 7.5.18, Omni OpenACC compiler 1.1
	MVAPICH2 2.1

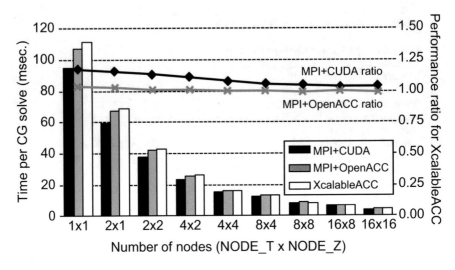

Fig. 19 Performance results

use the MPI+CUDA implementation type because it provides a balance of versatility and performance.

Figure 19 shows the performance results that indicate the time required to solve one CG iteration as well as the performance ratio values that indicate the comparative performance of XACC and other languages. When the performance ratio value of a language is greater than 1.00, the performance result of the language is better than that of XACC. Figure 19 shows that the performance ratio values of MPI+CUDA are between 1.04 and 1.18, and that those of MPI+OpenACC are between 0.99 and 1.04. Moreover, Fig. 19 also shows that the performance results of both MPI+CUDA and MPI+OpenACC become closer to those of XACC as the number of nodes increases.

5.2 Discussion

To examine the performance levels in detail, we measure the time required for the halo updating operation for two nodes and more. The halo updating operation consists of the communication and pack/unpack processes for non-contiguous regions in the XACC runtime.

While Fig. 20 describes communication time of the halo updating time of Fig 19, Fig. 21 describes pack/unpack time of it. Figure 20 shows that the communication performance levels of all implementations are almost the same. However, Fig. 21 shows that the pack/unpack performance levels of MPI+CUDA are better than those of XACC, and that those of MPI+OpenACC are worse than those of XACC. The reason for the pack/unpack operation performance level difference is that the XACC

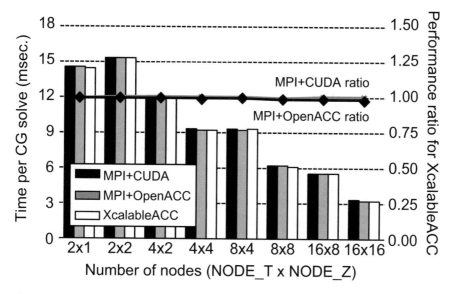

Fig. 20 Communication time

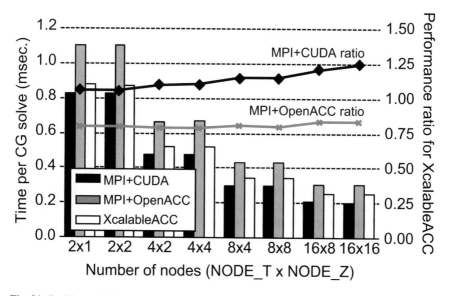

Fig. 21 Pack/unpack time

operation is implemented in CUDA at XACC runtime. Thus, some performance levels of XACC are better than those of MPI+OpenACC in Fig. 19. However, the performance levels of XACC in Fig. 21 is worse than those of MPI+CUDA because XACC requires the cost of XACC runtime calls.

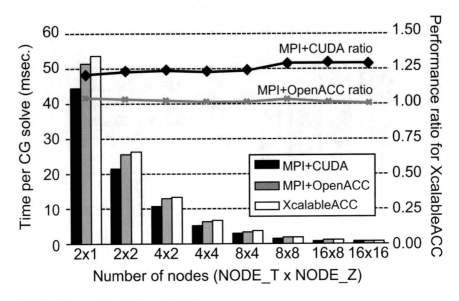

Fig. 22 Time excluding halo updating time

Figure 22 shows the overall time excluding the halo updating time, where performance levels of MPI+CUDA are the best, and those of XACC are almost the same as those of MPI+OpenACC. The reason for the difference is due to how to use GPU threads. In the CUDA implementation, we assign loop iterations to GPU threads in a cyclic-manner manually. In contrast, in the OpenACC and XACC implementations, how to assign GPU threads is an implementation dependent on an OpenACC compiler. In the Omni OpenACC compiler, initially loop iterations are assigned to GPU threads by a gang (threadblock) in a block manner, and then are also assigned to them by a vector (thread) in a cyclic manner. With the **gang** clause with the **static** argument proposed in the OpenACC specification version 2.0, programmers can determine how to use GPU threads to some extent, but the Omni OpenACC compiler does not yet support it.

Figure 23 shows the ratio of the halo updating time to overall time. As can be seen, as the number of nodes increases, the ratio increases as well. Therefore, when a large number of nodes are used, there is little difference in performance level of Fig. 19 among the three implementations. The reason why the ratio of MPI+CUDA is slightly larger than those of the others is that the time excluding the halo communication of MPI+CUDA in Fig. 20 is relatively small.

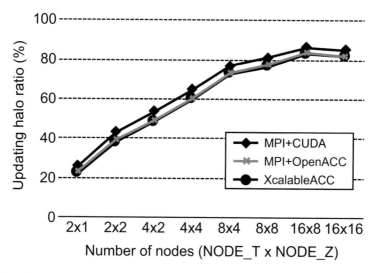

Fig. 23 Updating halo ratio

6   Productivity Improvement

6.1   *Requirement for Productive Parallel Language*

In Sect. 5, we developed three Lattice QCD codes using MPI+CUDA, MPI+OpenACC, and XACC. Figure 24 shows our procedure for developing each code where we first develop the code for an accelerator from the serial code, and then extend it to handle an accelerated cluster.

To parallelize the serial code for an accelerator using CUDA requires large code changes ("a" in Fig. 24), most of which are necessary to create new kernel functions and to make 1D arrays out of multi-dimensional arrays. By contrast, OpenACC accomplishes the same parallelization with just small code changes ("b"), because OpenACC's directive-based approach encourages reuse of an existing code. Besides, to parallelize the code for a distributed memory system, MPI also requires large changes ("c" and "d"), primarily to convert global indices into local indices.

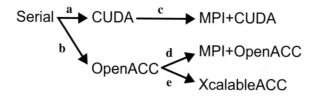

Fig. 24 Application development order on accelerated cluster

By contrast, XACC requires smaller code changes ("e") because XACC is also directive-based language as OpenACC.

In many cases, a parallel code for an accelerated cluster is based on an existing serial code. The code changes to the existing serial code are likely to trigger program bugs. Therefore, XACC is designed to reuse an existing code as possible.

6.2 Quantitative Evaluation by Delta Source Lines of Codes

As one of metrics for productivity, Delta Source Lines of Codes (DSLOC) is proposed[10]. The DSLOC indicates how the codes change from a corresponding implementation. The DSLOC is the sum of three components: how many lines are added, deleted, and modified. When the DSLOC is small, the programming costs and the possibility of program bugs will be small as well. We use the DSLOC to count the amount of change required to implement an accelerated cluster code from a serial code.

Table 2 shows the DSLOC where lowercase characters correspond to Fig. 24. The DSLOC of XACC (b + e) is smaller than MPI+CUDA (a + c) and MPI+OpenACC (b + d). The difference between XACC and MPI+CUDA is 420.0%, and that between XACC and MPI+OpenACC is 39.4%.

6.3 Discussion

In "e" of Table 2, four lines for modification are required to implement the XACC code from the OpenACC code. Figures 25 and 26 show the modification, which is a part of $WD()$ of Fig. 17. A variable tt is used to be an index for halo region. The tt is modified from line 6 of Fig. 25 to line 7 of Fig. 26. In Fig. 25, when a value of a variable t is "NT-1," that of the variable tt becomes "0" which is the lower bound index of the first dimension of the array v_out. On the other hand, in Fig. 26, communication of the halo is performed before execution of $WD()$ by the **reflect** directive shown in Fig. 16. Thus, the variable tt need only be incremented in Fig. 26. There are four such modifications in $WD()$. Note that XACC does not keep the semantics of the base code perfectly in this case in exchange for simplified

Table 2 DSLOC of Lattice QCD implementations

	a	b	c	d	e	a + c	b + d	b+e
DSLOC	552	22	280	201	138	832	223	160
Add	137	20	185	140	134	322	160	154
Delete	73	0	0	0	0	73	0	0
Modify	342	2	95	61	4	437	63	6

```
1  #pragma acc parallel loop collapse(4) present(v_out, u, v)
2  for(int t=0;t<NT;t++)
3   for(int z=0;z<NZ;z++)
4    for(int y=0;y<NY;y++)
5     for(int x=0;x<NX;x++){
6      int tt = (t + 1) % NT;
7      v_out[tt][z][y][x].v[0][0][0] = ... ;
```

Fig. 25 Code modification of *WD()* in OpenACC

```
1  #pragma xmp loop (t,z) on t[t][z]
2  #pragma acc parallel loop collapse(4) present(v_out, u, v)
3  for(int t=0;t<NT;t++)
4   for(int z=0;z<NZ;z++)
5    for(int y=0;y<NY;y++)
6     for(int x=0;x<NX;x++){
7      int tt = t + 1;
8      v_out[tt][z][y][x].v[0][0][0] = ... ;
```

Fig. 26 Code modification of *WD()* in XcalableACC

Table 3 SLOC of Lattice QCD implementations

	MPI+CUDA	MPI+OpenACC	XcalableACC
SLOC	1091	1002	996
#XcalableMP	–	–	122
#OpenACC	–	26	16
#XcalableACC	–	–	3
#MPI function	39	39	–

parallelization. In addition, there are two lines for modification shown in "b" of Table 2. It is a very fine modification for OpenACC constraints, which keeps the semantics of the base code.

As basic information, we count the source lines of codes (SLOC) of each of the Lattice QCD implementations. Table 3 shows the SLOC excluding comments and blank lines, as well as the numbers of each directive and MPI functions included in their SLOC. For reader information, SLOC of the serial version Lattice QCD code is 842. Table 3 shows that the 122 XMP directives are used in the XACC implementation, many of which are declarations for function arguments. To reduce the XMP directives, we are planning to develop a new syntax that combines declarations with the same attribute into one directive. Figure 27 shows an example of the new syntax applied to the declarations in Fig. 17. Since the arrays *v_out* and *v* have the same attribute, they can be declared into a single XMP directive. Moreover, the **shadow** directive attribute is added to the **align** directive as its clause. When applying the new directive to XACC implementation, the number of XMP directives

```
1  void WD(Quark_t v_out[NT][NZ][NY][NX], const Gluon_t u[4][NT][NZ][NY][NX],
              const Quark_t v[NT][NZ][NY][NX])
2  {
3  #pragma xmp align [i][j][*][*] with t[i][j] shadow [1:1][1:1][0][0] :: v_out, v
4  #pragma xmp align [*][i][j][*][*] with t[i][j] shadow [0][1:1][1:1][0][0] :: u
```

Fig. 27 New directive combination syntax that applies to Fig. 17

decreases from the 122 shown in Table 3 to 64, and the XACC DSLOC decreases from the 160 shown in Table 2 to 102.

References

1. M. Nakao et al., Evaluation of XcalableACC with tightly coupled accelerators/InfiniBand hybrid communication on accelerated cluster. Int. J. High Perform. Comput. Appl. **35**, 109434201882116 (2019)
2. XcalableMP Language Specification, http://xcalablemp.org/specification.html (2017)
3. The OpenACC Application Programming Interface, http://www.openacc.org (2015)
4. XcalableACC Language Specification, https://xcalablemp.org/download/XACC/xacc-spec-1.0.pdf (2017)
5. Lattice QCD code Bridge++, http://bridge.kek.jp/Lattice-code/index_e.html
6. K.G. Wilson, Confinement of quarks. Phys. Rev. D **10**, 2445 (1974)
7. HA-PACS, https://www.ccs.tsukuba.ac.jp/supercomputer/
8. A. Tabuchi et al., A source-to-source OpenACC compiler for CUDA, in *Euro-Par Workhops* (2013)
9. M. Nakao et al., XcalableACC: extension of XcalableMP PGAS language using OpenACC for accelerator clusters, in *Proceedings of the First Workshop on Accelerator Programming Using Directives* (2014)
10. A.I. Stone et al., Evaluating coarray Fortran with the CGPOP miniapp, in *Proceedings of the Fifth Conference on Partitioned Global Address Space Programming Models* (2011)

Mixed-Language Programming with XcalableMP

Masahiro Nakao

Abstract This chapter presents the mixed-language programming with Xcal-ableMP and other programming languages. It is supported by the linkage functions between XcalableMP and MPI library. We also demonstrate how to call XcalableMP program from Python program (M. Nakao et al., Linkage of XcalableMP and Python languages for high productivity on HPC cluster system, Proceedings of Workshops of HPC Asia, No .9, pp.39–47, 2018).

1 Background

To develop applications on high-performance computing (HPC) cluster systems, Partitioned Global Address Space (PGAS) languages that can demonstrate high productivity are used [2–5]. Because the use of PGAS languages is familiar in one-sided communication, applications in PGAS languages can sometimes exhibit higher performance than those using MPI library by directly using a communication layer close to hardware [5, 6]. Examples of PGAS languages include XcalableMP (XMP) [5, 7, 8]; XcalableACC [9–11]; Coarray Fortran [12], PCJ [13], Unified Parallel C,[1] UPC++ [14], HabaneroUPC++ [15], X10 [16], Chapel [17], and DASH [18].

Although PGAS languages have many advantages, re-implementing an existing MPI application using a PGAS language is often not realistic for the following reasons: (1) since the number of lines of a real-world application code may reach several million, the programming cost for re-implementing is excessive, and (2) cases where productivity and performance have been improved by PGAS languages are limited. Moreover, since each programming language generally has its own

---

[1] https://upc-lang.org/assets/Uploads/spec/upc-lang-spec-1.3.pdf

M. Nakao (✉)
RIKEN Center for Computational Science, Kobe, Hyogo, Japan
e-mail: masahiro.nakao@riken.jp

M. Sato (ed.), *XcalableMP PGAS Programming Language*,
https://doi.org/10.1007/978-981-15-7683-6_5

147

strong and weak points, it is difficult to develop all parallel applications using just one programming language.

In order to exploit the advantages of a PGAS language, it is important to consider the linkage between the PGAS language and other languages. For example, modifying only a part where the performance or code outlook will be better using a PGAS language has the potential to partially alleviate the two problems listed in the previous paragraph because the programming cost of partial re-implementation is smaller than that of whole re-implementation.

We have designed an XMP language, and developed Omni compiler described in Chapter 2. This chapter describes the development of linkage functions between XMP and MPI library for Omni compiler. Moreover, it also describes how to call XMP program from Python program. Especially, since Python has numerous scientific computing libraries, we believe that linking Python and XMP will lead to a significant reduction in programming cost when developing HPC applications.

2 Translation by Omni Compiler

Figure 1 shows an example of a code translation for XMP in C language, where the code of the left figure is translated into that of the right figure.[2] Omni compiler inserts **xmp_init_all()** and **xmp_finalize_all()** automatically to perform the initialization and finalization processes, respectively. These functions are defined in Omni compiler runtime library. Since **xmp_init_all()** calls **MPI_Init()** and **MPI_Comm_dup()** internally to duplicate **MPI_COMM_WORLD**. Since the newly duplicated communicator is used to perform XMP communication, user MPI communication does not conflict with XMP communication. Additionally, **xmp_finalize_all()** calls **MPI_Finalize()** function internally.

In an XMP program, the **task** directive can divide a node set. The implementation of the **task** directive creates a new communicator based on the duplicated communicator by **MPI_Comm_split()**. If communication occurs within the range of the **task** directive, then the new communicator is used to perform the communication.

Omni compiler renames a user **main()** as **xmpc_main()** in order to place the **xmpc_main()** between **xmp_init_all()** and **xmp_finalize_all()**. New **main()** calls **xmpc_main()**. The above special translation is performed only for **main()**. For other functions (such as **foo()**), renaming is not performed.

---

[2]Since Omni compiler performs almost the same operation for an XMP in Fortran code, these examples are omitted in this chapter.

```
void foo(){
  printf("Hello\n");
}

int main(){
  foo();
  return 0;
}
```

```
void foo(){
  printf("Hello\n");
}

static int xmpc_main(int argc, char **argv){
  foo();
  return 0;
}

int main(int argc, char **argv){
  xmp_init_all(argc, argv);
  int r = xmpc_main(argc, argv);
  xmp_finalize_all();
  return r;
}
```

Fig. 1 Example of translation in Omni compiler [19]

3 Functions for Mixed-Language

For a mixed-language programming with XMP, Omni compiler has the following functions.

- Calling an MPI program from an XMP program
- Calling an XMP program from an MPI program
- Calling an XMP program from a Python program

3.1 Function to Call MPI Program from XMP Program

Table 1 shows the functions to call an MPI program from an XMP program. These functions are defined in Appendix A.1 of the XMP specification version 1.4.[3] Figure 2 also shows an example of how to use these functions. In line 1 of the left figure, an XMP header file (xmp.h) is included to use the functions in Table 1. In line 2, an MPI header file (mpi.h) is included to obtain the information of the MPI communicator type that is used in line 7. In line 6, **xmp_init_mpi()** initializes an MPI environment. In line 8, **xmp_get_mpi_comm()** returns an MPI communicator from the information of the executing XMP node set. In line 9, **foo()** which is defined in right figure is called. In line 10, **xmp_finalize_mpi()** finalizes the MPI

---

[3]https://xcalablemp.org/download/spec/xmp-spec-1.4.pdf

Table 1 Functions to call MPI program from XMP program [19]

Language	Return value type	Function	Description
XMP/C	Void	xmp_init_mpi(int*, char***)	Initialize MPI environment
XMP/F	(None)	xmp_init_mpi()	
XMP/C	MPI_Comm	xmp_get_mpi_comm(void)	Create MPI communicator from
XMP/F	Integer	xmp_get_mpi_comm()	XMP node set
XMP/C	Void	xmp_finalize_mpi(void)	Finalize MPI environment
XMP/F	(None)	xmp_finalize_mpi()	

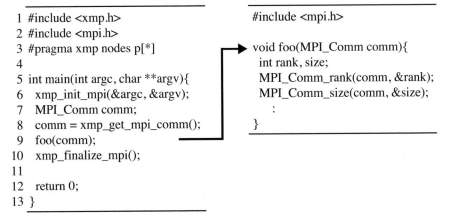

```
 1 #include <xmp.h>                       #include <mpi.h>
 2 #include <mpi.h>
 3 #pragma xmp nodes p[*]                  void foo(MPI_Comm comm){
 4                                           int rank, size;
 5 int main(int argc, char **argv){         MPI_Comm_rank(comm, &rank);
 6   xmp_init_mpi(&argc, &argv);            MPI_Comm_size(comm, &size);
 7   MPI_Comm comm;                           :
 8   comm = xmp_get_mpi_comm();            }
 9   foo(comm);
10   xmp_finalize_mpi();
11
12   return 0;
13 }
```

Fig. 2 Example of calling MPI program (mpi.c) from XMP program (xmp.c) [19]

environment. Note that **xmp_get_mpi_comm**() and other MPI functions must be placed between **xmp_init_mpi**() and **xmp_finalize_mpi**().

The implementations of **xmp_init_mpi**() and **xmp_finalize_mpi**() are empty because, as shown in Fig. 1, the **xmp_init_all**() and **xmp_finalize_all**() are always invoked at the beginning and the end of the program, and these functions initialize and finalize the MPI environment. Next, an implementation of **xmp_get_mpi_comm**() will be described. As shown in Sect. 2, the **task** directive creates a new MPI communicator. Thus, an MPI communicator is stored at a stack data architecture in Omni compiler runtime library. The **xmp_get_mpi_comm**() returns an MPI communicator at the top of the stack.

An example of compilation using Omni compiler is as follows:

```
$ mpicc mpi.c -c -o mpi.o
$ xmpcc xmp.c -c -o xmp.o
$ xmpcc mpi.o xmp.o -o a.out
```

Since Omni compiler uses an MPI compiler as a native compiler internally, MPI programs can also be compiled with the "xmpcc" command as follows:

```
$ xmpcc mpi.c -o mpi.o
```

Thus, it is also possible to execute all the compilation work using a single command as follows:

```
$ xmpcc mpi.c xmp.c -o a.out
```

The execution binary is executed using the execution command provided by user's MPI environment as follows:

```
$ mpirun -np 4 a.out
```

3.2 Function to Call XMP Program from MPI Program

Table 2 shows the functions to call an XMP program from an MPI program. These functions are defined in Appendix A.2 of the XMP specification version 1.4. Figure 3 shows an example of how to use these functions. In line 1 of the left figure, an XMP header file is included to use functions in Table 2. In line 7, **xmp_init()** initializes an XMP environment, and creates the XMP node set based on the communicator specified in its argument. In line 8, **foo()** in the right figure is called. In line 9, **xmp_finalize()** finalizes the XMP environment. Note that the XMP functions must be placed between **xmp_init()** and **xmp_finalize()**.

Though the **xmp_init()** is implemented to call the **xmp_init_all()** function described in Sect. 2, it also performs the following ingenuities:

Table 2 Functions to call XMP program from MPI program [19]

Language	Return value type	Function	Description
XMP/C	Void	xmp_init(MPI_Comm)	Initialize XMP environment
XMP/F	(None)	xmp_init(Integer)	
XMP/C	Void	xmp_finalize(void)	Finalize XMP environment
XMP/F	(None)	xmp_finalize()	

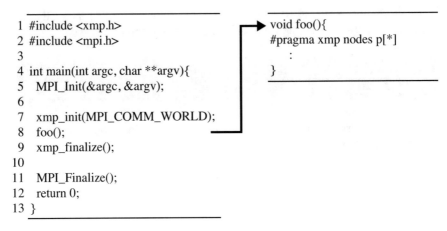

```
 1 #include <xmp.h>                          void foo(){
 2 #include <mpi.h>                          #pragma xmp nodes p[*]
 3                                                :
 4 int main(int argc, char **argv){          }
 5   MPI_Init(&argc, &argv);
 6
 7   xmp_init(MPI_COMM_WORLD);
 8   foo();
 9   xmp_finalize();
10
11   MPI_Finalize();
12   return 0;
13 }
```

Fig. 3 Example of calling XMP program from MPI program [19]

- Before calling **xmp_init()**, **MPI_Init()** must be called in the MPI program. Therefore, we added a procedure that ensures **MPI_Init()** is not called in **xmp_init_all()**.
- As shown in Sect. 2, **xmp_init_all()** duplicates **MPI_COMM_WORLD** to perform XMP communication. We also added a procedure that ensures the communicator specified in **xmp_init()** is duplicated instead of **MPI_COMM_WORLD**.

Basically, **xmp_finalize()** is also implemented to call **xmp_finalize_all()** in Sect. 2. As with **xmp_init()**, after calling **xmp_finalize()**, **MPI_Finalize()** is called in an MPI program. Therefore, we added a procedure to ensure that **MPI_Finalize()** is not called in **xmp_finalize_all()**.

The method to compile and execute is the same as Sect. 3.1.

3.3 Function to Call XMP Program from Python Program

There are two types of calling an XMP program from a Python program in Omni compiler; the one is "calling from a parallel Python program," the other is "calling from a sequential Python program."

3.3.1 From Parallel Python Program

Figure 4 shows an example of calling an XMP program from a parallel Python program. We assume the use of "mpi4py" for a Python MPI environment. In line 2 of the left figure, an XMP package is imported which is in Omni compier. In line 4, the shared library (**bar.so**) created from the right figure is read. In line 8,

```
1 from mpi4py import MPI                          void foo(long a[3], long b[3]){
2 import xmp                                       #pragma xmp nodes p[*]
3                                                       :
4 lib = xmp.Lib("bar.so")                          }
5 comm = MPI.COMM_WORLD
6 args = ([1,2,3], [4,5,6])
7
8 job = lib.call(comm, "foo", args)
```

Fig. 4 Example of calling XMP program (bar.c) from parallel Python program (bar.py) [19]

xmp.Lib.call() calls a parallel XMP program. This function performs initialization and finalization for an XMP environment internally.

To use the features, the Omni compiler runtime library must be a shared library. Therefore, we develop a new compile process to create a shared library for Omni compiler. When adding an option "--enable-shared" to "./configure" as follows, shared libraries are created.

```
$ ./configure --enable-shared
```

An example of compilation and execution using Omni compiler is as follows. A shared library is created by "xmpcc" command from a user program. Compile options used to create the shared library depend on a native compiler (e.g., "-fPIC -shard" if the native compiler is gcc). The execution binary is executed via Python.

```
$ xmpcc -fPIC -shared bar.c -o bar.so
$ mpirun -np 4 python bar.py
```

3.3.2 From Sequential Python Program

Figure 5 shows an example of calling an XMP program from a sequential Python program. In line 6, **xmp.Lib.spawn()** calls a parallel XMP program. The first argument is number of nodes in XMP. The last argument is an option for asynchronous operation. If it is true, processing may return to python before "**foo()**" completes. In line 7, **xmp.Lib.wait()** waits until "**foo()**" completes. In line 9, **xmp.Lib.elapse_time()** returns processing time for "**foo()**".

```
1 import xmp
2
3 lib = xmp.Lib("test.so")
4 args = ([1,2,3], [4,5,6])
5
6 job = lib.spawn(4, "foo", args, async = True)
7 job.wait()
8
9 print ("elapsed_time:{0}".format(job.elapsed_time()) + "[sec]")
```

Fig. 5 Example of spawning XMP program from sequential Python program [19]

An example of execution using Omni compiler is as follows. Note that a python program executes with one process, but an XMP program is executed with number of processes specified in code.

```
$ mpirun -np 1 python bar.py
```

4 Application to Order/Degree Problem

4.1 What Is Order/Degree Program

The order/degree problem is a problem that minimizes the diameter and average shortest path length (ASPL) among vertices in an undirected graph with a given number of vertices and degrees. The problem is useful for designing low latency interconnection networks (http://research.nii.ac.jp/graphgolf).

From the number of vertices (n) and degrees (d), the theoretical lower bounds of the diameter ($K_{n,d}$) and the ASPL ($L_{n,d}$) are calculated as follows [20]:

$$
K_{n,d} = \begin{cases} \lceil \frac{n-1}{2} \rceil & \text{if } d = 2 \\ \lceil \log_{d-1}(\frac{(n-1)(d-2)}{d}) + 1 \rceil & \text{if } d > 2 \end{cases}
$$

$$
L_{n,d} = \begin{cases} 1 & \text{if } K_{n,d} = 1 \\ \frac{S_{n,d} + K_{n,d} R_{n,d}}{n-1} & \text{if } K_{n,d} \geq 2 \end{cases}
$$

$$
S_{n,d} = \sum_{i=1}^{K_{n,d}-1} id(d-1)^{i-1}
$$

$$R_{n,d} = n - 1 - \sum_{i=1}^{K_{n,d}-1} d(d-1)^{i-1}$$

Figures 6 and 7 show examples of graphs with $n = 10$ and $d = 3$ and their distance matrices. The distance matrix indicates the shortest hop count between vertices. The diameter is the maximum value of the elements in the distance matrix. ASPL is the value obtained by dividing the total value of all elements by the number of elements $(n^2 - n)/2$. While the graph in Fig. 6 has random edges, the graph in Fig. 7 has edges optimized by our algorithm, which is described in Sect. 4.2. The diameter and ASPL of Fig. 7 are theoretical lower bounds.

In an effort to expand the order/degree problem into open science, the National Institute of Informatics has held a "Graph Golf" competition every year since 2015 to search for the smallest diameter and ASPL. A combination of several vertices and degrees is provided in each of those events. The competition has two categories: one is the General Graph Category, where vertices are placed freely, and the other is the Grid Graph Category, where vertices are placed on a two-dimensional grid. This section deals with the General Graph Category. Table 3 shows the combination of vertices and degrees used in 2017.

A python program "create-random.py" for the order/degree problem is available on the official Graph Golf website. The program outputs follow from the number of vertices and degrees. These calculations use the Python networkx package (https://networkx.github.io).

- Initial graph with random edges (the graph of Fig. 6 is created by this function)
- Calculation of diameter and ASPL
- Graph figure in Portable Network Graphics (PNG) format (the graphs shown Figs. 6 and 7 are created by this function)

4.2 Implementation

The "create-random.py" does not search out the smallest diameter and ASPL. Moreover, to obtain diameter and ASPL of a graph, it is necessary to calculate all of the shortest paths among its vertices. Although the "create-random.py" calculates the shortest paths using the **shortest_path_length** method of the networkx package, this method requires a significant amount of time.

To search for the smallest diameter and ASPL, we developed a GraphGolf code in both Python and XMP/C based on "create-random.py." A Simulated Annealing (SA) [21, 22] algorithm is used for optimization. The shortest paths calculation is parallelized by XMP directives. Figure 8 shows a flow chart for the algorithm. While Python is used to create initial graph and output the figure, XMP/C is used to implement other parts.

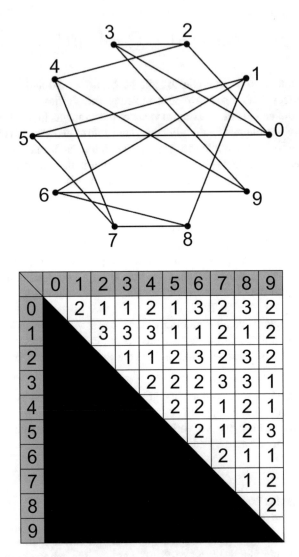

	0	1	2	3	4	5	6	7	8	9
0		2	1	1	2	1	3	2	3	2
1			3	3	3	1	1	2	1	2
2				1	1	2	3	2	3	2
3					2	2	2	3	3	1
4						2	2	1	2	1
5							2	1	2	3
6								2	1	1
7									1	2
8										2
9										

Fig. 6 Diameter = 3, ASPL = 1.89

Figures 9 and 10 show a portion of our codes. In lines 6–10 of Fig. 9, the number of vertices and degrees are transformed to allow their use in the program. In lines 12–17, an initial graph is created and set a variable *arr*. The first element of the variable *arr* stores the number of vertices and the degree. In lines 19–20, the initial graph is passed to the **xmp_graphgolf** function of Fig. 10, which optimizes it. The result is saved in a variable *arr*, which is the same as one of the arguments. After line 22, the result is transformed into a figure. In lines 1–3 of Fig. 10, the XMP directives declare the template and node set, and then distributes the template onto

Fig. 7 Diameter = 2, ASPL
=1.67

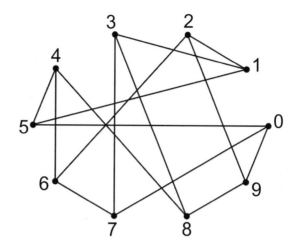

	0	1	2	3	4	5	6	7	8	9
0		2	2	2	2	1	2	1	2	1
1			1	1	2	1	2	2	2	2
2				2	2	2	1	2	2	1
3					2	2	2	1	1	2
4						1	1	2	1	2
5							2	2	2	2
6								1	2	2
7									2	2
8										1
9										

Table 3 Combination of vertices and degrees of General Graph Category in 2017

Number of vertices	32	256	576	1344	4896	9344	88,128	98,304	100,000	100,000
Number of degrees	5	18	30	30	24	10	12	10	32	64

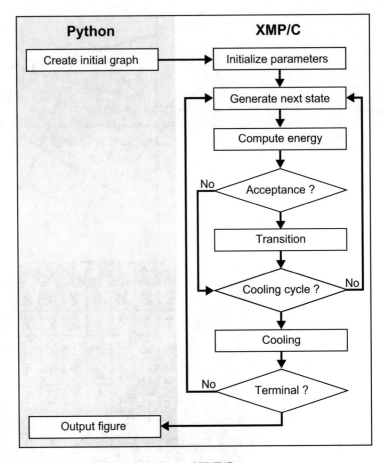

Fig. 8 Flow chart of an algorithm in Python and XMP/C

the node set in a block manner. In line 1, the "[:]" means that the template size is
not fixed at this point. In line 9, the **template_fix** directive determines the template
size *vertices*, which is the number of vertices. In lines 11–13, a diameter and ASPL
are calculated. The calculation is a state of the "Compute energy" shown in Fig. 8.
This calculation uses the top-down approach of the breadth-first search. In line 10,
the **loop** directive parallelizes the loop statement to calculate each shortest path in
parallel. In lines 14–15, the **reduction** directives aggregate a diameter and ASPL
stored at each node.

```
1   import ctypes
2   import xmp
3   import networkx as nx
4   import argparse
5
6   argumentparser = argparse.ArgumentParser()
7   argumentparser.add_argument('vertex', type=int)
8   argumentparser.add_argument('degree', type=int)
9   vertex = args.vertex
10  degree = args.degree
11
12  arr = ((c_int * 2) * (vertex * degree / 2 + 1))()
13  arr[i][0] = vertex
14  arr[i][1] = degree
15  for i, l in enumerate(nx.generate_edgelist(g, data=False)):
16      arr[i+1][0] = int(l.split()[0])
17      arr[i+1][1] = int(l.split()[1])
18
19  lib = xmp.Lib("xmp_graphgolf.so")
20  lib.spawn(4, "xmp_graphgolf", arr, async = False)
21
22  image_name = "n"+str(vertex)+"d"+str(degree)+".png"
23  lines = []
24  for line in arr:
25      lines.append(str(line[0]) + "␣" + str(line[1]))
26      G = nx.parse_edgelist(lines, nodetype = int)
27      save_image(G, image_name)
28
29  def save_image(g, filepath):
30      import matplotlib as mpl
31      mpl.use('Agg')
32      import matplotlib.pyplot as plt
33      layout = nx.circular_layout(g)
34      nx.draw(g, with_labels=False, node_size=50, linewidths=0, alpha=0.5, node_color='
                #3399ff', edge_color='#666666', pos=layout)
35      plt.draw()
36      plt.savefig(filepath)
```

Fig. 9 Code in Python

4.3 Evaluation

To evaluate the performance of the Graph Golf application, we used the "coma" system located in University of Tsukuba, the specifications of which are shown in Table 4.

We measured the time required to calculate all of the shortest paths once by changing the number of nodes. We assigned 20 XMP nodes to each compute node, and used a medium-sized number of vertices and degrees ($n = 9344$, $d = 10$), as shown in Table 3.

```
 1   #pragma xmp template t[:]
 2   #pragma xmp nodes p[*]
 3   #pragma xmp distribute t[block] onto p
 4
 5   void xmp_graphgolf(int *edge)
 6   {
 7      :
 8   int vertices = edge[0];
 9   #pragma xmp template_fix t[vertices]
10   #pragma xmp loop on t[i]
11      for(int i=0;i<vertices;i++){
12         : // Calculate diameter and ASPL
13         }
14   #pragma xmp reduction(+:ASPL)
15   #pragma xmp reduction(max:diameter)
16      :
17   }
```

Fig. 10 Code in XMP/C

Table 4 Coma system specifications

CPU	Intel Xeon-E5 2670v2 2.5 GHz 10 Cores × 2 Sockets
Memory	DDR3 1866 MHz 59.7 GB/s 64 GB
Network	InfiniBand FDR 7 GB/s
Software	intel/16.0.2, intelmpi/5.1.1, Omni compiler 1.2.1
	Python 2.7.9, networkx 1.9

Figure 11 shows performance results where the bar graph shows the time measurements, and the line graph shows the parallel efficiency of one XMP node. The time for one XMP node is 123.17 s, while the time for 1280 XMP nodes (using 64 compute nodes) is 0.13 s, which is 921 times faster. Since the time using the Python networkx package is 148.83 s in one CPU core, XMP achieved a performance improvement of 21%.

From an examination of Fig. 11, we found that the parallel efficiency decreases as the number of nodes increases. We consider that the following reasons are responsible for the decrease:

- The ratio of communication time increases. Figure 12 shows the ratio of communication time and calculation time to the total time. As the number of nodes increases, the proportion of communication time also increases.
- The parallelized loop lengths are non-uniform. The length of the loop statement in line 11 of Fig. 10 is 9344, which is the same as the number of vertices. Since the length is divided by the number of nodes, the length non-uniformity increases as the number of nodes increases.

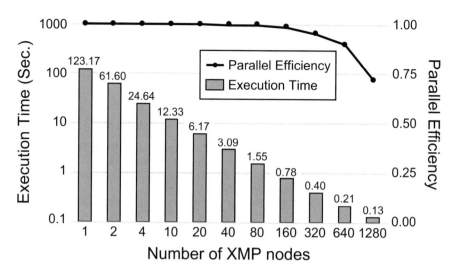

Fig. 11 Performance evaluation

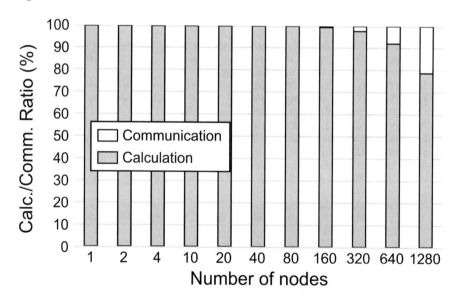

Fig. 12 Calculation and communication ratio

5 Conclusion

This chapter describes how to use linkage functions between XMP and MPI library in Omni compiler. Moreover, it also describes how to call an XMP program from a Python program. Users can call functions written in these languages with a simple procedure. Since many existing parallel applications are written in MPI library, these functions can be useful for extending existing applications. Furthermore, it will be possible to effectively use the high functionality of Python.

References

1. M. Nakao et al., Linkage of XcalableMP and Python languages for high productivity on HPC cluster system, in *Proceedings of Workshops of HPC Asia, No .9* (2018), pp.39–47
2. F. Cantonnet et al., Productivity analysis of the UPC language, in *18th International Parallel and Distributed Processing Symposium* (2004), pp.254–260
3. K. Yelick et al., Productivity and performance using partitioned global address space languages, in *Proceedings of the International Workshop on Parallel Symbolic Computation* (2007)
4. A.I. Stone et al., Evaluating coarray Fortran with the CGPOP Miniapp, in *Proceedings of the Fifth Conference on Partitioned Global Address Space Programming Models* (2011)
5. M. Nakao et al., Implementation and evaluation of the HPC challenge benchmark in the XcalableMP PGAS language. Int. J. High Perform. Comput. Appl. **33**, 110–123 (2017)
6. J. Jithin et al., Unifying UPC and MPI runtimes: experience with MVAPICH, in *Proceedings of the Fourth Conference on Partitioned Global Address Space Programming Model* (2010), pp. 5:1–5:10
7. M. Nakao et al., Productivity and performance of the HPC challenge benchmarks with the XcalableMP PGAS language, in *Proceedings of the Fourth Conference on Partitioned Global Address Space Programming Model* (2013), pp. 157–171
8. M. Nakao et al., Productivity and performance of global-view programming with XcalableMP PGAS language, in *Proceedings of the 2012 12th IEEE/ACM International Symposium on Cluster, Cloud and Grid Computing* (2012), pp. 402–409
9. M. Nakao et al., XcalableACC: extension of XcalableMP PGAS language using OpenACC for accelerator clusters, in *Proceedings of the First Workshop on Accelerator Programming Using Directives* (2014), pp.27–36
10. M. Nakao et al., Implementing lattice QCD application with XcalableACC language on accelerated cluster, in *IEEE International Conference on Cluster Computing (CLUSTER)* (2017), pp. 429–438
11. M. Nakao et al., Evaluation of XcalableACC with tightly coupled accelerators/InfiniBand hybrid communication on accelerated cluster. Int. J. High Perform. Comput. Appl. **33**, 109434201882116 (2019)
12. R.W. Numrich et al., Co-array Fortran for parallel programming. SIGPLAN Fortran Forum **17**(2), 1–31 (1998)
13. M. Nowicki et al., PCJ - Java library for high performance computing in PGAS model, in *International Conference on High Performance Computing & Simulation* (2014), pp. 202–209
14. Y. Zheng et al., UPC++: A PGAS Extension for C++, in *IEEE 28th International Parallel and Distributed Processing Symposium* (2014), pp. 1105–1114
15. K. Vivek et al., HabaneroUPC++: a compiler-free PGAS library, in *Proceedings of the 8th International Conference on Partitioned Global Address Space Programming Models, No. 5* (2014), pp. 5:1–5:10
16. C. Philippe et al., X10: an object-oriented approach to non-uniform cluster computing, in *OOPSLA '05 Proceedings of the 20th Annual ACM SIGPLAN Conference on Object-Oriented Programming, Systems, Languages, and Applications*, vol. 40, No. 10 (2005), pp. 519–538
17. B.L. Chamberlain et al., Parallel programmability and the Chapel language. Int. J. High Perform. Comput. Appl. **21**(3), 291–312 (2007)

18. K. Fürlinger et al., DASH: a C++ PGAS library for distributed data structures and parallel algorithms, in *IEEE 18th International Conference on High Performance Computing and Communications; IEEE 14th International Conference on Smart City; IEEE 2nd International Conference on Data Science and Systems (HPCC/SmartCity/DSS)* (2016), pp. 983–990
19. M. Nakao et al., Linkage of XcalableMP and Python languages for high productivity on HPC cluster system, in *Workshop on PGAS Programming Models: Experiences and Implementations* (2018)
20. V.G. Cerf et al., A lower bound on the average shortest path length in regular graphs. Networks **4**(4), 335–342 (1974)
21. M. Nicholas et al., Equation of state calculations by fast computing machines. J. Chem. Phys. **21**(6), 1087–1092 (1953)
22. S. Kirkpatrick et al., Optimization by simulated annealing. Science **220**(4598), 671–680 (1983)

Three-Dimensional Fluid Code
with XcalableMP

Hitoshi Sakagami

Abstract In order to adapt parallel computers to general convenient tools for computational scientists, a high-level and easy-to-use portable parallel programming paradigm is mandatory. XcalableMP, which is proposed by the XcalableMP Specification Working Group, is a directive-based language extension for Fortran and C to easily describe parallelization in programs for distributed memory parallel computers. The Omni XcalableMP compiler, which is provided as a reference XcalableMP compiler, is currently implemented as a source-to-source translator. It converts XcalableMP programs to standard MPI programs, which can be easily compiled by the native Fortran compiler and executed on most of parallel computers. A three-dimensional Eulerian fluid code written in Fortran is parallelized by XcalableMP using two different programming models with the ordinary domain decomposition method, and its performances are measured on the K computer. Programs converted by the Omni XcalableMP compiler prevent native Fortran compiler optimizations and show lower performance than that of hand-coded MPI programs. Finally almost the same performances are obtained by using specific compiler options of the native Fortran compiler in the case of a global-view programming model, but performance degradation is not improved by specifying any native compiler options when the code is parallelized by a local-view programming model.

1 Introduction

Computational scientists usually want to concentrate their attention on their essential research. Parallel programming is never an objective for them even if computational powers of parallel computers are necessary to advance their subjects, and this dilemma is annoying them. In order to adapt the parallel computer from a

H. Sakagami (✉)
National Institute for Fusion Science, Toki, Japan
e-mail: sakagami.hitoshi@nifs.ac.jp

165

special kind of machines to general convenient tools for computational scientists, a high-level and easy-to-use portable parallel programming paradigm is mandatory. XcalableMP (XMP) [1], which is proposed by the XcalableMP Specification Working Group, is directive-based language extensions for Fortran and C to easily describe parallelization in programs for distributed memory parallel computers. The XMP/F compiler [2], which is provided as a reference XMP Fortran compiler, is currently implemented as a source-to-source translator. It converts XMP Fortran programs to standard MPI Fortran programs, which can be easily compiled by the native Fortran compiler and executed on most of parallel computers.

XMP supports typical data/task parallelization methods with simple directives under a "global-view" programming model, which is partially based on experiences of High Performance Fortran [3, 4] and Fujitsu XPF (VPP FORTRAN) [5]. XMP also supports PGAS (Partitioned Global Address Space) features like Coarray Fortran [6] as a "local-view" programming model. In addition, combinations of XMP and OpenMP directives are consistently maintained by the XMP/F compiler. An essential design principle of XMP is "performance awareness," which means that all communications or synchronizations are taken by explicit directives or Coarray statements and no implicit actions are taken.

First, we used XMP Fortran to parallelize the code using the global-view programming model, and measured its performance on the K computer. We found that programs converted by the XMP/F compiler prevent optimizations by the native Fortran compiler and show lower performance than that of hand-coded MPI programs, but finally almost the same performances are obtained by using specific compiler options of the native Fortran compiler. Next we parallelized the code using the local-view programming model, and also measured its performance on the K computer. We found that translated programs prevent optimizations by the native Fortran compiler and show lower performance than that of the global-view programming model programs. This degradation cannot be solved by simply specifying native compiler options at this moment, and improvements of the XMP/F compiler are expected.

2　Global-View Programming Model

IMPACT-3D is a three-dimensional Eulerian fluid code written in Fortran and it performs compressible and inviscid fluid computation to simulate convergent asymmetric flows related to laser fusion [7]. A Cartesian coordinate system is employed and an explicit 5-point stencil in one direction is used in IMPACT-3D with uniform grid spacing. So it is easy to parallelize the code with the ordinary domain decomposition method. Communications between neighboring subdomains are needed to exchange boundary data.

As the global-view programming model is a directive oriented approach, programs can be incrementally parallelized and different parallelization methods can be easily tried. Although IMPACT-3D is actually parallelized by three different methods, original source codes are completely same and there are a few directive differences among three methods.

2.1 Domain Decomposition Methods

The code is parallelized by three different domain decomposition methods, namely the domain is divided in (a) only Z direction, (b) both Y and Z directions, and (c) all of X, Y, and Z directions, which are shown in Fig. 1.

Assume *LX, LY,* and *LZ* are system mesh sizes of the code in X, Y, and Z directions, and *NX, NY,* and *NZ* are division numbers in X, Y, and Z directions, respectively. In the case of only Z domain decomposition method, total amount of communicated data per domain is proportional to $LX \cdot LY$, which is not depended on any division numbers, and communication occurs twice per time step. On the other hand, data proportional to $(LX \cdot LY) \div NY$ must be communicated twice and that of $(LZ \cdot LX) \div NZ$ is also communicated twice per domain per time step in both Y and Z domain decomposition method. In the case of all of X, Y, and Z domain decomposition method, data proportional to $(LX \cdot LY) \div (NX \cdot NY)$, $(LZ \cdot LX) \div (NZ \cdot NX)$, and $(LY \cdot LZ) \div (NY \cdot NZ)$ must be communicated per domain per time step twice, twice and three times, respectively. Thus total communication costs in three different domain decomposition methods are depended on a trade-off between latency and speed. Additional communication is one reduction operation to obtain a maximum scalar value in whole simulation system.

A node array that corresponds with physical compute units in parallel computer is defined by *node* directive, three-dimensional Fortran arrays are decomposed with *template, distribute,* and *align* directives, corresponding DO loops are parallelized by *loop* directive and communications between neighboring subdomains are implemented by *shadow* and *reflect* directives. The code can be parallelized by using the "global-view" programming model directives only. Typical XMP Fortran programs are shown for each decomposition method, in Listing 1 for only Z direction, Listing 2 for both Y and Z directions, and Listing 3 for all of X, Y, and Z directions.

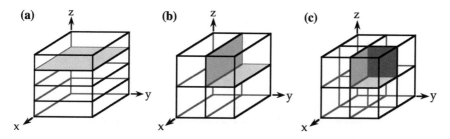

Fig. 1 IMPACT-3D is parallelized by three different domain decomposition methods. The domain is divided in (**a**) only Z direction, (**b**) both Y and Z directions, and (**c**) all of X, Y, and Z directions

lx, ly, lz are Fortran array size of first, second, third dimension, and *nx, ny, nz* are a number of division in X, Y, Z directions, respectively. These are also variable names in the program shown in Listings.

The code is also hand-coded with MPI using the same domain decomposition methods to compare performances.

Listing 1 Typical XMP programs using the global-view programming model for only Z domain decomposition method

```
 1  integer parameter :: lx=..., ly=..., lz=...
 2  integer parameter :: nz=...
 3  !$XMP NODES proc(nz)
 4  !$XMP TEMPLATE t(lx,ly,lz)
 5  !$XMP DISTRIBUTE t(*,*,BLOCK) ONTO proc
 6  real*8 :: physval(6,lx,ly,lz)
 7  real*8 :: ram
 8  !$XMP ALIGN (*,*,*,k) WITH t(*,*,k) :: physval
 9  !$XMP SHADOW (0,0,0,1) :: physval
10  ...
11  !$XMP LOOP (iz) ON t(*,*,iz)
12  !$OMP PARALLEL DO PRIVATE(iy,ix)
13  do iz = 1, lz
14   do iy = 1, ly
15    do ix = 2, lx-1
16     ...
17     physval(..,ix,iy,iz) = ... &
18        physval(..,ix-1,iy,iz) ... physval(..,ix+1,iy,iz)
19     ...
20  ...
21  !$XMP LOOP (iz) ON t(*,*,iz)
22  !$OMP PARALLEL DO PRIVATE(iy,ix)
23  do iz = 1, lz
24   do iy = 2, ly-1
25    do ix = 1, lx
26     ...
27     physval(..,ix,iy,iz) = ... &
28        physval(..,ix,iy-1,iz) ... physval(..,ix,iy+1,iz)
29     ...
30  ...
31  !$XMP REFLECT (physval)
32  !$XMP LOOP (iz) ON t(*,*,iz)
33  !$OMP PARALLEL DO PRIVATE(iy,ix)
34  do iz = 2, lz-1
35   do iy = 1, ly
36    do ix = 1, lx
37     ...
38     physval(..,ix,iy,iz) = ... &
39        physval(..,ix,iy,iz-1) ... physval(..,ix,iy,iz+1)
40     ...
41  ...
42  !$XMP LOOP (iz) ON t(*,*,iz) REDUCTION(max:ram)
43  !$OMP PARALLEL DO REDUCTION(max:ram) PRIVATE(iy,ix)
```

```
44 do iz = 1, lz
45  do iy = 1, ly
46   do ix = 1, lx
47    ram = max( ram, ... )
```

Listing 2 Typical XMP programs using the global-view programming model for both Y and Z domain decomposition methods

```
 1 integer parameter :: lx=..., ly=..., lz=...
 2 integer parameter :: ny=..., nz=...
 3 !$XMP NODES proc(ny,nz)
 4 !$XMP TEMPLATE t(lx,ly,lz)
 5 !$XMP DISTRIBUTE t(*,BLOCK,BLOCK) ONTO proc
 6 real*8 :: physval(6,lx,ly,lz)
 7 real*8 :: ram
 8 !$XMP ALIGN (*,*,j,k) WITH t(*,j,k) :: physval
 9 !$XMP SHADOW (0,0,1,1) :: physval
10 ...
11 !$XMP LOOP (iy,iz) ON t(*,iy,iz)
12 !$OMP PARALLEL DO PRIVATE(iy,ix)
13 do iz = 1, lz
14  do iy = 1, ly
15   do ix = 2, lx-1
16    ...
17    physval(..,ix,iy,iz) = ... &
18       physval(..,ix-1,iy,iz) ... physval(..,ix+1,iy,iz)
19    ...
20 ...
21 !$XMP REFLECT (physval) width(0,0,1,0)
22 !$XMP LOOP (iy,iz) ON t(*,iy,iz)
23 !$OMP PARALLEL DO PRIVATE(iy,ix)
24 do iz = 1, lz
25  do iy = 2, ly-1
26   do ix = 1, lx
27    ...
28    physval(..,ix,iy,iz) = ... &
29       physval(..,ix,iy-1,iz) ... physval(..,ix,iy+1,iz)
30    ...
31 ...
32 !$XMP REFLECT (physval) width(0,0,0,1)
33 !$XMP LOOP (iy,iz) ON t(*,iy,iz)
34 !$OMP PARALLEL DO PRIVATE(iy,ix)
35 do iz = 2, lz-1
36  do iy = 1, ly
37   do ix = 1, lx
38    ...
39    physval(..,ix,iy,iz) = ... &
40       physval(..,ix,iy,iz-1) ... physval(..,ix,iy,iz+1)
41    ...
42 ...
43 !$XMP LOOP (iy,iz) ON t(*,iy,iz) REDUCTION(max:ram)
44 !$OMP PARALLEL DO REDUCTION(max:ram) PRIVATE(iy,ix)
```

```
45 do iz = 1, lz
46  do iy = 1, ly
47   do ix = 1, lx
48    ram = max( ram, ... )
```

Listing 3 Typical XMP programs using the global-view programming model for all of X, Y, and Z domain decomposition method

```
 1 integer parameter :: lx=..., ly=..., lz=...
 2 integer parameter :: nx=..., ny=..., nz=...
 3 !$XMP NODES proc(nx,ny,nz)
 4 !$XMP TEMPLATE t(lx,ly,lz)
 5 !$XMP DISTRIBUTE t(BLOCK,BLOCK,BLOCK) ONTO proc
 6 real*8 :: physval(6,lx,ly,lz)
 7 real*8 :: ram
 8 !$XMP ALIGN (*,i,j,k) WITH t(i,j,k) :: physval
 9 !$XMP SHADOW (0,1,1,1) :: physval
10 ...
11 !$XMP REFLECT (physval) width(0,1,0,0)
12 !$XMP LOOP (ix,iy,iz) ON t(ix,iy,iz)
13 !$OMP PARALLEL DO PRIVATE(iy,ix)
14 do iz = 1, lz
15  do iy = 1, ly
16   do ix = 2, lx-1
17    ...
18    physval(..,ix,iy,iz) = ... &
19       physval(..,ix-1,iy,iz) ... physval(..,ix+1,iy,iz)
20    ...
21 ...
22 !$XMP REFLECT (physval) width(0,0,1,0)
23 !$XMP LOOP (ix,iy,iz) ON t(ix,iy,iz)
24 !$OMP PARALLEL DO PRIVATE(iy,ix)
25 do iz = 1, lz
26  do iy = 2, ly-1
27   do ix = 1, lx
28    ...
29    physval(..,ix,iy,iz) = ... &
30       physval(..,ix,iy-1,iz) ... physval(..,ix,iy+1,iz)
31    ...
32 ...
33 !$XMP REFLECT (physval) width(0,0,0,1)
34 !$XMP LOOP (ix,iy,iz) ON t(ix,iy,iz)
35 !$OMP PARALLEL DO PRIVATE(iy,ix)
36 do iz = 2, lz-1
37  do iy = 1, ly
38   do ix = 1, lx
39    ...
40    physval(..,ix,iy,iz) = ... &
41       physval(..,ix,iy,iz-1) ... physval(..,ix,iy,iz+1)
42    ...
43 ...
44 !$XMP LOOP (ix,iy,iz) ON t(ix,iy,iz) REDUCTION(max:ram)
```

```
45  !$OMP PARALLEL DO REDUCTION(max:ram) PRIVATE(iy,ix)
46  do iz = 1, lz
47   do iy = 1, ly
48    do ix = 1, lx
49     ram = max( ram, ... )
```

2.2 Performance on the K Computer

As one node consists of 8 cores in the K computer, one MPI process is dispatched onto each node and each process performs computations with 8 threads. We run both XMP and MPI codes with three different decomposition methods and evaluate the weak scaling on the K computer using Omni XcalableMP 0.7.0 and Fujitsu Fortran K-1.2.0.15. A number of cores for execution and corresponding simulation parameters are summarized in Table 1.

Performance are measured by a hardware monitor installed on the K computer, and MFLOPS/PEAK, Memory throughput/PEAK and SIMD execution usage are obtained.

2.2.1 Comparison with Hand-Coded MPI Program

MFLOPS/PEAK values for all six cases, namely (MPI, XMP) × (only Z, both Y and Z, all of X, Y, and Z) are shown in Fig. 2.

Performances of XMP codes are the same as those of MPI codes, and small differences among three decomposition methods are found. But we can get only 8~9% of peak performance of the K computer. From the hardware monitor, we found that SIMD execution usage was less than 5% in all cases, and this could degrade the performance. Most cost intensive DO loops in IMPACT-3D include IF statements, which are needed to correctly treat extremely slow fluid velocity regardless of XMP and MPI codes, and the IF statement interrupts the native Fortran compiler to generate SIMD instructions inside the DO loop. Thus relatively low performance is obtained.

Table 1 Simulation parameters for global-view programming model

#Core	lx=ly=lz	Only Z	Both Y and Z		All of X, Y and Z		
		nz	ny	nz	nx	ny	nz
256	1024	32	8	4	4	4	2
2048	2048	256	16	16	8	8	4
16,384	4096		64	32	16	16	8
131,072	8192		128	128	32	32	16

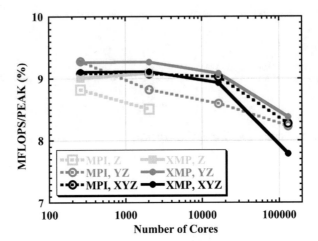

Fig. 2 MFLOPS/PEAK measured by the hardware monitor installed on the K computer. Solid and dash lines indicate performances of XMP and MPI codes, respectively. Colors of light gray, gray, and black indicate only Z domain decomposition, both Y and Z domain decomposition, and all of X, Y, and Z domain decomposition methods, respectively

2.2.2 Optimization for SIMD

As the *true* rate of the IF statement is nearly 100% in IMPACT-3D, speculative execution of SIMD instruction causes almost no overhead. So forcing the compiler to generate the SIMD instructions could be useful to enhance the performance, and it can be done with *simd=2* compiler option. All codes are recompiled with that option and rerun. SIMD execution usage increases up to around 50% in all cases, and we can expect performance improvement. MFLOPS/PEAK values for all cases are shown in Fig. 3.

Small differences among three decomposition methods are also found with this compiler option. MPI code performance is improved and we can get up to 20% of the peak performance. XMP code performance is also improved, but these are below 15% even MPI and XMP code performance is almost same without *simd=2* option. According to compiler diagnostic of the native Fortran compiler, the software pipelining is adopted for cost intensive DO loops in the MPI code, but it is not applied for the source code converted by the XMP/F compiler from the XMP code. As the XMP/F compiler converts a simple DO statement of "do i = is, ie" to more general form "do i1 = xmp_s1, xmp_e1, xmp_d1" and the native Fortran compiler cannot optimize the DO loop because do increment is given by a variable and it is unknown at compilation time. So we improved the XMP/F compiler to generate "do i1 = xmp_s1, xmp_e1, 1" form when the do increment is not given and supposed to be one in the XMP code. As a result, the software pipelining is also adopted for cost intensive DO loops converted by the XMP/F compiler, but no performance improvement is obtained. Although Memory throughput/PEAK values

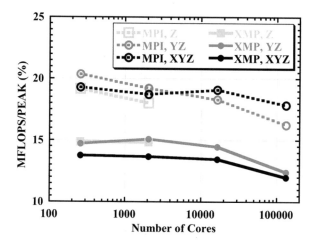

Fig. 3 MFLOPS/PEAK measured by the hardware monitor installed on the K computer with SIMD optimization by *simd=2* compiler option. Solid and dash lines indicate performances of XMP and MPI codes, respectively. Colors of light gray, gray, and black indicate only Z domain decomposition, both Y and Z domain decomposition, and all of X, Y, and Z domain decomposition methods, respectively

of MPI codes are 55%, those of XMP codes are only 37% and this low memory throughput is one of candidates for low sustained performance.

2.2.3 Optimization for Allocatable Arrays

In the converted code by the XMP/F compiler, all Fortran arrays are treated as allocatable arrays even the original code uses static arrays. The allocatable array prevents the native Fortran compiler from optimizing the DO loop with prefetch instructions because the array size cannot be determined at compilation time, and it could cause low memory throughput. All Fortran arrays in the hand-coded MPI code for XYZ decomposition are just replaced by allocatable arrays and we check a performance difference. Performance of the MPI code are shown in Fig. 4 for static arrays (light gray dash) and allocatable arrays (gray dash).

MFLOPS/PEAK values are dropped from 20% to 15%, and this performance degradation without the prefetch instructions is confirmed. To force the native Fortran compiler to perform the prefetch optimization, we can use *prefetch_stride* compiler option. All codes are recompiled with *prefetch_stride* compiler option and rerun. Performance improvements by this compiler option are shown in Fig. 4 for both MPI (gray dash to black dash) and XMP (gray solid to black solid) codes. MFLOPS/PEAK values are improved by 2~3% with the prefetch optimization. Finally we can get almost the same performance with XMP as that of MPI when allocatable arrays are used, but efforts to shrink the performance gap between static and allocatable arrays are still needed.

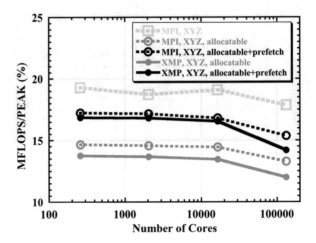

Fig. 4 IMFLOPS/PEAK measured by the hardware monitor installed on the K computer with prefetch optimization by *prefetch_stride* compiler option. Solid and dash lines indicate performances of XMP and MPI codes, respectively. Colors of light gray, gray, and black indicate static arrays, allocatable arrays, and allocatable arrays with prefetch optimization, respectively

3 Local-View Programming Model

In the local-view programming model, communications among domains are written by Fortran Coarray assignment statements, with which two types of one-sided communications for local data, namely *put* and *get*, are adopted. For the sake of simplicity, we focus on the all of X, Y, and Z domain decomposition method in this section.

3.1 Communications Using Coarray

Just same as the MPI program, DO loop boundaries in the original source code must be modified and communications must be explicitly written by Coarray assignment statements. Typical XMP Fortran programs using *put* communications are shown in Listing 4, which is corresponding to Listing 3. Division numbers are defined just as variables, not parameters to easily change them by input data without recompilations. As Coarray features in Fortran 2008, which is supported by the XMP/F compiler at that time, do not include reduction operations, the code to obtain the maximum value of the scalar variable in whole simulation system must be hand-coded. But Coarray features in Fortran 2015 support reduction operations by intrinsic subroutines, and these codes are simply replaced with *co_max* intrinsic subroutine, which is shown in Listing 5. These intrinsic subroutines are partially supported by the current XMP/F compiler.

Listing 4 Typical XMP programs using the local-view programming model with *put* communications for all of X, Y, and Z domain decomposition method

```
 1 integer, parameter :: lx=..., ly=..., lz=...
 2 real*8 :: ram
 3 real*8, allocatable :: rami(:)
 4 real*8, allocatable :: physval(6,:,:,:)[:]
 5 real*8 :: ramc[*]
 6 ...
 7 limgn = THIS_IMAGE()
 8 lsx = lx / nx
 9 lsy = ly / ny
10 lsz = lz / nz
11 linxp = limgn + 1
12 linxm = limgn - 1
13 linyp = limgn + nx
14 linym = limgn - nx
15 linzp = limgn + (nx*ny)
16 linzm = limgn - (nx*ny)
17 allocate( physval(6,0:lsx+1,0:lsy+1,0:lsz+1)[*] )
18 allocate( rami(nx*ny*nz) )
19 ...
20 physval(:,lsx+1,:,:)[linxm] = physval1(:,1,:,:)
21 physval(:,0,:,:)[linxp] = physval1(:,lsx,:,:)
22 SYNC ALL
23 !$OMP PARALLEL DO PRIVATE(iy,ix)
24 do iz = 1, lsz
25  do iy = 1, lsy
26   do ix = 1, lsx
27    ...
28    physval(..,ix,iy,iz) = ... &
29      physval(..,ix-1,iy,iz) ... physval(..,ix+1,iy,iz)
30    ...
31 ...
32 physval(:,:,lsy+1,:)[linym] = physval1(:,:,1,:)
33 physval(:,:,0,:)[linyp] = physval1(:,:,lsy,:)
34 SYNC ALL
35 !$OMP PARALLEL DO PRIVATE(iy,ix)
36 do iz = 1, lsz
37  do iy = 1, lsy
38   do ix = 1, lsx
39    ...
40    physval(..,ix,iy,iz) = ... &
41      physval(..,ix,iy-1,iz) ... physval(..,ix,iy+1,iz)
42    ...
43 ...
44 physval(:,:,:,lsz+1)[linzm] = physval1(:,:,:,1)
45 physval(:,:,:,0)[linzp] = physval1(:,:,:,lsz)
46 SYNC ALL
47 !$OMP PARALLEL DO PRIVATE(iy,ix)
48 do iz = 1, lsz
49  do iy = 1, lsy
50   do ix = 1, lsx
```

```
51    ...
52    physval(..,ix,iy,iz) = ... &
53       physval(..,ix,iy,iz-1) ... physval(..,ix,iy,iz+1)
54    ...
55 ...
56 !$OMP PARALLEL DO REDUCTION(max:ram) PRIVATE(iy,ix)
57 do iz = 1, lsz
58  do iy = 1, lsy
59   do ix = 1, lsx
60    ram = max( ram, ... )
61 ...
62 ramc = ram
63 SYNC ALL
64 if( limgn .eq. 1 ) then
65  rami(1) = ram
66  do i = 2, nx*ny*nz
67   rami(i) = ramc[i]
68  end do
69  ram = max( rami )
70  ramc = ram
71 end if
72 SYNC ALL
73 if( limgn .ne. 1 ) then
74  ram = ramc[1]
75 end if
```

Listing 5 Reduction operations can be replaced by an intrinsic subroutine

```
1 ...
2 call CO_MAX( ram )
3 ...
```

Differences of programs between *put* and *get* communications are only in Coarray assignment and related *sync all* statements, and the other parts are completely same. Ttypical XMP Fortran programs related with *get* communications are shown in Listing 6. Note that related *sync all* statement must be written after *put* or before *get* communications.

Listing 6 Typical XMP programs using the local-view programming model with *get* communications for all of X, Y, and Z domain decomposition method

```
1 ...
2 SYNC ALL
3 physval(:,lsx+1,:,:) = physval1(:,1,:,:) [linxp]
4 physval(:,0,:,:)     = physval1(:,lsx,:,:) [linxm]
5 ...
6 SYNC ALL
7 physval(:,:,lsy+1,:) = physval1(:,:,1,:) [linyp]
8 physval(:,:,0,:)     = physval1(:,:,lsy,:) [linym]
```

```
 9  . . .
10  SYNC ALL
11  physval(:,:,:,lsz+1) = physval1(:,:,:,1) [linzp]
12  physval(:,:,:,0) = physval1(:,:,:,lsz) [linzm]
13  . . .
```

3.2 Performance on the K Computer

We run three XMP codes using the global-view programming model, and the local-view programming model with *put* and *get* communications, and local-view communications are implemented on Fujitsu RDMA. Each process performs computations with 8 threads just like before and we evaluate the weak scaling on the K computer using Omni XcalableMP 0.9.1 and Fujitsu Fortran K-1.2.0.18. A number of cores for execution and corresponding simulation parameters are summarized in Table 2 and performance are also measured by the hardware monitor installed on the K computer. As versions of both Omni XcalableMP and Fujitsu Fortran compilers are different from those of previous section, we also rerun the global-view programming model code. MFLOPS/PEAK values for all cases are shown in Fig. 5.

Performances using the global-view programming model are almost same as those in previous section, but the local-view programming model shows very low performances, namely 3% of peak performance of the K computer. From the hardware monitor, we found that SIMD execution usage was less than 0.2% in local-view programming model cases, this means that cost intensive DO loops in IMPACT-3D are not SIMDized at all even with *simd=2* and *prefetch_stride* native Fortran compiler options. All Fortran allocatable coarrays in the local-view programming model codes are converted to pointer arrays by the XMP/F compiler. The pointer array prevents the native Fortran compiler from SIMDizing the DO loop even it is forced to SIMDize the loop by *simd=2* compiler option because the compiler thinks that variables may be overlapped and SIMD execution causes incorrect calculations. To tell the compiler that variables are not overlapped, we can specify *noalias* option and SIMD execution usage is improved to 15%. But prefetch instructions are still suppressed and the pointer array may prevent other compiler optimizations, performances are not improved at all.

Table 2 Simulation parameters for local-view programming model

#Core	$lx=ly=lz$	All of X, Y and Z		
		nx	ny	nz
256	1024	4	4	2
2048	2048	8	8	4
16,384	4096	16	16	8

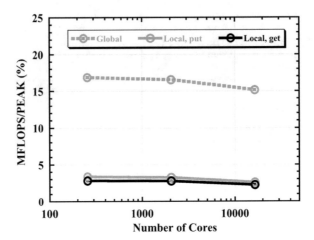

Fig. 5 MFLOPS/PEAK measured by the hardware monitor installed on the K computer. Gray dash line indicates performance of the global-view programming model. Gray and black solid lines indicate performances of the local-view programming model with *put* and *get* communications, respectively

4 Summary

We have parallelized a three-dimensional fluid code with XMP Fortran using the global-view programming model and compared XMP performances with those of the hand-coded MPI program on the K computer. We found that performances of XMP programs are the same as those of MPI programs but these are only 8~9% of peak performance of the K computer. It was found that this relative low performance is due to lack of SIMD execution according to SIMD execution usage by the hardware monitor. We forced the native Fortran compiler to SIMDize loops with the specific compiler option, and found that performance of MPI programs reach to 20% of peak performance even those of XMP programs remain around 15%. It was found that this relative low performance is due to low memory throughput according to Memory throughput/PEAK by the hardware monitor. Finally we could get almost the same performance of XMP codes as those of MPI codes by using additional specific compiler option of the native Fortran compiler.

Next we parallelized the code using the local-view programming model, and also measured its performance on the K computer. We found that translated programs prevent SIMDization by the native Fortran compiler and show only 3% of peak performance of the K computer, much lower performance than that of the global-view programming model programs. This degradation cannot be solved by simply specifying native compiler options at this moment, and improvements of the XMP/F compiler are expected.

These kinds of advanced performance optimization techniques of the native Fortran compiler are not clear and may be somewhat difficult for computational scientists, but XMP programming still requires much less efforts than those for MPI programming.

Acknowledgments This work was partially supported by JSPS Grant-in-Aid for Scientific Research (C) (25400539). Part of the research was funded by MEXT's program for the Development and Improvement for the Next Generation Ultra High-Speed Computer System, under its Subsidies for Operating the Specific Advanced Large Research Facilities.

References

1. XcalableMP, http://www.xcalablemp.org/
2. Omni XMP compiler, http://omni-compiler.org/xcalablemp.html
3. High Performance Fortran, http://hpff.rice.edu/
4. K. Kennedy, C. Koelbel, H. Zima, *Proceedings of the 3rd ACM SIGPLAN Conference on History of Programming Languages* (2007), pp. 7-1–7-22
5. Y. Zhang, H. Iwashita, K. Ishii, M. Kaneko, T. Nakamura, K. Hotta, *Proceedings of the 6th International Workshop on OpenMP* (2010), pp. 133–148
6. J. Reid, *Coarrays in the Next Fortran Standard*, ISO/IEC JTC1/SC22/WG5 N1787 (2009)
7. H. Sakagami, H. Murai, Y. Seo, M. Yokokawa, *IEEE/ACM SC2002 Conference*, pap147 (2002)

Hybrid-View Programming of Nuclear Fusion Simulation Code in XcalableMP

Keisuke Tsugane, Taisuke Boku, Hitoshi Murai, Mitsuhisa Sato, William Tang, and Bei Wang

Abstract XcalableMP(XMP) supports a global-view model that allows programmers to define global data and to map them to a set of processors, which execute the distributed global data as a single thread. In XMP, the concept of a coarray is also employed for local-view programming. In this study, we port Gyrokinetic Toroidal Code - Princeton (GTC-P), which is a three-dimensional gyrokinetic PIC code developed at Princeton University to study the microturbulence phenomenon in magnetically confined fusion plasmas, to XMP as an example of hybrid memory model coding with the global-view and local-view programming models. In local-view programming, the coarray notation is simple and intuitive compared with Message Passing Interface (MPI) programming, while the performance is comparable to that of the MPI version. Thus, because the global-view programming model is suitable for expressing the data parallelism for a field of grid space data, we implement a hybrid-view version using a global-view programming model to compute the field and a local-view programming model to compute the movement of particles. The performance is degraded by 20% compared with the original MPI version, but the hybrid-view version facilitates more natural data expression for static grid space data (in the global-view model) and dynamic particle data (in the local-view model), and it also increases the readability of the code for higher productivity.

K. Tsugane
Fujitsu Laboratories Ltd., Kawasaki, Kanagawa, Japan
e-mail: tsugane.keisuke@fujitsu.com

T. Boku
Center for Computational Sciences, University of Tsukuba, Tsukuba, Ibaraki, Japan
e-mail: taisuke@ccs.tsukuba.ac.jp

H. Murai · M. Sato (✉)
RIKEN Center for Computational Science, Kobe, Hyogo, Japan
e-mail: h-murai@riken.jp; msato@riken.jp

W. Tang · B. Wang
Princeton Institute for Computational Science and Engineering, Princeton University, Princeton, NJ, USA

M. Sato (ed.), *XcalableMP PGAS Programming Language*,
https://doi.org/10.1007/978-981-15-7683-6_7

1 Introduction

In XMP, the global-view model allows programmers to define global arrays, which are distributed to processors by adding the directives. Some typical communication patterns are supported by directives, such as data exchange between neighbor processors in stencil computations. In contrast to the global-view model, the local-view model describes remote memory access using the node (processor) index. This operation is implemented as one-sided communication. XMP employs the coarray concept from Coarray Fortran as a local-view programming model. A coarray is a distributed data object, which is indexed by the coarray dimension that maps indices to processors. In XMP, the coarray is defined in C as well as Fortran. In the local-view model, a thread on each processor executes its own local computations independently with remote memory access to data located in different processors by coarray access. The local-view model requires that programmers define their algorithms by explicitly decomposing the data structures and controlling the flow in each processor. The data view is similar to that in MPI, but coarray remote access provides a more intuitive view of accessing the data in different processors, thereby increasing productivity.

In this chapter,[1] we consider a hybrid-view programming approach, which combines the global-view and local-view models in XMP according to the characteristics of the distributed data structure of the target application. The global-view model allows programmers to express regular parallel computations such as domain decomposition with stencil computation in a highly intuitive manner simply by adding directives to a serial version of code. However, it is difficult to describe parallel programs in the global-view model when more irregular communication patterns and complex load balancing are required on the processing. Thus, local-view programming is necessary in these situations.

We apply this hybrid-view programming for Gyrokinetic Toroidal Code - Princeton (GTC-P)[4], which is a large-scale plasma turbulence code that can be applied at the International Thermonuclear Experimental Reactor (ITER [13]) scale and beyond for next-generation nuclear fusion simulation. The GTC-P is an improved version of the original GTC[2] and it is a type of gyrokinetic Particle-in-Cell (PIC) code with two basic data arrays: global grid data that corresponds to the physical problem space and particle data that corresponds to particles moving around the grid space. The original GTC-P was written in C as a form of hybrid programming with OpenMP and MPI. In this code, the grid data and particle data are mapped onto MPI processes and exchanged. As found with most codes of this type, it is difficult to manage complex data distributions and communication for both grid data and particle data during code development. Furthermore, to simulate the

---

[1]The original version of this chapter was published in: Keisuke Tsugane, Taisuke Boku, Hitoshi Murai, Mitsuhisa Sato, William M. Tang, Bei Wang, "Hybrid-view programming of nuclear fusion simulation code in the PGAS parallel programming language XcalableMP." Parallel Computing 57: 37–51 (2016).

microturbulence phenomenon in plasmas for magnetically confined fusion devices, non-flat domain decomposition is necessary in one dimension, as well as parallelizing multiple dimensions, to obtain accurate large-scale simulations. Therefore, the number of computations becomes extremely large for next-generation and large-scale reactors such as ITER.

We consider both types of data models in XMP, i.e., global-view and local-view models, which are suitable for representing grid space data and particle data, respectively, because of their data distribution and communication pattern. In this study, we implement the GTC-P code in two ways: using XMP with a local-view only model, and with a combination of local-view and global-view models, where we evaluate the performance and productivity of these approaches. As the preliminary result, we implemented and evaluated the GTC-P in XMP hybrid-view model[15]. Moreover, we indicate the causes of performance degradation for GTC-P in XMP and evaluate the GTC-P of hybrid versions written in XMP+OpenMP and MPI+OpenMP in this study.

The remainder of this chapter is organized as follows. Next, we briefly describe the GTC-P nuclear fusion simulation code in Sect. 2. Section 3 describes the implementation of GTC-P using Hybrid programing model of XMP. We report the performance and productivity evaluation in Sect. 4, and related works in Sect. 5. Finally, we conclude our study in Sect. 6.

2 Nuclear Fusion Simulation Code

Typical methods used to simulate the microturbulence phenomenon in magnetically confined fusion plasmas include the Monte Carlo method and the PIC method. In this study, we only consider the gyrokinetic PIC method among them as a target application to explain the GTC and GTC-P code briefly.

2.1 Gyrokinetic PIC Simulation

The simulation of the gyrokinetic PIC method uses a space grid to calculate the field and for the particle trajectory calculation, which does not depend on the grid when moving in the free space. Figure 1 shows an image of a gyrokinetic PIC simulation with a two-dimensional block distribution. The typical behavior of the gyrokinetic PIC code is as follows.

1. Add the charge of the particle to the nearby grid points.
2. Solve the electric field affected by the electrostatic potential by calculating the charge density of the nearby grid points using Poisson's equation.
3. Interpolate the electric field in the current position based on each particle in the nearby grid points and move the position of the particle in the space.

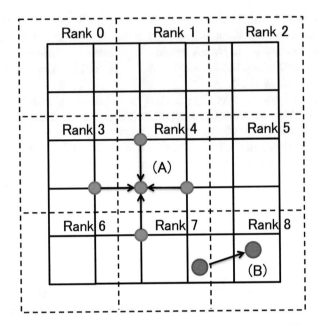

Fig. 1 Image from a gyrokinetic PIC simulation with a two-dimensional block distribution; (A) Calculation of the field using the nearby grid points and (B) the movement of a particle. The dashed lines indicate processor boundaries

During each step, a process must communicate with another if that process holds the data for the space in the grid that is affected, as shown in Fig. 1 (A), or if the particle data move from or to that process, as shown in Fig. 1 (B). Based on the above, if the size of the distributed domain, e.g., the grid in Fig. 1, is not changed, the data distribution employed in the global-view programming model is suitable and the communication between nearby grid points can be described by the `reflect` directive in XMP coding. In contrast, if the number of particles on each distributed domain changes dynamically during each time step of the simulation, such as particle motion, coarray communication is required using local-view programming.

2.2 GTC

GTC is a three-dimensional (3D) gyrokinetic PIC code, which was developed by DOE SciDAC, UC Irvine, etc.[2] for studying the microturbulence phenomenon in plasmas for magnetically confined fusion devices. Figure 2 shows a conceptual image of a 3D torus physical space. GTC treats the physical space and the movement of particles in three directions: the toroidal direction around the major axis, the poloidal direction around the magnetic axis, and the radial direction of the minor radius from the magnetic axis. The cross-section of the toroidal direction is known

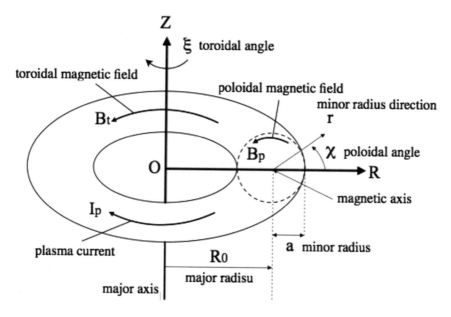

Fig. 2 Conceptual image of the three-dimensional torus space in GTC-P[10]

as the poloidal plane. GTC-P is a modified version of GTC, where there are several differences in the parallelization scheme. Moreover, GTC-P is implemented as two versions in the C and Fortran languages, whereas the original GTC is coded in Fortran. In this study, we focus on the C implementation of GTC-P.

GTC parallelizes the problem according to three levels. Processing on the space grid domain in the toroidal direction and the processing of particles in each domain are mapped onto MPI processes. Also, the grid-related calculation and particles in each distributed domain are further subdivided using OpenMP for each process. GTC-P has four levels of parallelism with additional parallelism in the radial direction. The total number of MPI processes that need to be executed is $N_t \times N_r \times N_{rp}$, where N_t is the number of domains decomposed in the toroidal direction, N_r is the number of domains decomposed in the radial direction, and N_{rp} is the number of particles decomposed in each of the distributed domains.

There is a difference in the number of grid points on the poloidal plane, as demonstrated in Fig. 3 (left). The toroidal domain can be distributed with equally sized intervals, but the radial domain cannot be distributed with equally sized intervals due to the large difference in the domain size depending on its position in space. Therefore, in order to align as much as possible the number of grid points to be mapped on each process, the outer area of the radial domain is distributed as short radial interval and its inner area is distributed as long radial interval, such as Fig. 3 (right).

GTC-P has mainly six computational kernels. The `charge` kernel deposits the charge from particles onto the grid using the four-point approximation of nearby

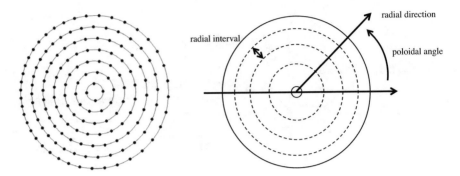

Fig. 3 Example showing the grid points on the poloidal plane in GTC-P[3] (left). Image of the radial domain decomposition on poloidal plain. The dashed line shows the border of the decomposition (right)

grid points. The `poisson`, `field`, and `smooth` kernels solve the gyrokinetic Poisson's equation, compute an electric field, and smooth the charge and potential with a filter on the grid, respectively. The `push` kernel interpolates the electric field onto particles using the field. The `charge` and `push` kernels account for large percentage of the elapsed time in this simulation [4, 16].

3   Implementation of GTC-P by Hybrid-view Programming

In this section, we describe how to implement GTC-P using hybrid programming model of XMP.

3.1   Hybrid-View Programming Model

XMP allows the use of hybrid-view programming, which combines the global-view and local-view models. The global-view model allows programmers to express regular parallel computations, such as domain decomposition with stencil computation, in a highly intuitive manner simply by adding directives to a serial version of the code. On the other hand, when the data distribution cannot be simply described in domain decomposition manner or the communication pattern is complicated, the global-view model is not suitable, and more dynamism is required to express the code naturally. Thus, the coarray notation provided by the local-view model is required in this case, and it is possible to program in a flexible manner using these models.

Figure 4 shows a skeleton code of the implementation of a gyrokinetic PIC simulation with XMP. In this example, the grid uses a two-dimensional block

```
1   double f[X][Y]; /* Electric field data */
2   double p[N]; /* Particle data */
3   double send[N], recv[N]:[*];
4   #pragma xmp align f[i][j] with T(i, j)
5   #pragma xmp shadow f[1:1][1:1]
6
7   for(t=0; t<TIME; t++) {
8     /* Calculate the grid−related work */
9     #pragma xmp reflect(f)
10    /* Calculate the particle−related work */
11    /* Pack the communication elements from array "p" to array "send" */
12    /* Calculate the destination process "pe" and communication size "icount" */
13    recv[0:icount]:[pe] = send[0:icount];
14    xmp_sync_all(NULL); /* Synchronization */
15  }
```

Fig. 4 Example showing the implementation of a gyrokinetic PIC simulation with XMP

distribution and each block has a sleeve area, which is used to calculate the field with the nearby grid points based on the shadow directive. The particle movement is represented by the coarray notation where the communication elements are packed in the array send. Based on the above, we describe the two implementations of GTC-P using XMP. First, we implement the XMP-localview version using coarray communication, which is equivalent to using MPI point-to-point communication with the exception of MPI collective communication (as shown below). Next, the XMP-hybridview version is implemented by describing the fields using a distributed array with the reflect directive for overlapped sleeve area communication and the distributed data in the global-view programming model, as well as using the coarray notation to move the particle data. In addition, we use the bcast and reduction directives instead of MPI collective communication (MPI_Bcast and MPI_Allreduce) in both versions.

3.2 Implementation Based on the XMP-Localview Model: XMP-localview

In GTC-P, the communication processes required to move particles between grids and to exchange grid points are represented by MPI_Sendrecv or MPI_Isend/Irecv, where most of the communication is performed between adjacent processes in one dimension. GTC-P has the steady state exchange of particles between neighboring subdomains. Because the number of particles changes dynamically, this implementation uses the coarray notation in the local-view programming model.

Figures 5 and 6 show the particle data movement using MPI and the corresponding the coarray notation in GTC-P, respectively. In the exchange of coarray notation for particle data movement, it communicates the number of particles and the particle data, i.e., nsendright and sendright, with the adjacent process on the neighbor to the right. In addition, Figs. 7 and 8 show the exchange of grid points using MPI and the corresponding coarray notation in GTC-P, respectively. In the example of the coarray notation for the exchange of grid points, after copying a value to a one-dimensional array, i.e., sendr or Xsendr, it communicates with the adjacent process on the neighbor to the right. Because the coarray notation is non-blocking communication, xmp_sync_image on the sixth line of Fig. 6 and the seventh line of Fig. 8 are required to guarantee that communication has been completed between two processes, in this case, the neighboring (right_pe) and current processes.

```
1   /* send # of particles to right neighbor and recv from left neighbor */
2   MPI_Sendrecv(&nsendright, 1, MPI_INT, right_pe, sendtag,
3                       &nrecvleft, 1, MPI_INT, left_pe, recvtag, comm, &status);
4   /* send particles to right neighbor and recv from left neighbor */
5   MPI_Sendrecv(sendright, nsendright, MPI_DOUBLE, right_pe, sendtag,
6                       recvleft, nrecvleft, MPI_DOUBLE, left_pe, recvtag, comm, status);
```

Fig. 5 Particle data movement using MPI point-to-point communication in GTC-P

```
1   /* send # of particles to right neighbor */
2   nrecvleft:[right_pe] = nsendright;
3   /* send particles to right neighbor */
4   recvleft[0:nsendright]:[right_pe] = sendright[0:nsendright];
5   /* synchronization */
6   xmp_sync_image(right_pe, NULL);
```

Fig. 6 Particle data movement using the coarray notation in GTC-P

```
1   double *sendr, *recvl;
2
3   for(i=0;i<nloc_over;i++)
4     sendr[i]=phitmp[i*(mzeta+1)+mzeta];
5
6   MPI_Sendrecv(sendr,nloc_over,MPI_DOUBLE,right_pe,
7         isendtag,recvl,nloc_over,MPI_DOUBLE,left_pe,
8         irecvtag,toroidal_comm,&istatus);
```

Fig. 7 Exchange of grid points using MPI point-to-point communication in GTC-P

```
1   double Xsendr[nloc_over],Xrecvl[nloc_over]:[*];
2
3   for(i=0;i<nloc_over;i++)
4     Xsendr[i]=phitmp[i*(mzeta+1)+mzeta];
5
6   Xrecvl[0:nloc_over]:[right_pe]=Xsendr[0:nloc_over];
7   xmp_sync_image(right_pe, NULL);
```

Fig. 8 Exchange of grid points using the coarray notation in GTC-P

3.3   Implementation Based on the XMP-Hybridview Model: XMP-Hybridview

In the XMP-hybridview implementation, all of the space grid data are denoted by a global-view model with compile-time mapping and the sleeve data are exchanged by XMP directives, whereas the particle data movements are denoted by a local-view model with the coarray notation, as shown Fig. 6. It is necessary to represent an unequal block size for domain decomposition in the radial dimension. Because this dimension's space grid is denoted in the global-view model, we apply the gblock notation to represent it correctly in the same manner as the original MPI implementation. The gblock notation can control the variable block size of each domain on the mapped space position. This feature is especially important for porting GTC-P onto XMP with a global-view model. Figure 10 shows an example of the GTC-P implementation with the XMP global-view programming model using gblock. The 11th line of this example denotes the block size distribution in the radial dimension. Because of describing the data distribution by global-view model, we can describe the loop distribution only to insert loop directive onto the serial code that is from the 28th to 30th lines of this example. In addition, OpenMP directives can be combined with XMP such as the 27th line.

The calculation of the grid-related works, such as the deposit of the charge from particles onto the grid using a four-point approximation of grid points, the computation of an electronic field, and the interpolation of the electronic field onto particles, are similar to four-point stencil calculation on the poloidal plain. In these codes, we can describe the loop parallelization by inserting loop directive onto the serial version. Appropriate directives are used for each dimension of the distributed array in XMP, and we further synchronize the sleeve data that overlap at each end of the distributed domain, which we can describe simply using the reflect directive. Figure 9 shows an example of the reflect directive, which is the same as the communication described in Figs. 7 and 8. Thus, we can describe it using a directive on one line, which is much simpler compared with the MPI notation in Figs. 7 and 8. When the width clause is specified, it can be designated as part of the sleeve elements and the periodic is used to update the sleeve area of the global lower (upper) bound based on the global upper (lower) bound (Fig. 10).

```
1   #define n_t 2
2   /* Number of the toroidal domain decomposition */
3   #define n_r 4
4   /* Number of the radial domain decomposition. */
5   #define n_rp 2
6   /* Number of the particle decomposition. */
7
8   #define nloc_over 107722
9
10  double phitmp[nloc_over_all][2*n_t];
11  int b[n_r*n_rp]
12    = {10967,10967,14086,14086,16164,16164,12644,12644};
13  /* Block size of each process in the "gblock" distribution. */
14
15  #pragma xmp nodes P2(n_r * n_rp, n_t)
16  /* Number of processes (nodes). */
17  #pragma xmp template T(0:nloc_over-1, 0:2*n_t-1)
18  /* Template length. */
19  #pragma xmp distribute T(gblock(b), block) onto P2
20  /* Distribution format of the template. */
21  #pragma xmp align phitmp[i][j] with T(i, j)
22  /* Alignment of an array with a template.*/
23  #pragma xmp shadow phitmp[0][1:0]
24  /* Assignment of the sleeve area. */
25  /* ... */
26  #pragma xmp loop (i, j) on T(i, j)
27  #pragma omp parallel for
28    for (i = 0; i < nloc_over; i++)
29      for (j = 0; j < mzeta; j++)
30        phitmp[i][j] = func(i, j);
```

Fig. 9 Exchange of grid points using the `reflect` directive in GTC-P

```
1   #pragma xmp reflect (phitmp) width (0,/periodic/1:0)
```

Fig. 10 Example showing GTC-P implementation using the XMP global-view programming model

4 Performance Evaluation

4.1 Experimental Setting

We evaluated the performance of our two implementations using a massively parallel GPU cluster: HA-PACS[1] at the Center for Computational Sciences, University of Tsukuba. Table 1 shows the computing environment employed for one node. HA-PACS is a GPU cluster, but we only utilized CPUs in this study. We have a plan to extend this research using a GPU-enabled version of XcalableMP, XcalableACC [9] to make use of GPU of HA-PACS. We apply the optimization option for NUMA with 'numactl -localalloc', and disable the CPU affinity setting of MVAPICH2 with MV2_ENABLE_AFFINITY=0.

As preliminary evaluations, we investigate the amount of the memory usage and the performance of communication using XMP and MPI. First, we indicate the comparison of the memory usage when one array is allocated in the local-view model, global-view model, and MPI. They are evaluated with 'getpid()' and 'grep VmHWM /proc/[pid]/status' from C program during execution. An array size is 1 MB. We show the minimum size in the each amount of the memory usage when four node execution. The tests showed that the amount of memory usage of all programming models is almost same according to Table 2. Then, we evaluate the performance of XMP and MPI communication with Ping-Pong program, which is defined by a power of two communication size, because XMP coarray is implemented by GASNet[6] which is a communication library optimized for some interconnections specifies, e.g., InfiniBand and Gemini. Figure 11 shows the performance of XMP coarray and MPI_Send/Recv communication. XMP is a good performance if the transfer size is about 65,536 Bytes or less, whereas MPI is a good performance if it is more than about 65,536 Bytes. We used a parameter of GASNet GASNET_IBV_PORTS="mlx4_0:1+mlx4_0:2" which specifies

Table 1 Machine environment (HA-PACS cluster)

CPU	Intel Xeon E5-2670 × 2 (2.6 GHz)
	CPU (8 cores/CPU) × 2 = 16 cores
Memory	128 GB, DDR3 1600 MHz
Interconnection	InfiniBand : Mellanox Connect-X3
	Dual-port QDR
OS	CentOS 6.4
C Compiler	gcc 4.4.7
MPI	MVAPICH2 2.0
GASNet	1.24.0

Table 2 The amount of the memory usage for several different programming models (KB)

MPI	Local-view	Global-view
19,488	19,532	19,888

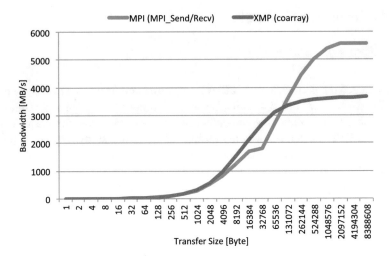

Fig. 11 Ping-Pong communication bandwidth with MPI (MPI_Send/Recv) and XMP (coarray)

Table 3 Evaluation of the weak scaling of decomposition for each domain using problems ranging from 16 to 512 processes	Problem size A	Default	Toroidal	Radial	Particle
	mstep	100	20	20	20
	mpsi	90	90	90–2880	90
	mzetamax	64	2–64	2	2
	Particles per cell	100	100	100	100–3200

to use two ports of Infiniband, but we could get the performance of only single port of Infiniband. It may be an issue with GASNet library.

The GTC-P simulation size is determined by several important numerical parameters. Table 3 shows the default parameters for problem size A provided by GTC-P, where we modified the parameters to evaluate weak scaling based on problem size A. Strong scaling was evaluated using the minimum parameters in the decomposition of each domain shown in Table 3, where mstep is the number of calculation steps, mzetamax is the number of grid points in the toroidal dimension, and mpsi is the number of grid points in the radial domain. Because the number of grid points in the poloidal plane and in the toroidal domain must be the same during decomposition, this was also changed in the parameter set for problem size A.

First, we used up to 32 nodes of HA-PACS where 16 processes ran on each node and the total number of processes ranged from 16 to 512. The processes mapped to evaluate the decomposition on each domain are shown in Table 4. As described above, three problem dimensions were considered: toroidal, radial, and particle. When we decomposed these dimensions into parallel processes, we always fixed the decomposition number on two dimensions (e.g., toroidal and radial) as 2 × 2 and we varied the decomposition size in the other dimension (e.g., particle) from 4 to 128, thereby scaling the total number of processes from 16 to 512. However, during decomposition on the toroidal dimension, we fixed the decomposition number on the

Table 4 Process mapping to evaluate the scaling of decomposition for each domain (N_txN_rxN_{rp})

Processes	Toroidal	Radial	Particle
16	$2 \times 2 \times 4$	$2 \times 4 \times 2$	$2 \times 2 \times 4$
32	$4 \times 2 \times 4$	$2 \times 8 \times 2$	$2 \times 2 \times 8$
64	$8 \times 2 \times 4$	$2 \times 16 \times 2$	$2 \times 2 \times 16$
128	$16 \times 2 \times 4$	$2 \times 32 \times 2$	$2 \times 2 \times 32$
256	$32 \times 2 \times 4$	$2 \times 64 \times 2$	$2 \times 2 \times 64$
512	$64 \times 2 \times 4$	$2 \times 128 \times 2$	$2 \times 2 \times 128$

radial and particle dimensions as 2×4. This was due to variations in the number of calculations because increasing the toroidal dimension also changes the poloidal planes, as described above. We used this scheme to change the scaling dimension.

Second, we used 16 nodes where one process ran on each node and the number of threads ranged from 1 to 16 in each process. The processes mapped on each domain to evaluate the decomposition are $2 \times 4 \times 2$ and $2 \times 2 \times 4$.

4.2   Results

With weak scaling, Figs. 12, 13, and 14 shows the elapsed time for both calculation and communication of MPI, XMP-localview, and XMP-hybridview required to scale the number of processes from 16 to 512, where decomposition on the toroidal

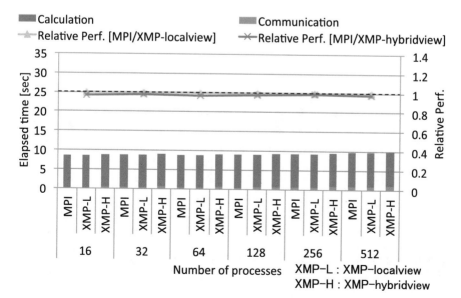

Fig. 12 Elapsed time of the decomposition on toroidal dimension from 16 to 512 processes in weak scaling

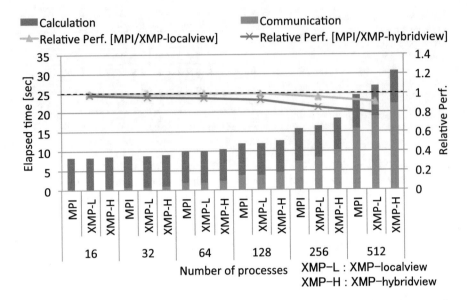

Fig. 13 Elapsed time of the decomposition on radial dimension from 16 to 512 processes in weak scaling

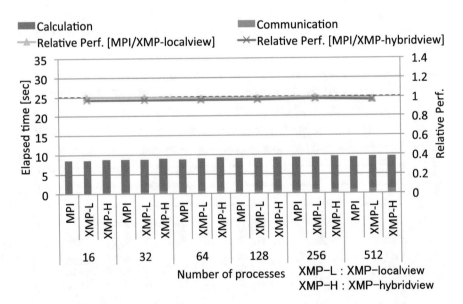

Fig. 14 Elapsed time of the decomposition on particle dimension from 16 to 512 processes in weak scaling

and particle dimensions exhibited good scalability, whereas scaling on the radial dimension was poor. Figure 13 shows that the performance of decomposition on the radial dimension decreased as the number of nodes increased compared with the other two types of domain decomposition, as shown in Figs. 12 and 14. Most of the communications are performed at the neighboring surface during decomposition on any dimension and the total amount of communication data does not vary greatly; thus, we focused on the calculation load balance between processes. Table 5 shows the difference between the maximum and minimum calculation times required for each type of decomposition, where the calculation time was defined as the computational time required for each process except the communication time. This table shows that the calculation time for processes differed greatly with radial dimension decomposition as the number of processes increased. This phenomenon occurred with all three implementations, including MPI.

This may be explained by the method used to decompose the domain in the radial dimension. For other dimensions, it is easy to decompose the domain completely and equally for all processes. However, decomposition is complicated in the radial dimension because the domain volume varies in the inner part and outer part due to the torus form of the problem space. The volume and the corresponding grid size

Table 5 Load imbalance: maximum and minimum times required to calculate the processes with toroidal, radial, and particle decomposition [s] (number of local grid points in each poloidal plane)

Processes	Toroidal	
	Minimum	Maximum
16	8.408406 (19805)	8.548204 (19916)
32	8.440145 (19805)	8.541321 (19916)
64	8.44846 (19805)	8.631631 (19916)
128	8.511492 (19805)	8.718713 (19916)
256	8.6418 (19805)	8.853517 (19916)
512	8.865397 (19805)	9.109388 (19916)
Processes	Radial	
	Minimum	Maximum
16	8.114932 (10967)	8.270015 (16164)
32	8.083982 (12104)	8.539186 (24200)
64	8.075058 (14130)	9.487029 (33462)
128	8.070919 (17422)	11.014277 (74745)
256	8.232447 (23198)	12.686402 (141700)
512	8.763279 (34522)	16.508915 (270844)
Processes	Particle	
	Minimum	Maximum
16	8.408406 (19805)	8.548204 (19916)
32	8.406107 (19805)	8.558563 (19916)
64	8.394203 (19805)	8.565195 (19916)
128	8.394159 (19805)	8.562974 (19916)
256	8.393343 (19805)	8.591214 (19916)
512	8.390172 (19805)	8.641762 (19916)

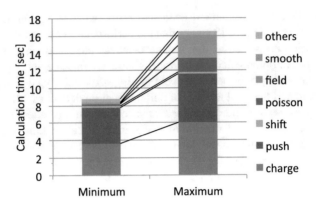

Fig. 15 Breakdown of the minimum and maximum calculation times on the radial domain decomposition using 512 processes

are calculated based on the formula used to describe the torus shape, which implies that an error is incurred during integer rounding to determine the number of grids. Table 5 shows that the number of total grid points assigned to the processes with the maximum and minimum calculation times differed greatly. Also, Fig. 15 shows the breakdown of the minimum and maximum calculation times on the radial domain decomposition 512 processes. The difference between the calculation times of the grid-related works, such as charge, push, poisson, field, and smooth, increased on radial domain decomposition. During each time step, the computation of all processes must be bounded as a barrier operation and the increase in the integer rounding error according to the problem size (i.e., weak scaling) causes a greater load imbalance, which degrades the overall performance.

On the other hand, the communication time of XMP-localview and XMP-hybridview on the radial dimension increases as the number of nodes increased compared with the MPI, as shown in Fig. 13. We explored the number of send calls and each communication size because the performance of communication on XMP and MPI are reversed at about 65,536 Bytes according to Fig. 11. Figure 16 shows the number of send calls in process number 0 on each domain decomposition classified as the communication size of more than 65,536 Bytes and 65,536 Bytes or less. In the radial domain decomposition, the number of send calls at more than 65,536 Bytes increases compared with the toroidal and particle decomposition. Therefore, the performance of XMP-localview and XMP-hybridview is degraded compared with MPI. The results were the XMP-localview implementation obtains approximately the same performance as the MPI implementation while the performance degradation using XMP-hybridview is increased by up to 20% compared with the MPI implementation.

With strong scaling, Figs. 17 and 18 show the elapsed time for both calculation and communication of MPI, XMP-localview, and XMP-hybridview, where the decomposition on the radial and particle dimensions, respectively. The performances of XMP-localview and XMP-hybridview on the particle dimension are

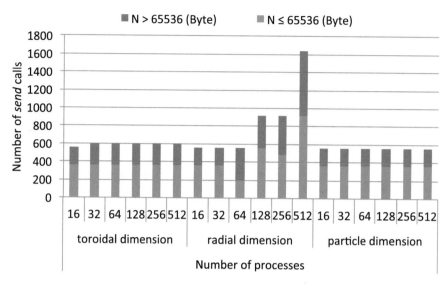

Fig. 16 Number of send calls in process number 0 on each domain decomposition from 16 to 512 processes in weak scaling

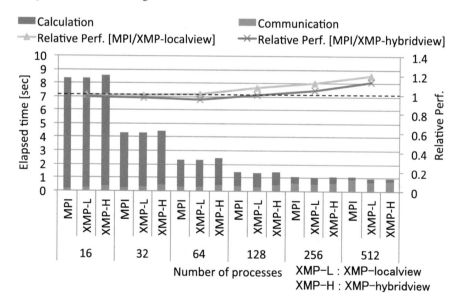

Fig. 17 Elapsed time of the decomposition on radial dimension from 16 to 512 processes in strong scaling

almost same compared with MPI, as shown Fig. 18, while the elapsed time of the decomposition on the radial dimension increases as the number of nodes increases, as shown Fig. 17.

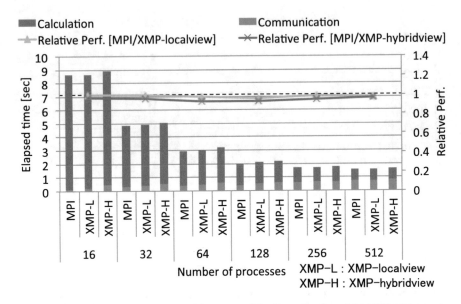

Fig. 18 Elapsed time of the decomposition on particle dimension from 16 to 512 processes in strong scaling

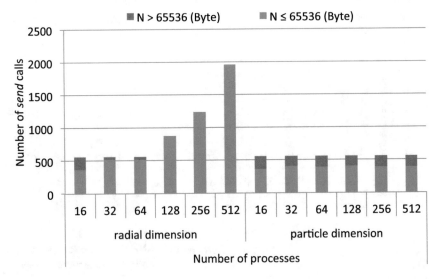

Fig. 19 Number of send calls in process number 0 on each domain decomposition from 16 to 512 processes in strong scaling

We explored the number of send calls and each communication size same as weak scaling. Figure 19 shows the number of send calls in process number 0 on radial and particle domain decomposition classified as the communication size of more than 65,536 Bytes and 65,536 Bytes or less. The number of send calls on the

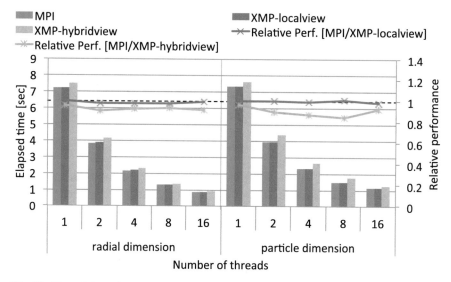

Fig. 20 Elapsed time of the decomposition on radial and particle dimension from 1 to 16 threads

radial domain decomposition at 65,536 Bytes or less increases compared with the particle decomposition. Therefore, the performance of XMP-localview and XMP-hybridview are increased compared with MPI on radial domain decomposition from 128 to 512 processes in strong scaling.

Figure 20 shows the elapsed time of the decomposition on radial and particle dimension, i.e., $2 \times 4 \times 2$ and $2 \times 2 \times 4$, ranged from 1 to 16 threads per process using 16 nodes where one process ran on each node. The results were the performance of XMP implementation with thread parallelization is scaled the same as MPI.

4.3   Productivity and Performance

A good programming environment should facilitate high performance and high productivity, but high performance is sometimes obtained by low-level programming such as MPI, which unfortunately yields low productivity.

The XMP-localview implementation is simple and intuitive compared with MPI because the coarray communication is expressed in the form of an array assignment statement, as shown Figs. 6 and 8. In coarray notation, the communication size and data are intuitively represented by array section and the data type is checked automatically. The performance of XMP-localview is comparable to that of the MPI version.

In XMP-hybridview, the global data structure required for the field data is described in the global-view model, which is almost the same as that in the serial code without particle calculation to communicate to the other process, and its data distribution is annotated by the directives, as shown in Fig. 10. This improves the readability of the code because it is unnecessary for users to describe the many arguments on a line such as MPI APIs, thereby facilitating the easy maintenance of the program and simple parallelization from the original sequential code. For the global data structure, the communication with the overlapped sleeve area in the distributed calculation domain can be described in only one line of the reflect directive, as shown in Fig. 9.

Table 6 shows the delta Source Lines of Code (SLOC) [14] for several implementations. This metric indicates how many lines of code changed from the serial implementation of GTC-P, which shows modified, added, and deleted lines. Due to the reasons described above, the amount of code added and modified from the serial implementation is smaller with the XMP-hybridview implementation than the MPI implementation. In both of XMP implementations, the deleted lines are larger than MPI implementation because the explicit memory free is unnecessary for the distributed array and communication buffer for coarray in the global scope. In summary, XMP-hybridview implementation increases productivity.

The difference in performance between XMP-hybridview and MPI is attributable to the increase in the communication size of the reflect directive. The reflect directive is responsible for the communication designated as the sleeve area by the width clause, but it cannot update partially the sleeve area. Figure 21 shows that the two-dimensional array is distributed to two nodes and exchanged the sleeve area in MPI and XMP implementations. In GTC-P, there is a communication pattern updated only in inner sleeve area which is represented as the hatching areas in Fig. 21 (left).

Table 6 Differences in the delta SLOC from Serial implementation for several different implementations of GTC-P

	Serial	MPI	XMP	
			Localview	Hybridview
SLOC	4110	5427	5398	5179
Modified	–	170	168	158
Added	–	1319	1303	1112
Deleted	–	2	15	43
Total delta SLOC	–	1491	1486	1313

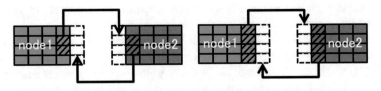

Fig. 21 Updating of the sleeve area with MPI and XMP-localview (left), and XMP-hybridview (right) in GTC-P. The hatching areas are communicated to nearby node

5   Related Research

GTC or GTC-P have been executed and optimized on some platforms. X. Liao et al.[7] optimized GTC to use offload-programming model for the Intel Xeon Phi accelerator, and evaluated the performance on MilkyWay-2 supercomputer. K. Madduri et al.[8] described the optimization for multi- and many-core systems, and evaluated on some systems including Graphic Processing Unit (GPU) based on NVIDIA Fermi architectures. In our study, we focus on the evaluation of not only the performance but also the productivity for GTC-P.

PIC method is often implemented some PGAS parallel programming languages. H. Sakagami and T. Mizuno[12] implemented 2D particle code, ESPAC2: 2D electrostatic plasma, based on PIC method using High Performance Fortran (HPF) [5] which is directive-based language similar to OpenMP and supports the global-view model. The particle data is distributed into the block, while the electrostatic field is replicated onto each process. After the distributed particle data is calculated in each process, the reduction operation is executed to update the particle data of electrostatic field on each time step. The data distribution is an easy expression which is annotated by directives in HPF. R. Preissl et al.[11] introduced hybrid PGAS+OpenMP approach for 3D PIC code, Gyrokinetic Tokamak Simulation (GTS) which is implemented in MPI+OpenMP. As PGAS parallel programming language, they used Coarray Fortran. The one-sided communication in Coarray Fortran is simple and more intuitive notation compared with MPI programming because it is expressed in the form of array assignment statement. However, the description of data distribution is same as MPI. To use simple coarray communication and easy data distribution by directives, we consider a hybrid-view approach, which combines the global-view and local-view models in XMP.

6   Conclusion

In this study, we implemented two versions of GTC-P, a large-scale nuclear fusion simulation code, using the global-view and local-view programming models in XMP for parallel programming languages, and we evaluated their performance and productivity. The first version, XMP-localview, only uses coarray communication in the local-view programming model, which simply replaces MPI point-to-point communication, except for collective communication such as MPI_Allreduce. The second version, XMP-hybridview, uses the distribution of the calculation domain and the `reflect` directive in the global-view programming model, as well as coarray communication for particle motion in the local-view programming model. Experimental evaluations showed that the XMP-localview implementation obtained approximately the same performance as MPI, whereas the XMP-hybridview implementation degraded the performance by 20%. In addition, we obtained high productivity with the XMP implementation. In XMP-localview, the coarray notation is simpler and more intuitive compared with MPI programming, and the XMP-hybridview allows more natural data expression for both static grid space data (in the global-view model) and dynamic particle data (in the local-view model), thereby increasing the readability of the code.

References

1. Center for Computational Sciences, University of Tsukuba, HA-PACS project, http://www. ccs.tsukuba.ac.jp/eng/research-activities/projects/ha-pacs/. Accessed 16 Mar 2009
2. DoE SCiDAC, UC Irvine, etc., Gyrokinetic toroidal code, http://phoenix.ps.uci.edu/GTC/. Accessed 16 Mar 2009
3. S. Ethier, W.M. Tang, Z. Lin, Gyrokinetic particle-in-cell simulations of plasma microturbulence on advanced computing platforms. J. Phys. Conf. Ser. **16**(1), 1–15 (2005)
4. S. Ethier, M. Adams, J. Carter, L. Oliker, Petascale parallelization of the gyrokinetic toroidal code, in *Proceedings of the 9th International Meeting on High Performance Computing for Computational Science (VECPAR)*, California (2010), pp. 1–9
5. C.H. Koelbel, M.E. Zosel, *The High Performance Fortran Handbook* (MIT Press, Cambridge, 1993)
6. LBNL FTG, U.C. Berkeley, GASNet specification version 1.8 (2006), http://gasnet.lbl.gov/ dist/docs/gasnet.pdf. Accessed 16 Mar 2009
7. X. Liao, L. Xiao, C. Yang, Y. Lu, Milkyway-2 supercomputer: system and application. Front. Comput. Sci. **8**(3), 345–356 (2014)
8. K. Madduri, K.Z. Ibrahim, S. Williams, E.-J. Im, S. Ethier, J. Shalf, L. Oliker, Gyrokinetic toroidal simulations on leading multi- and manycore HPC systems, in *Proceedings of 2011 International Conference for High Performance Computing, Networking, Storage and Analysis (SC)*, Seattle (2011), pp. 23:1–23:12
9. M. Nakao, H. Murai, T. Shimosaka, A. Tabuchi, T. Hanawa, Y. Kodama, T. Boku, M. Sato, XcalableACC: extension of XcalableMP PGAS language using OpenACC for accelerator clusters, in *Proceedings of the First Workshop on Accelerator Programming Using Directives (WACCPD)*, New Orleans (2014), pp. 27–36
10. H. Nuga, A. Fukuyama, Kinetic modeling of the heating processes in tokamak plasmas. PhD Thesis, Kyoto University (2011), pp. 1–111
11. R. Preissl, N. Wichmann, B. Long, J. Shalf, S. Ethier, A. Koniges, Multithreaded global address space communication techniques for gyrokinetic fusion applications on ultra-scale platforms, in *Proceedings of 2011 International Conference for High Performance Computing, Networking, Storage and Analysis (SC)*, Seattle (2011), pp. 78:1–78:11
12. H. Sakagami, T. Mizuno, Compatibility comparison and performance evaluation for Japanese HPF compilers using scientific applications. Concurr. Comput. Pract. Exp. **27**, 555–573 (2002)
13. Y. Shimomura, R. Aymar, V. Chuyanov, M. Huguet, R. Parker, Iter overview. Nucl. Fusion **39**(9Y), 1295–1308 (1999)
14. A. Stone, J. Dennis, M. Strout, Evaluating coarray Fortran with the CGPOP Miniapp, in *Proceedings of 5th International Conference on PGAS Programming Models*, Texas (2011), pp. 1–10
15. K. Tsugane, H. Nuga, T. Boku, H. Murai, M. Sato, W. Tang, B. Wang, Hybrid-view programming of nuclear fusion simulation code in the PGAS parallel programming language XcalableMP, in *Proceedings of the 20th IEEE International Conference on Parallel and Distributed Systems (ICPADS)*, Hsinchu (2014), pp. 640–647

16. B. Wang, S. Ethier, W. Tang, T. Williams, K.Z. Ibrahim, K. Madduri, S. Williams, L. Oliker, Kinetic turbulence simulations at extreme scale on leadership-class systems, in *Proceedings of the International Conference on High Performance Computing, Networking, Storage and Analysis*, Denver (2013), pp. 82:1–82:12

Parallelization of Atomic Image Reconstruction from X-ray Fluorescence Holograms with XcalableMP

Atsushi Kubota, Tomohiro Matsushita, and Naohisa Happo

Abstract X-ray fluorescence holography is a three-dimensional middle range local structure analysis method, which can provide three-dimensional atomic images around specific elements within a radius of a few nanometers. Three-dimensional atomic images are reconstructed by applying discrete Fourier transform (DFT) to hologram data. Presently, it takes long time to process this DFT. In this study, the DFT program is parallelized by using a parallel programming language XcalableMP. The DFT process, whose input is 21 holograms data of 179×360 points and output is a three-dimensional atomic image of 192^3 points, is executed on PC cluster which consists of 8 nodes of Intel Xeon X5660 processors and 96 cores in total and we confirmed that the parallelized DFT execution is 94 times faster than the sequential execution.

1 Introduction

X-ray fluorescence holography (XFH) is a three-dimensional middle range local structure analysis method, which can prove 3D atomic images around specific elements within a radius of a few nanometers[4]. Compared to other method such as X-ray diffraction, which has been widely used for structure analysis of crystals and other materials, XFH is more sensitive to atomic fluctuations, and therefore it is useful for characterization of local lattice distortions.

In the XFH method, hologram data are obtained by experiments done at large synchrotron facilities such as SPring-8 and KEK-PF. Three-dimensional atomic images are reconstructed from the obtained holograms by Barton's method[1, 2].

A. Kubota (✉) · N. Happo
Hiroshima City University, Hiroshima, Japan
e-mail: kubota@hiroshima-cu.ac.jp; happo@hiroshima-cu.ac.jp

T. Matsushita
Nara Institute of Science and Technology, Ikoma, Nara, Japan
e-mail: t-matusita@ms.naist.jp

© The Author(s) 2021
M. Sato (ed.), *XcalableMP PGAS Programming Language*,
https://doi.org/10.1007/978-981-15-7683-6_8

In Barton's method, it takes long time to reconstruct the atomic images from the obtained holograms.

In distributed-memory computing environment such as PC clusters and super-computers, hybrid parallelization is widely used by describing inter- and intra- node parallelism with Message-Passing Interface (MPI) [6] and OpenMP [7], respectively. However, it is pointed out that MPI programs tend to be complicated and error-prone. Therefore, in order to improve productivity of parallel programming, a variety of parallel programming languages, language extensions, and libraries have been proposed. Some examples of them are High Performance Fortran (HPF) [5], CoArray adopted in Fortran2008, UPC [9], which is based on C language, and XcalableMP [10], in which distribution of data and parallelization of loops are specified by directives. New parallel programming languages such as X10 [8] and Chapel [3] are also proposed.

We adopted a hybrid parallel programming approach, in which inter- and intra-node parallelism are described in XcalableMP and OpenMP, respectively, to paral-lelize the existing atomic image reconstruction program by Barton's method written in C language because it can be parallelized with small amount of modification.

In the rest of this chapter, X-ray fluorescence holography and reconstruction of atomic images are explained in Sect. 2. Parallelization of atomic image reconstruc-tion is explained in Sect. 3 and its performance results are shown in Sect. 4. Finally, concluding remarks are given in Sect. 5

2 X-ray Fluorescence Holography

There are two modes in XFH, namely the normal mode and the inverse mode. In this chapter, we focus on the inverse mode because it is mainly used in experiments of XFH recently. Please refer to the literatures such as [4] in details.

In the inverse mode, the angle of a sample material to the incident X-ray is varied as shown in Fig. 1 and intensity of X-ray fluorescence emitted from atoms in the sample is measured by the detector.

As shown in Fig. 2, the incident X-ray approaching atom A and another incident X-ray also approaching atom A after scattered by atom B form a constant wave of X-ray around atom A. The pattern of the constant wave from atom A varies according to the angle of the incident X-ray and resulted in the variation of the intensity of the X-ray fluorescence from atom A. Experimental data obtained by measuring the intensity of X-ray fluorescence make a hologram of the atomic image.

Incident X-ray wave approaching atom A directly corresponds to reference wave of ordinary hologram and incident X-ray wave approaching atom A after scattered by atom B corresponds to object wave.

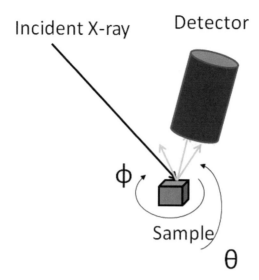

Fig. 1 Inverse mode of XFH

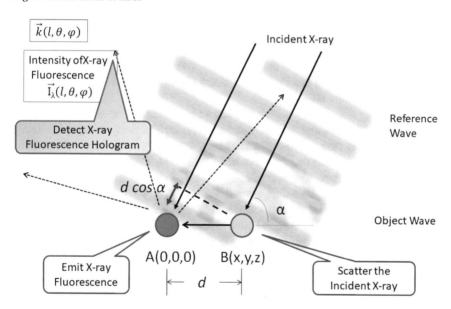

Fig. 2 Difference of optical path length in inverse mode

2.1 Reconstruction of Atomic Images

When the intensity $I_\lambda(l, \theta, \phi)$ measured at polar coordinate system $k(l, \theta, \phi)$ on a hologram on a sphere by incident X-ray of wave length λ, the position of an atom in the sample can be calculated as follows.

Suppose atom A and B are located at the origin and $r(x, y, z)$ in the sample, the atomic image of atom b can be reconstructed by calculation similar to three-dimensional discrete Fourier Transform. In atomic images reconstructed from holograms obtained by several wave lengths, real atomic images are enhanced and, at the same time, ghost images are reduced[4]. In order to reduce the processing time, atomic images are reconstructed from the hologram on the sphere of radius l as shown in Eq. (1):

$$\chi(x, y, z) = \sum_\theta \sum_\phi \sum_\lambda -I_\lambda(\theta, \phi) \exp(i2\pi(|r| - kr)/\lambda) \sin \theta \tag{1}$$

The input data are stored in double precision floating point number format. Coordinate on the sphere is represented in the polar coordinate system ranging from $\theta = 1°$ to $179°$ and from $\phi = 0°$ to $359°$ by $1°$ grid on each angle. The output data are grid points values on the rectangular coordinate system ranging from -10 to 10.0 Å by 0.1 Å grid on each axis. The complex numbers at grid points calculated by the reconstruction are stored in the output file.

192 grid points are laid on each axis on the rectangular coordinate system ranging from -9.6 to 9.6 Å by 0.1 Å grid in order to parallelize the reconstruction easily on PC cluster, it is explained in detail in Sect. 4.

Because the grid points of input data are located on the polar coordinate system and, on the other hand, those of output data are on the rectangular coordinate system, it is difficult to apply the fast Fourier transform (FFT) algorithm to DFT and it takes long time to calculate DFT.

We estimate that it may take a few days to reconstruct the three-dimensional atomic images from holograms measured by experiments. Because crystal structure of sample and its lattice constant are already known by other methods, in order to reduce the time required for reconstruct atomic images for crystal with a certain lattice constant, for example, 2 Å, three-dimensional atomic images are estimated with several two-dimensional atomic images on x–y planes at $z = -4, -2, 0, 2, 4$ Å. If needed, atomic images at $z = -1.9$ and 2.1 Å are reconstructed to analyze atomic fluctuations and lattice distortions.

Thus, it takes long time to analyze the crystal structure because reconstruction of two-dimensional atomic images and observation of the atomic images repeatedly.

2.2 Analysis Procedure of XFH

In XFH, experimental data are analyzed in the following procedure. The most time-consuming step is reconstruction while pre- and post- steps are also needed.

1. experiment
2. removal of background waves
3. completion of sphere data

4. reconstruction of atomic images and
5. display of them

Because it is known that low frequency noise called background wave is included in hologram data obtained by XFH experiments, the noise is removed before reconstruction.

In the experiment, the intensity of X-ray fluorescence emitted from sample is measured, while it is slanted from $\theta = 0$ to 75° and rotated from $\phi = 0$ to 360° at each θ in Fig. 1. For $\theta > 75°$, the meaningful intensity is not measured because the surface of the sample and the incident X-ray are nearly parallel. By making use of symmetry of crystal structure of the sample, the hologram data on the sphere ranging from $\theta = 0$ to 180° are completed. An example of hologram on the sphere shown in Fig. 3 is obtained by their pre-processes such as removal of background waves and completion of sphere data.

The values on grid points of the reconstructed atomic images are merely values proportional to existence probability of atom at each grid point on the x-y-z rectangular coordinate system. For a grid point, the value of low existence probability is noise and its atom image is not displayed if the value is less than threshold value and reconstructed images are displayed as shown in Fig. 4.

Fig. 3 An example hologram obtained by an experiment

Fig. 4 An example of reconstructed three-dimensional atom images

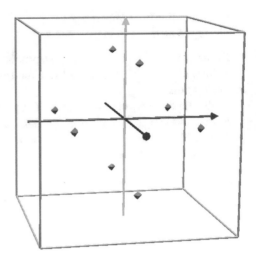

3 Parallelization

As pointed out in Sect. 2, it is an issue that it takes long time to analyze the crystal structure because reconstruction of two-dimensional atomic images and observation of the images are repeated several times. We therefore try to improve the reconstruction of three-dimensional atomic images by parallelizing DFT with parallel programming language XcalableMP and parallel API OpenMP on multi-node PC clusters.

OpenMP [7] is a parallel programming API which enables parallelization by inserting directives in sequential programs. It enables parallelization of loops with data parallelism easily and high performance on shared-memory machines can be achieved. Similar to OpenMP, XcalableMP [10] is a parallel programming language which also enables parallelization by inserting directives in sequential programs. Data distribution among distributed-memory computing environment such as multi-node PC clusters and supercomputers can be specified by inserting directives. Both OpenMP and XcalableMP are designed so that directives related to parallelization are ignored when the program is compiled to a sequential executable. Thus both sequential and parallel programs are maintained in one common source code. In addition, XcalableMP and OpenMP can be used at the same time for hybrid inter- and intra- node parallelization.

In this section, hybrid parallelization of reconstruction in two steps as follows:

1. parallelization of reconstruction of two-dimensional atomic images by OpenMP on single PC node and
2. parallelization of reconstruction of three-dimensional atomic images by XcalableMP and OpenMP on multi-nodes

3.1 Parallelization of Reconstruction of Two-Dimensional Atomic Images by OpenMP

Presently, according to the Eq. (1), in the loop of reconstruction of two-dimensional atomic images at certain z on x-y plane, five loops of x, y, θ, ϕ, and λ are nested from outer to inner loop. In this chapter, θ loop denotes the loop which accesses contiguous elements in a dimension of array θ for short.

The strategy of optimization and parallelization of two-dimensional reconstruction is as follows:

1. Replace trigonometric function calls with array references
2. Apply loop interchange and
3. Choose a loop to be parallelized

These optimization and parallelization are explained below.

In reconstruction of two-dimensional atomic images, some calls of trigonometric functions such as sin and cos in nested loops are replaced with references of arrays. The values of the trigonometric functions are stored in the arrays before entering the nested loops.

In this study, this nested loop is interchanged to λ, x, y, θ, and ϕ from outer to inner loop to improve the cache hit ratio. The size of the three-dimensional input array whose dimensions are λ, θ, and ϕ is about 10 MB and may not be stored on the secondary cache. In order to improve the cache hit ratio, when λ is fixed at the most outer loop, 500 KB data of the input array for a λ are stored on the cache and accessed repeatedly in the nested loop of x, y, θ, and ϕ. In the original loop nests, the index range of the inner-most λ loop is at most 20. After interchanging loops, the index range of the inner-most ϕ is 360 and it is expected that SIMD instructions in general purpose processors such as Intel AVX can be applied to the inner-most loop.

After these optimizations, the x loop in the nested loops is parallelized by OpenMP directive so that the performance of reconstruction of two-dimensional atomic images is improved.

3.2 Parallelization of Reconstruction of Three-dimensional Atomic Images by XcalableMP

In reconstruction of three-dimensional atomic images, according to the Eq. (1), by extending the optimized and parallelized nested loop of reconstruction of two-dimensional atomic images as described in Sect. 3.1, the six loops of λ, z, x, y, θ, and ϕ are nested from outer to inner loop. Similar to the two-dimensional loop, the values of some trigonometric functions are calculated in advance before entering the six nested loop.

Among the six nested loops, the outer z loop and the inner x loop are parallelized by XcalableMP and OpenMP. In other words, the nested loops are parallelized among inter-nodes by the z loop level and also parallelized within each node by the x loop level. The parallelized kernel loop of three-dimensional atomic image reconstruction is shown in Fig. 5. Other combinations of parallelizing x, y, and z loops are also performed and discussed in Sect 4.

In this study, z loop is parallelized by XcalableMP directives and the output arrays are distributed contiguously, namely BLOCK distribution, among nodes in z dimension as shown in Fig. 6. All of the input data are read on every node simultaneously and stored replicated. The data of atomic images, which are distributed among nodes in z dimension, are calculated on each node, aggregated to one root node as shown in Fig. 7, and finally written to the output file on the root node.

4 Performance Evaluation

In this section, we show the performance results of parallel runs of reconstruction of two-dimensional atomic images parallelized by OpenMP executed on a single node and reconstruction of three-dimensional atomic images parallelized by XcalableMP and OpenMP on a multi-node PC cluster. Comparison of XcalableMP and MPI for multi-node parallelization with respect to the performance and productivity of programming are also demonstrated.

The PC cluster consist of eight nodes and each node has two sockets of six-core Intel Xeon X5660 2.8 GHz and 24 GB main memory. The nodes are connected with InfiniBand DDR (4 Gbps) and Gigabit Ethernet. The size of smart cache on Xeon X5660 is 12 MB. The program is compiled with XcalableMP 1.2.2 and Intel Compiler 18.0.1 with -O3 -XHOST optimization option.

4.1 Performance Results of Reconstruction of Two-Dimensional Atomic Images

The program of reconstruction of two-dimensional atomic images is executed on a single node of the PC cluster. The input data are obtained in an experiment in which lead zirconate titanate (PZT) is used as a sample in the experiment and 21 types of incident X-rays are entered to the sample while varying angles ranging from $\theta = 1$ to $179°$ and from $\phi = 0$ to $359°$. The output is an two-dimensional array $[x][y] = [192][192]$ for a certain z.

In Table 1, the execution time of the original, array reference of trigonometric function calls, and loop interchange on one node. Execution time and speed-up ratio

```
for (l=0; l<No_Incident; l++) {
  input_hologram(l, Xi);
#pragma xmp loop on t(z)
  for (iz=0; iz<NZ; iz++) {
    z = position(iz);
#pragma omp parallel for private(...)
    for (ix=0; ix<NX; ix++) {
      x = position(ix);
      for (iy=0; iy<NY; iy++) {
        y = position(iy);
        r_norm = norm(x,y,z);
        sum1r = 0.0;
        sum1i = 0.0;
        for (th=1; th<NTHETA; th++) {
          sum2r = 0.0;
          sum2i = 0.0;
          for (phi=0; phi<NPHI; phi++) {
            d = r_norm
              - tab_kx[th][phi]*x
              - tab_ky[th][phi]*y
              - tab_kz[th]*z;
            a = k[l]*d;
            sum2r += Xi[th][phi]*cos(a);
            sum2i += Xi[th][phi]*sin(a);
          } /* end for phi */
          sum1r += sum2r * tab_sin[th];
          sum1i += sum2i * tab_sin[th];
        } /* end for theta */
        Ur_r[z][x][y] += sum1r * wt[l];
        Ur_i[z][x][y] += sum1i * wt[l];
      } /* end for y */
    } /* end for x */
  } /* end for z */
} /* end for l */
```

Fig. 5 Kernel loop of three-dimensional atomic image reconstruction

Fig. 6 Input and output arrays and specification of their distribution by XcalableMP directives

```
#pragma xmp nodes p(1)
#pragma xmp template t(0:191)
#pragma xmp distribute t(block) onto p

/* input array */
double Xi[NTHETA][NPHI];

/* output arrays */
double Ur_r[NZ][NX][NY];
#pragma xmp align Ur_r[n][*][*] with t(n)
double Ur_i[NZ][NX][NY];
#pragma xmp align Ur_i[n][*][*] with t(n)
double Ur_r1[NZ][NX][NY];
double Ur_i1[NZ][NX][NY];
```

Fig. 7 Aggregation of arrays by XcalableMP

```
#pragma xmp gmove
Ur_r1[:][:][:] = Ur_r[:][:][:];
#pragma xmp gmove
Ur_i1[:][:][:] = Ur_i[:][:][:];
```

Table 1 Performance results of reconstruction of two-dimensional atomic images by OpenMP on Xeon X5660

Original (s)	Array references and loop exchange (s)	OpenMP(s) 12 threads	Speed-up ratio
972.473	914.301	75.814	12.8

of the program parallelized by OpenMP with 12 threads on two sockets of six-core Xeon are 75.814 s and 12.8, respectively.

Here, let us consider the effect of the loop interchange. The size of input three-dimensional double precision array (λ, θ, ϕ) is about 10 MB. Before the loop interchange, loops x and y are the outer loops and 10 MB input data is repeatedly referenced in the nest of inner three loops λ, θ, and ϕ. Because the size of smart cache is 12 MB, it is assumed that the input data are spilled out of the cache and cache misses are occurred frequently. On the contrary, λ loop is placed at the outermost the loop nests by the loop interchange and a part of the input data is repeatedly referenced in the inner loops θ and ϕ. This fragment of the input data is about 500 KB and can be stored in the smart cache.

4.2 Performance Results of Reconstruction of Three-dimensional Atomic Images

The reconstruction of three-dimensional atomic images is executed mainly on the six nested loops of λ, z, x, y, θ, and ϕ.

The input and output data are stored in three-dimensional arrays of $[\lambda][\theta][\phi] = [21][179][360]$ and $[z][x][y] = [192][192][192]$, respectively. The output array is divided in z dimension and distributed among nodes on the PC cluster.

The z loop and x loop in the reconstruction program are parallelized by XcalableMP and OpenMP, respectively. The performance results of parallel execution on the PC cluster are shown in Tables 2 and 3. For the size of output $[z][x][y] = [192][192][192]$, because the estimation time of the sequential execution is too long, it is executed when the total number of threads is greater than or equal to eight as shown in Table 2. The #Threads columns of both Tables 2 and 3 stand for the total number of threads, which is the product of the number of nodes and the number threads per node. In addition to the total execution time, time for reading from the input file, aggregating the atomic images distributed among nodes, and writing to the output file.

The performance results of reconstruction of only for eight $x-y$ planes at $Z = 0, 1 \ldots 7$ are shown in Table 3. Because it takes a few hours in the sequential execution, this reconstruction is executed with threads ranging from 1 to 96.

The speed-up ratio of reconstruction of atomic images of both 192 and 8 $x-y$ planes are depicted in Fig. 8. Both horizontal and vertical axes are logarithmic scales. The Z8 graph is the speed-up ratio to the one thread execution in Table 3. The Z192 graph is the speed-up ratio to the eight thread execution in Table 2 multiplied by 8. In both lines in Fig. 8, it is confirmed that nearly ideal speed-up is achieved. The speed-up ratio values at 96 threads for Z8 and Z192 are 94.21 and 94.23, respectively.

Table 2 Performance results for reconstruction (z:192) parallelized by XcalableMP

#Threads	Execution (s)	Input (s)	Aggregation (s)	Output (s)
8 (8 × 1)	21,683.076	0.781	0.176	9.772
48 (8 × 6)	3,623.352	0.721	0.163	9.731
96 (8 × 12)	1,840.942	0.767	0.174	9.701

Table 3 Performance results for reconstruction (z:8) parallelized by XcalableMP

#Threads	Execution (s)	Input (s)	Aggregation (s)	Output (s)
1 (1 × 1)	7,214.325	0.745	0.007	0.301
8 (8 × 1)	923.830	0.473	0.009	0.303
12 (1 × 12)	603.962	0.459	0.005	0.310
48 (8 × 6)	151.574	0.458	0.008	0.303
96 (8 × 12)	76.576	0.455	0.009	0.310

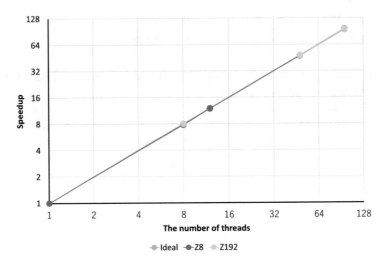

Fig. 8 The speed-up ratio of execution parallelized by XcalableMP

Because the sizes of input and output data are small, the ratio of the file I/O time to the total execution time is very small and the time of aggregation of distributed data to one root node by gmove construct of XcalableMP is also very short. Therefore, high performance is achieved without parallel file I/O.

4.3 Comparison of Parallelization with MPI

In order to compare the productivity of parallel programming, we also implemented the reconstruction of three-dimensional atomic images with MPI. The number of lines of the program in C already parallelized by OpenMP is 350 and the number of modified or inserted lines for multi-node parallelization by XcalableMP is 32, while that by MPI is 53. This program can be parallelized with less effort in XcalableMP than in MPI.

Table 4 summarizes the execution time and the number of modified and inserted lines. The size of the reconstructed atomic images is $[z][x][y] = [192][192][192]$ and 96 threads are used in total on the eight-node PC cluster. The difference of the execution time parallelized by XcalableMP and MPI is small. We confirmed that the higher productivity of parallel programming is achieved by XcalableMP than MPI without sacrificing performance.

Table 4 Execution parallelized by XcalableMP and MPI (z:192, 96 threads)

Parallelization	Time (s)	#Modifed lines
XcalableMP	1, 840.942	32
MPI	1, 817.042	53

Data aggregation of the reconstructed atomic images distributed among nodes is described by gmove statement by XcalableMP, while called MPI_Gatherv library function by MPI. We confirmed XcalableMP compiler transfers gmove to appropriate MPI library functions.

5 Conclusion

This chapter describes parallelization of reconstruction of three-dimensional atomic images in X-ray fluorescence holography, which is an analysis method of material science. In order to execute it on large-scale PC clusters and supercomputer, we adopt hybrid parallelization, or inter- and intra-node parallelization by XcalableMP and OpenMP.

The program, whose input is 21 holograms data of 179×360 points and output is a three-dimensional atomic image of 192^3 points, is executed on PC cluster which consists of eight nodes of Intel Xeon X5660 processors and 96 cores in total, is executed in 1841 s, or about half an hour. We estimated that it would take a few days to execute this reconstruction sequentially. We confirmed that the performance is improved by parallelization to the practical use.

We also confirmed that the higher productivity of parallel programming is achieved by XcalableMP than MPI without sacrificing performance.

Acknowledgments The part of this work was supported by JSPS Grant-in-Aid for Scientific Research on Innovative Areas "3D Active-Site Science," Grant Number 26105013.

References

1. J.J. Barton, Photoelectron holography. Phys. Rev. Lett. **61**(12), 1356–1359 (1988)
2. J.J. Barton, Removing multiple scattering and twin images from holographic images. Phys. Rev. Lett. **67**(22), 3106–3109 (1991)
3. B.L. Chamberlain, Chapel, chapter 6, in *Programming Models for Parallel Computing*, ed. by P. Balaji (The MIT Press, Cambridge, 2015)
4. K. Hayashi, N. Happo, S. Hosokawa, Evaluation of local lattice distortion by X-ray fluorescence holography. JSSRR **26**(4), 195–205 (2013) [in Japanese]
5. High Performance Fortran Forum, *High Performance Fortran Language Specification (Ver. 2.0)* (1997)
6. Message Passing Interface Forum, *MPI: Message Passing Interface Version 3.1* (2015), https://www.mpi-forum.org/docs/mpi-3.1/mpi31-report.pdf
7. OpenMP Architecture Review Board, *OpenMP Application Program Interface Version 5.0* (2018), https://www.openmp.org/wp-content/uploads/OpenMP-API-Specification-5.0.pdf

8. V. Saraswat, B. Bloom, I. Peshansky, O. Tardieu, D. Grove, *X10 Language Specification Version 2.6.2* (2019), http://x10.sourceforge.net/documentation/languagespec/x10-latest.pdf
9. UPC Consortium, *Berkeley UPC – Unified Parallel C Version 2019.4.2* (2019), http://upc.lbl.gov
10. XcalableMP Specification Working Group, *XcalableMP Language Specification Version 1.4* (2018), https://xcalablemp.org/download/spec/xmp-spec-1.4.pdf

Multi-SPMD Programming Model with YML and XcalableMP

Miwako Tsuji, Hitoshi Murai, Taisuke Boku, Mitsuhisa Sato,
Serge G. Petiton, Nahid Emad, Thomas Dufaud, Joachim Protze,
Christian Terboven, and Matthias S. Müller

Abstract This chapter describes a multi-SPMD (mSPMD) programming model and a set of software and libraries to support the mSPMD programming model. The mSPMD programming model has been proposed to realize scalable applications on huge and hierarchical systems. It has been evident that simple SPMD programs such as MPI, XMP, or hybrid programs such as OpenMP/MPI cannot exploit the postpeta- or exascale systems efficiently due to the increasing complexity of applications and systems. The mSPMD programming model has been designed to adopt multiple programming models across different architecture levels. Instead of invoking a single parallel program on millions of processor cores, multiple SPMD programs of moderate sizes can be worked together in the mSPMD programming model. As components of the mSPMD programming model, XMP has been supported. Fault-tolerance features, correctness checks, and some numerical libraries' implementations in the mSPMD programming model have been presented.

M. Tsuji (✉) · H. Murai · M. Sato
RIKEN Center for Computational Science, Kobe, Japan
e-mail: miwako.tsuji@riken.jp; h-murai@riken.jp; msato@riken.jp

T. Boku
Center for Computational Sciences, University of Tsukuba, Tsukuba, Japan
e-mail: taisuke@ccs.tsukuba.ac.jp

S. G. Petiton
LIFL, Université de Lille, Lille, France
e-mail: serge.petiton@univ-lille.fr

N. Emad · T. Dufaud
Li-Parad, UVSQ, Versailles, France
e-mail: nahid.emad@uvsq.fr; thomas.dufaud@uvsq.fr

J. Protze · C. Terboven · M. S. Müller
RWTH Aachen University, Aachen, Germany
e-mail: protze@itc.rwth-aachen.de; terboven@itc.rwth-aachen.de; mueller@itc.rwth-aachen.de

219

M. Sato (ed.), *XcalableMP PGAS Programming Language*,
https://doi.org/10.1007/978-981-15-7683-6_9

1 Introduction

From petascale, post-petascale to exascale, supercomputers will be larger, denser, and more complicated. A huge number of cores will be arranged in a multi-level hierarchy, such as a group of cores in a node, a group or cluster of nodes tightly linked, and a cluster of clusters. Because it is not easy to fully utilize such systems for current programming models such as simple SPMD, OpenMP+MPI, it is essential to adopt multiple programming models across different architecture levels. In order to exploit the performance of such systems, we have proposed a new programming model called the multi-SPMD (mSPMD) programming model, where several MPI programs and OpenMP+MPI programs work together conducted by a workflow programming[14]. To develop each of the mSPMD components in a workflow, XcalableMP (XMP) has been supported. In this chapter, we introduce the mSPMD programming model, and a development and execution environment implemented to realize the mSPMD programming model.

2 Background: International Collaborations for the Post-Petascale and Exascale Computing

There were two important international collaborative projects to plan, implement, and evaluate the multi-SPMD programming model. In this section, we describe the projects briefly.

Firstly, Framework and Programming for Post-Petascale Computing (FP3C) project conducted during September 2010–March 2013 aimed to exploit efficient programming and method for future supercomputers. The FP3C project was a French-Japan research project, where more than ten Universities and research institutes participated. Featured topics of the project were new programming paradigms, languages, methods, and systems for the existing and future supercomputers. The mSPMD programming had been proposed in the FP3C project. Many important features in the mSPMD programming model had been implemented during the project period.

The priority program "Software for Exascale Computing" (SPPEXA) had been conducted to address fundamental research on the various aspects of HPC software during 2013–2015 (phase-I) and 2016–2018 (phase-II). The project "MUST Correctness Checking for YML and XMP Programs (MYX)" had been selected as a phase-II program of the SPPEXA. As the name of the project suggested, the MYX project combined MUST, developed in Germany, YML, developed in France, and XMP, developed in Japan, to investigate the application of scalable correctness checking methods. The deliverable from the MYX project will be described in Sect. 8.

3 Multi-SPMD Programming Model

3.1 Overview

While most programming models consider MPI+X such as MPI+OpenMP, or MPI+X_1+X_2 $\cdots$, we consider X_1+MPI (or XMP) +X_2 and propose a multi-SPMD (mSPMD) programming model where MPI programs and OpenMP+MPI programs work together in the context of a workflow programming model. In other words, tasks in a workflow are parallel programs written in XMP, MPI, or their hybrid with OpenMP.

Figure 1 shows the overview of the mSPMD programming model. In the target systems we have expected, there should be non-uniform memory access (NUMA), general-purpose many-core CPUs, and accelerators such as GPU. We employ a shared memory programming model within a node, or a group of cores, and GPGPU programming on an accelerator. In a group of nodes, we have considered a distributed parallel programming model. Between these groups of nodes, there is a workflow programming model to manage and control several distributed parallel programs and hybrid programs of the distributed parallel and shared programming models. To realize this framework, we support XcalableMP (XMP) to describe the distributed parallel programs in a workflow as well as MPI, which is a de-facto standard for distributed parallel programming. For the shared programming and GPGPU, as well as XMP+OpenMP, MPI+OpenMP, MPI+GPGPU such as CUDA, OpenACC, we support a runtime library called StarPU. The StarPU library[1], which is a task programming library for hybrid architectures, enables us to implement heterogeneous applications in a uniform way. XMP provides an extension to enable work-sharing among CPU cores and GPU [7]. YML[2–4]—a development and execution environment for a scientific workflow—is used for the workflow execution.

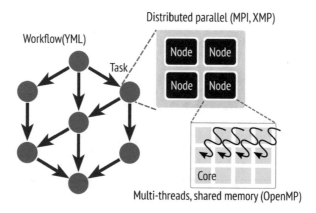

Fig. 1 An overview of multi-SPMD programming model

3.2   YML

YML[2–4] is a workflow programming environment for a scientific workflow. YML had been developed to execute a workflow application in a grid and P2P environment and provides the following software:

- Component (task) generator,
- Workflow compiler, and
- Workflow scheduler.

The YML workflow compiler supports an original workflow language called YvetteML, which allows us to describe dependency between tasks easily. Some details of the YvetteML are described later, in Sect. 4.2. A workflow written in the YvetteML would be compiled by the YML workflow compiler into a DAG of tasks. The YML workflow scheduler interprets the DAG to execute the defined workflow. Depending on the available systems, the scheduler uses different middleware, such as XtremWeb for a P2P, OmniRPC[9] for a grid. The YML component generator generates executable programs from "abstract" and "implementation" descriptions of a component. Figures 2 and 3 show examples of "abstract" and "implementation," respectively. Note that in Fig. 3, while we show an example using XMP, the original YML had supported neither XMP nor MPI. The XMP and MPI supports were added by extending YML and middleware.

3.3   OmniRPC-MPI

YML has been designed to execute workflow applications over various environments, such as clusters, P2P, and single processors. During the execution, the YML workflow scheduler dynamically loads a backend library for its environment. Each of the backend libraries calls APIs defined in middleware libraries. For example, in

```xml
<?xml version="1.0" ?>
<component type="abstract" name="add_mat">
<params>
<param name="A" type="Matrix" mode="in" />
<param name="B" type="Matrix" mode="in" />
<param name="C" type="Matrix" mode="out" />
</params>
</component>
```

Fig. 2   An example of "Abstract" in YML

```
<?xml version="1.0" ?>
<component type="impl" name="add_mat">
<impl lang="XMP" nodes="CPU:(4x4)">
<templates>
<template name="t" format="block" size="(256,256)" />
</templates>
<distribute>
<param template="t" name="A(256,256)" align="[i][j],(j,i)" />
<param template="t" type="B(256,256)" align="[i][j],(j,i)" />
<param template="t" type="C(256,256)" align="[i][j],(j,i)" />
</distribute>
<source>
<![CDATA[
   ....
#pragma xmp loop(j,i) on t(j, i)
  for(i=0; i<256; i++){
     for(j=0; j<256; j++)
        C[i][j] = A[i][j]+B[i][j];
]]>
</source>
</component>
```

Fig. 3 An example of "Implementation" in YML

a grid environment, the OmniRPC backend linked with the OmniRPC middleware library should be loaded.

The OmniRPC [9] is a grid RPC facility for cluster systems. The OmniRPC supports a master-worker programming model, where remote serial programs (rexs) are executed by exec, rsh or ssh.

To realize the mSPMD programming model, we have implemented an MPI backend and extended the OmniRPC to OmniRPC-MPI for a large scale cluster environment. The OmniRPC-MPI library provides the following functions:

- invoke a remote program (worker program) over a specified number of nodes.
- communication between the workflow scheduler and the remote programs.

  - the scheduler sends a request to execute a certain task to a remote program.
  - the scheduler listens to the communicator and receives a termination message from a remote program.

- manage remote programs and computational resources.

4 Application Development in the mSPMD Programming Environment

In this section, we describe how to develop applications in the mSPMD programming environment.

4.1 Task Generator

Figure 4 shows the YML Component generator extended for the mSPMD programming environment. The generator takes an implementation source code, such as the one shown in Fig. 3. Then, combining the implementation and abstract source codes, it generates several intermediate files: (1) an XMP source code, which extracts task procedure itself defined by a user and (2) an interface definition file, which includes some communication functions used to communicate with a workflow scheduler. The YML Component generator calls (1) an XMP compiler to translate the XMP source code to a C-source code with XMP runtime library calls and (2) a C-compiler to compile the C-source code generated by the XMP compiler. The YML Component generator calls (1) an OmniRPC-generator to translate the interface definition to a C-source code and (2) a C-compiler to compile the C-source code generated by the OmniRPC-generator. Finally, the YML Component generator calls a linker to link the compiled object files and external libraries such as an MPI library.

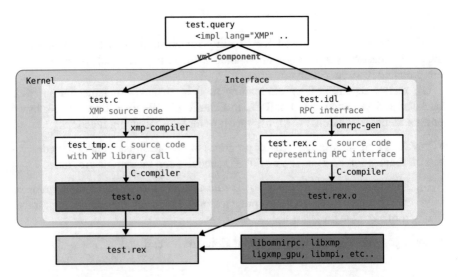

Fig. 4 YML Component (task) generator extended for the mSPMD programming environment

During a workflow application execution, the remote programs generated by the YML Component generator are invoked and managed by the YML workflow scheduler and the OmniRPC-MPI middleware.

4.2 Workflow Development

A workflow application in the mSPMD is defined by a workflow description language called YvetteML. The YvetteML allows us to define the dependencies between tasks easily. Figure 5 shows an example of the YvetteML, which computes an inversion of a matrix by the Block Gauss–Jordan method. In the YvetteML, the following directives are supported:

compute call a task

par parallel loop or region
each index of the loop can be executed in parallel, or

```
<?xml version="1.0" ?>
<application name="Gauss-Jordan">
<graph>

par(k:=0;nBlocks-1); do
  par
    if (k neq 0) then
      wait(prodDiffA[k][k][k-1]);
    endif
    compute inversion(A[k][k],
        B[k][k]); #step0:inversion
    notify(bInversed[k][k]);
//
    if (k neq nBlocks-1) then
      par (i:=k+1; nBlocks-1)
      do
        wait(bInversed[k][k]);
        compute prodMat(B[k][k],
                        A[k][i]);
        notify(prodA[k][i]);
      enddo
    endif
//
    wait(bInversed[k][k]);
    par(i:=0;nBlocks-1); do
      if(i neq k) then
        compute mProdMat
          (A[i][k],B[k][k],B[i][k]);
        notify(mProdB[k][i][k]);
      endif
```

```
    if(k gt i) then
      compute prodMat(
                B[k][k],B[k][i]);
      notify(prodB[k][i]);
    endif
  enddo
//
  par(i:= 0;nBlocks-1)
  do
    if(i neq k) then
      if(k neq nBlocks - 1) then
        par(j:=k+1; nBlocks-1); do
          wait(prodA[k][j]);
          compute prodDiff(A[i][k],
                    A[k][j],A[i][j]);
          notify
            (prodDiffA[i][j][k]);
        enddo
      endif
      if (k neq 0) then
        par(j:=0;k - 1); do
          wait(prodB[k][j]);
          compute prodDiff(A[i][k],
                    B[k][j],B[i][j]);
        enddo
      endif;endif;enddo;endpar;enddo
</graph>
</application>
```

Fig. 5 An example of an application written in YvetteML

each code block defined by **//** in a **par** region can be executed in parallel

ser   serial loop

wait   wait until the corresponding signal has been issued by **notify**

notify   issues a specific signal for **wait**

4.3 Workflow Execution

The YML workflow compiler compiles the YvetteML into a directed acyclic graph (DAG), and the YML workflow scheduler interprets the DAG to execute a workflow application.

Figure 6 illustrates a workflow execution in the mSPMD programming model. First, mpirun kicks the YML workflow scheduler. The YML workflow scheduler, which has been linked with the OmniRPC-MPI library, interprets the DAG of a workflow application and asks the invocation a task specified by YvetteML **compute (task-name)** to the OmniRPC-MPI library. The OmniRPC-MPI library finds a remote program which includes the specified task, and invokes the remote program over the specified number of nodes by calling MPI_Comm_spawn, and sends a request to perform the specific task.

While actual communications, node management, and task scheduling have been supported by the OmniRPC-MPI library, the YML workflow scheduler schedules a "logical" order of tasks based on the DAG of an application.

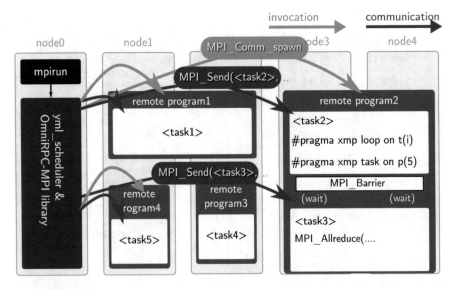

Fig. 6 A workflow execution of the mSPMD

5 Experiments

In this section, we demonstrate the performance of the mSPMD programming model and our implementation.

Table 1 shows the specification of the K computer, which has been used for the experiments.

In our experiments, the Block Gauss–Jordan (BGJ) method, which computes the inversion of a matrix A, has been considered. Figure 7 shows the algorithm of the BGJ method. The workflow for the BGJ method written in YvetteML has been shown in Fig. 5. As shown in Table 2, tasks in the workflow process block(s). In order to investigate the performance over different levels of hierarchical parallelism:

- the total size of the matrix A is fixed to 32,768 × 32,768, but the number of blocks is varied from 1 × 1 to 16 × 16.
- the total number of processes (cores) for a workflow is fixed to 4096, but the number of processes for each task is varied from 8 to 4096.

Table 1 Specification of K computer

CPU	Fujitsu SPARC64VIIIfx, 8 core, 2.00 GHz
Memory	16 GB , 64 GB/s
Cache	L1: 32 + 32 KB/core, L2: 6 MB/core
Network	Tofu (6D mesh/torus) Interconnect
	5 GB/s × 2

$$
\begin{aligned}
&\textbf{for } k \textbf{ from } 0 \textbf{ to } p-1 \textbf{ do} \\
&\quad (1)\ Inv^{(k)} = [A_{k,k}^{(k)}]^{-1} \\
&\quad (2)\ \boldsymbol{b}_k^{(k+1)} = Inv^{(k)} \cdot \boldsymbol{b}_k^{k} \\
&\quad \textbf{if } k \neq p-1 \textbf{ then} \\
&\quad\quad \textbf{for } i \textbf{ from } 0 \textbf{ to } p-1 \textbf{ do} \\
&\quad\quad\quad \textbf{if } i \neq k \textbf{ then} \\
&\quad\quad\quad\quad (3)\ A_{k,i}^{(k+1)} = Inv^{(k)} \cdot A_{k,i}^{(k)} \\
&\quad\quad\quad\quad (4)\ \boldsymbol{b}_i^{(k+1)} = b_i^{(k+1)} - A_{i,k}^{(k)} \cdot \boldsymbol{b}_k^{(k+1)} \\
&\quad\quad\quad\quad \textbf{for } j \textbf{ from } k+1 \textbf{ to } p-1 \textbf{ do} \\
&\quad\quad\quad\quad\quad (5)\ A_{i,j}^{(k+1)} = A_{i,j}^{(k)} - A_{i,k}^{(k+1)} \cdot A_{k,j}^{(k)} \\
&\quad\quad\quad\quad \textbf{end for} \\
&\quad\quad\quad \textbf{end if} \\
&\quad\quad \textbf{end for} \\
&\quad \textbf{end if} \\
&\textbf{end for}
\end{aligned}
$$

Fig. 7 Algorithm of the Block Gauss–Jordan method

Table 2 Tasks in the Block Gauss–Jordan workflow application. The input/output of the tasks such as $A_{i,j}$, $B_{i,j}$, $C_{i,j}$, $\cdots$ are blocks of a matrix

Task	Description
inversion($A_{i,j}$)	Compute the inversion of a block $A_{i,j}$
prodMat($A_{i,j}$, $B_{i,j}$)	Compute $B_{i,j} = A_{i,j}B_{i,j}$
mProdMat($A_{i,j}$, $B_{i,j}$,$C_{i,j}$)	Compute $C_{i,j} = -A_{i,j}B_{i,j}$
prodDiff($A_{i,j}$, $B_{i,j}$,$C_{i,j}$)	Compute $C_{i,j} = C_{i,j} - A_{i,j}B_{i,j}$

Table 3 # of blocks, block sizes and # of tasks in the Block Gauss–Jordan method

# of blocks	1×1	2×2	4×4	8×8	16×16
Block size	$32{,}768^2$	$16{,}384^2$	8192^2	4096^2	2048^2
# of tasks	3	18	108	696	4848

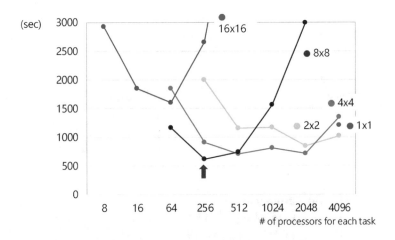

Fig. 8 Execution time of the BGJ workflow applications

Therefore, if we have a single block and assign all processes for a task, then it is almost equivalent to a distributed parallel application. On the other hand, if we divide a matrix into many small blocks and assign a process for each block, it is almost a traditional workflow application. Table 3 shows the block size and the number of tasks for each number of blocks. If we assign 512 processes for each task, then at most eight tasks can be executed simultaneously.

Figure 8 shows the execution time of the BGJ workflow applications for the number of blocks and the number of processes per task. The results show that the best performance has been realized when we divide a matrix into 8×8 blocks and assign 256 processes for each task. Our framework of the mSPMD programming model can realize such an appropriate combination of different parallelisms and can allow application developers to control the different parallelism levels easily. On the other hand, the extreme cases—1×1 block and 16×16 blocks—have not performed well. Also, assigning too many processes for small tasks, for example,

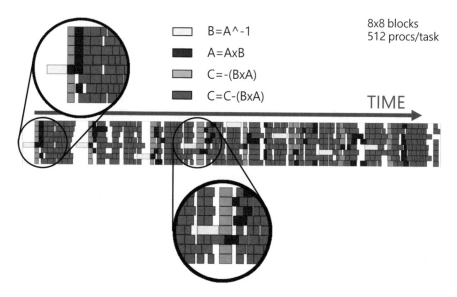

Fig. 9 Execution timeline of the BGJ workflow application with 8×8 blocks

2048 processes for 8×8 blocks, more than 256 processes for 16×16 processes, show poor performance.

Figure 9 shows the execution timeline (from left to right) of the BGJ workflow application with 8×8 blocks. As shown in the figure, at the first step, the task of inversion ($B = A^{-1}$) must be executed solely since the other tasks on the first step use the result of the inversion. After the second step, some of the matrix calculations such as $A = A \times B, C = -(B \times A), C = C - (B \times A)$ on the kth step and the inversion on $k + 1$th step can be overlapped. For other programming models such as flat-MPI, it is not easy to execute tasks or functions on different steps simultaneously. On the other hand, the mSPMD programming model and our programming environment allow application developers to describe this sort of applications easily.

6 Eigen Solver on the mSPMD Programming Model

In this section, as a use case of the mSPMD programming model, we introduce an eigen solver implemented on the mSPMD programming model.

6.1 Implicitly Restarted Arnoldi Method (IRAM), Multiple Implicitly Restarted Arnoldi Method (MIRAM) and Their Implementations for the mSPMD Programming Model

The iterative methods are widely used to solve eigenvalue programs in scientific computation. Implicitly Restarted Arnoldi Method (IRAM) [10] is one of the iterative methods to search the eigen elements λ s.t. $Ax = \lambda x$ of a matrix A.

Figure 10 shows the algorithm of IRAM. IRAM is a technique that combines the implicitly shifted QR mechanism with an Arnoldi factorization and the IRAM can be viewed as a truncated form of the implicitly shifted QR-iteration. After the first m-step Arnoldi factorization, the eigen pairs of a Heisenberg matrix H are computed. If the residual norm is small enough, the iteration is stopped. Otherwise, the shifted QR by selecting shifts based on eigenvalues of the Heisenberg matrix is computed. Using these new vectors and H as a starting point, we can apply p additional steps of the Arnoldi process to obtain an m-step Arnoldi factorization.

Multiple IRAM (MIRAM) is an extension of IRAM, which introduces two or more instances of IRAM. The instances of IRAM work on the same problem, but they are initialized with different subspaces $m_1, m_2, \cdots$. At the restarting point, each instance selects the best $(m_{best}, H_{best}, V_{best}, f_{best})$ from l IRAM instances.

In the mSPMD programming model, MIRAM has been implemented, as shown in Fig. 11. The source code written in YvetteML is shown in Fig. 12. The YML workflow scheduler invokes l IRAM instances and a data server. Each of IRAM

Input: A, V_m, H_m, F_m with $AV_m = V_m H_m + f_m e_m$
  A is a matrix of order n,
  m is krylov subspace size s.t. $m \ll n$,
  k is the number of desired eigen pairs s.t. $k < m$.
for i **from** 0 **to** convergence **do**
  (1) compute the eigenvalue σ and eigenvectors of H_m
  compute residual norm. If converge, stop.
  (2) Select a set of $p = m - k$ shifts $(u_1, \cdots, u_p)$ and set $q^T := e_m^T$
  (3) **for** j **from** 1 **to** p
      (1) Factor$[Q_j, R_j]$ = qr$(H_m - u_j I)$
      (2) $H_m = Q_j^T H_m Q_j$, $V_m = V_m Q_j$
      (3) $q^H = q^H Q_j$
  end for
  (4) $f_k = v_{k+1}\beta_k + f_m\sigma_k$, $V_k = V_m(1:n, 1:k)$, $H_k = H_m(1:k, 1:k)$
  (5) Apply p additional steps of Arnoldi process to obtain a new m step Arnoldi
      factorization $AV_m = V_m H_m + f_m e_m^T$
end for

Fig. 10 Algorithm of IRAM

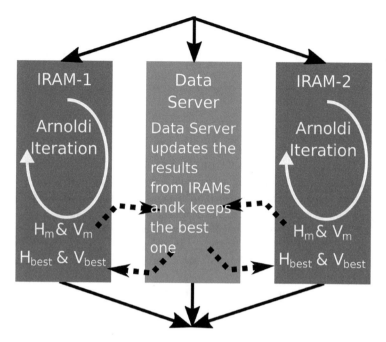

Fig. 11 Overview of MIRAM on the mSPMD programming model

```
<?xml version="1.0" ?>
<application name="MIRAM">
<graph>
    niram:=3;
    par
       par(eid:=0;niram-1); do
         compute iram_main(eid,...);
       enddo
       //
       compute iram_dsrv(niram,...);
    endpar
</graph>
</application>
```

Fig. 12 MIRAM workflow

instances computes an Arnoldi iteration asynchronously over n nodes and sends the resulting (m, H, V, f) to the data server. The data server keeps the best result and sends it to each IRAM. Each IRAM restarts with the (m, H, V, f) sent by the data server.

6.2 Experiments

Here, we show the result of experiments on the T2K-Tsukuba supercomputer. The specification of the T2K Tsukuba is shown in Table 4. In the experiments, we use a matrix called *Schenk/nlpkkt240* from the SuiteSparse Matrix Collection [11], where $n = 27,993,600$ and the number of non-zero elements are 760,648,352.

Figure 13 shows the results of MIRAM with IRAM solvers of $m = 24, 32, 40$ (left) and 3 independent runs of IRAM solvers of the $m = 24, 32, 40$ (right). While MIRAM converged around 450 iterations, none of 3 IRAMs could not converge until 500 iterations.

This MIRAM example shows that by using the mSPMD programming model, two different accelerations can be achieved. While the workflow programming model of the mSPMD accelerates the convergence of the Arnoldi iterations, the distributed parallel programming model speeds up each iteration of the Arnoldi method.

Table 4 Specification of T2K Tsukuba

CPU	Opteron Barcelona B8000, 4 cores, 4 sockets, 2.3 GHz
Memory	32 GB
Network	Fat-tree, full-bisection interconnection quad-rail of InfiniBand

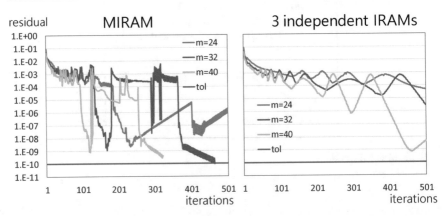

Fig. 13 Results of MIRAM with 3 IRAM solvers (right) and 3 independent runs of IRAM (left)

7 Fault-Tolerance Features in the mSPMD Programming Model

7.1 Overview and Implementation

As well as scalability and programmability, reliability is an important issue in exascale computing. Since the number of components of an exascale supercomputer should be tremendously large, it is evident that the mean time between failure (MTBF) of a system decreases as the number of the system's components increases. Therefore, fault tolerance becomes essential for systems and applications. Here, we develop a fault-tolerance mechanism in an mSPMD programming model, and its development and execution environment. The fault tolerance in the mSPMD programming model can be realized without modifying applications' source codes[13].

Figure 14 illustrates the fault-tolerant mechanism in the mSPMD programming model. If the workflow scheduler can find an error in a task and execute the task again on different nodes, then we can realize a fault-tolerance and resilience mechanism automatically.

We have extended the OmniRPC-MPI described in Sect. 3.3 to detect errors in remote programs and notify the errors to the YML workflow scheduler. For these purposes, heartbeat messages between master and remote programs have been introduced in the OmniRPC-MPI library. If an error is detected in a remote program, then it is reported to the YML workflow scheduler as a return value of existing APIs. The `OmniRpcProbe(Request r)` API has been designed to listen to the status of a requested task in a remote program. This returns `success` if the remote program sends a signal to indicate the requested task `r` has successfully finished. On the other hand, if heartbeat messages from the remote program executing the task `r` have stopped, `OmniRpcProbe(Request r)` returns `fail`.

The YML scheduler re-schedules the failed task if it receives `fail` signal from the OmniRPC-MPI library. The re-scheduling method is simple; The YML scheduler puts the failed task at the head of the "ready" task queue.

7.2 Experiments

We have performed some experiments to investigate the overhead of the fault detection and the elapsed time when errors occur on a cluster shown in Table 5. The BGJ method shown in Sect. 5 had been used. The size of a matrix is 20,480 × 20,480 and divided into

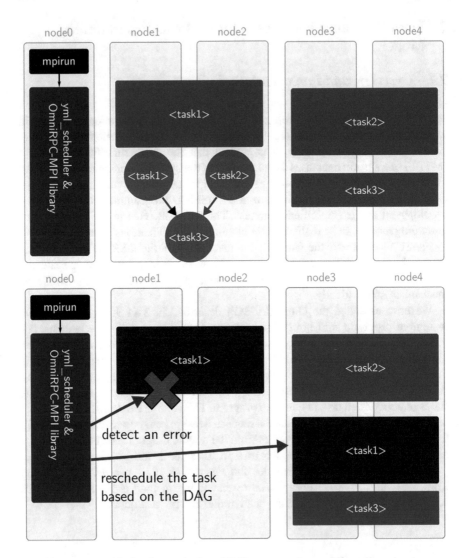

Fig. 14 Overview of fault tolerance in the mSPMD programming model

Table 5 Specification of a FX10 cluster

CPU	Fujitsu SPARC64VIIIfx, 16 core, 1.65 GHz
Memory	32 GB, 85 GB/s
Cache	L1: 32 + 32 KB/core, L2: 6 MB/core
Network	Tofu (6D mesh/torus) Interconnect
	5 GB/s × 2

# of blocks	1×1	2×2	4×4	8×8
Block size	$20,480^2$	$10,240^2$	5120^2	2560^2

1024 cores (64 nodes) are used for each workflow, and 64–1024 cores are assigned for each task in a workflow.

Firstly, we have considered the overhead of the heartbeat messages used to detect errors in remote programs. Figure 15 shows the performance of the normal and fault-tolerant mSPMD programming executions using between 64 and 1024 compute cores per task. The dotted lines are the results of fault-tolerant mSPMD programming executions, and the solid lines are those of the regular mSPMD programming executions. As shown in the figure, the best combination of the number of blocks and the number of processes per task is 4×4 blocks and 512 processes for both cases of with and without fault-tolerance support. The overhead of using a heartbeat message is very small and is 2.3% on average and 4.7% at a maximum.

Then, we have investigated the behavior and performance of the fault-tolerant mSPMD programming execution when errors occur. Instead of waiting for real errors, we have inserted fake errors that stop heartbeat messages from remote programs randomly with a certain error probability computed by an expected

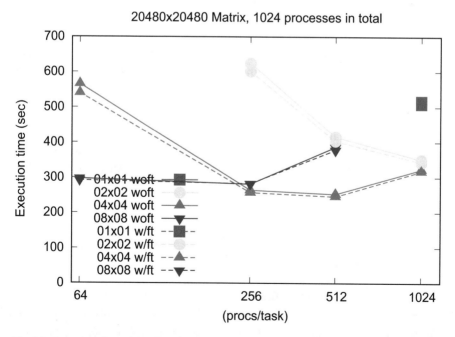

Fig. 15 Execution time with and without FT for the number of cores for each task. The graph legends show the number of blocks

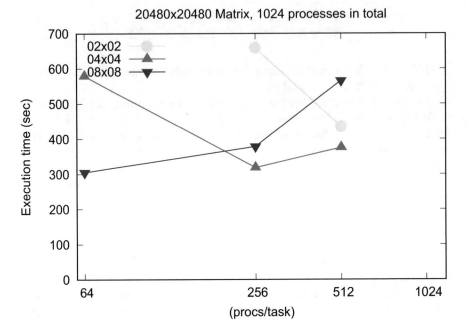

Fig. 16 Execution time with FT for the number of cores for each task under fake errors. The graph legends show the number of blocks

MTBF (90,000 s). Figure 16 shows the performance of the fault-tolerant mSPMD programming execution under fake errors. Unfortunately, for the case of 1×1 block and 1024 processes per task, it was not possible to complete the workflow, since the face error ratio used in the experiment is higher than real systems. For the other cases, the applications can be completed. The best combination of the number of blocks and the number of processes per task is 4×4 blocks and 256 processes, while it was 512 processes under the "no-error" condition. This is because the tasks executed on a relatively small number of nodes are relatively easy to recover when they fail.

8 Runtime Correctness Check for the mSPMD Programming Model

8.1 Overview and Implementation

The mSPMD programming model has been proposed to realize scalability for large scale systems. Additionally, as we discussed in Sect. 7, we support fault-tolerant features in the mSPMD programming model. In this section, we discuss another important issue in large scale systems, productivity.

One of the reasons for the low productivity in distributed parallel programs is the difficulty of debugging. Several libraries and tools have been proposed to help and debug parallel programs. MUST (Marmot Umpire Scalable Tool) [5, 6, 12] is a runtime tool that provides a scalable solution for efficient runtime MPI error checking. The MUST has supported not only MPI but also XcalableMP (XMP) [8].

In this section, we discuss how to adapt the MUST library to the SPMD programs in the mSPMD programming model and enable the MUST correctness checking for the mSPMD. Computational experiments have been performed to confirm MUST's operation in the mSPMD and to estimate the overhead of the correctness checking.

The mSPMD programming model consists of workflow scheduler, middleware, remote programs, and so on. Each of the remote programs includes user-defined tasks and control sections where the remote program communicates with the workflow scheduler. In this work, we focus on the user-defined tasks within the remote programs, and the correctness check by the MUST library should be applied only to the user-defined tasks. Figure 17 shows an overview of the application execution in the mSPMD programming model and the target of the correctness check by the MUST library in the mSPMD programming model. While MUST checks the MPI and XMP communications shown in orange letters, MPI_Comm_spawn used to invoke remote programs, MPI_Send used to send a request to the remote programs, must be ignored.

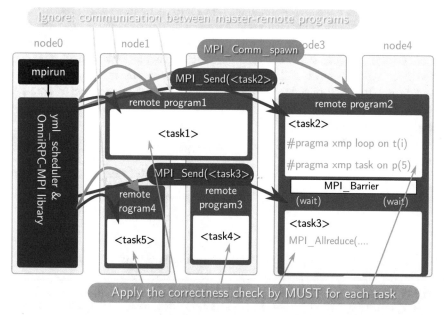

Fig. 17 Applying MUST to the mSPMD programming model. Only communication functions written in red letters are checked, MPI functions written in black letters are not checked

MUST replaces MPI functions starting with MPI_ such as MPI_Send with their own MPI functions, including correctness check and actual communication. The functions starting with MPI_ such as MPI_Send in standard MPI libraries wrap the functions starting with PMPI_ which perform communication. In order to avoid the correctness check for the control sections, we define some macro to use PMPI functions directly (Fig. 18). Moreover, to reserve an additional process for MUST in remote programs, we define the macro to invoke remote programs (Fig. 19).

The original MUST creates an output file named MUST_Output.html for each of parallel applications. On the other hand, in the mSPMD programming model, there are one or more parallel applications simultaneously. Therefore, we modify the MUST library to generate different MUST_Output_<id>.html files for different remote programs. So far, we give a process id of the rank-0 of a remote program as the <id> the output file. Figure 20 shows an example of the output file generated by MUST in the mSPMD programming model.

8.2 Experiments

We have performed some experiments to evaluate the execution times and to investigate applications' behaviors with and without the MUST library. In these experiments, the Oakforest-PACS (OFP) system has been used. Table 6 shows the specification of the OFP. For remote programs, we adopt the flat-MPI programming model where each MPI process runs on each core.

We focus on collective communication (MPI_Allreduce) and point to point communication (Pingpong) and consider codes with and without error for each. Figure 21 shows the tasks used in the experiments. From the top to bottom, allreduce (w/o error), allreduce (w/ error, type mismatch), pingpong (w/o error), pingpong (w/ error, type mismatch), allreduce (w/ error, operation mismatch), and allreduce (w/ error, buffer size mismatch). Also, we consider different numbers of iterations

Fig. 18 The Macro to disable the MUST correctness check

```
#define MYX

#ifdef MYX
#define MPI_Comm_rank(comm, rank)\
            PMPI_Comm_rank(comm, rank)

#define MPI_Barrier(comm)\
            PMPI_Barrier(comm)

....

#endif // #ifdef MYX
```

Fig. 19 The Macro to invoke remote programs with $n + 1$ processes where "+1" is kept for MUST

```
#define MPI_Comm_spawn(command, argv, maxprocs,\
    info, root, comm, intercomm, array_of_errcodes)\
        PMPI_Comm_spawn(command, argv, maxprocs+1,\
    info, root, comm, intercomm, array_of_errcodes)
```

MUST Output, starting date: Tue Jul 16 17:34:45 2019.

Rank(s)	Type	Message
0	Error	Two collective calls cause a type mismatch! This call sends data to the c⋯

Details:

Message	From	References
Two collective calls cause a type mismatch! This call sends data to the call in reference 1. The mismatch occurs at (MPI_UNSIGNED_LONG) in the send type and at (MPI_LONG) in the receive type (consult the MUST manual for a detailed description of datatype positions). (Information on communicator: MPI_COMM_WORLD) (Information on send transfer of count 1 with type:MPI_UNSIGNED_LONG) (Information on receive of count 1 with type:MPI_LONG	Representative location: call MPI_Allreduce (1st occurrence)	References of a representative process: reference 1 rank 5: call MPI_Allreduce (1st occurrence)
5	Error	Two collective calls cause a type mismatch! This call sends data to the c⋯
1	Error	Two collective calls cause a type mismatch! This call sends data to the c⋯
9	Error	Two collective calls cause a type mismatch! This call sends data to the c⋯
56	Error	Two collective calls cause a type mismatch! This call sends data to the c⋯
15	Error	Two collective calls cause a type mismatch! This call sends data to the c⋯

Fig. 20 Screenshot of the output file generated by MUST in the mSPMD programming model

Table 6 The specification of the Oakforest-PACS

CPU	Intel Xeon Phi 7250 (KNL), 68 core, 1.4 GHz
Memory	96 GB(DDR) + 16 GB(MCDRAM)
Network	Intel Omni-Path Network, 100 Gpbs
Compiler	intel/2018.1.163
MPI library	impi/2018.1.163
OS	CentOS 7

and different interval seconds between MPI function calls in each test code for the overhead evaluations.

Table 7 shows the applications' behaviors and the statuses of error reports, when applying or not applying MUST. While the datatype conflict and operation conflict errors are reported when we apply the MUST, the applications are completed without any report when we do not apply the MUST even though the results of the reduction should be wrong.

Figure 22 shows the execution time of the mSPMD programming executions with and without the MUST library. Workflow applications include between 1 and 32 tasks of MPI_Allreduce. Figure 23 shows the results for MPI_Send/Recv. Each task uses 32 processes in all experiments. As shown in Fig. 22, the overhead to check and record errors of collective communication is ignorable if we do not perform communication very intensively. On the other hand, if collective communication functions called very frequently, then the overheads become large even if there is no error. As shown in Fig. 23, the overhead of the MUST library is small if there is no error in point to point communication functions. However, it takes more time if there are some errors. The fact indicates that there is almost no overhead to check point to point communication, but it takes some time to analyze and record errors in the point to point communication functions.

```
for(i=0; i<Niter; i++){
  MPI_Allreduce(buf, rbuf, 1, MPI_LONG, MPI_SUM, MPI_COMM_WORLD);
  usleep(Usec);
}
for(i=0; i<Niter; i++){
  if(myrank==0)
  MPI_Allreduce(buf, rbuf, 1, MPI_UNSIGNED_LONG,
                                    MPI_SUM, MPI_COMM_WORLD);
  else
  MPI_Allreduce(buf, rbuf, 1, MPI_LONG, MPI_SUM, MPI_COMM_WORLD);
  usleep(Usec);
}
 for(i=0; i<Niter; i++){
  if(myrank%2==0)
  MPI_Send(buf, 1, MPI_LONG, dest, tag, MPI_COMM_WORLD);
  else
  MPI_Recv(buf, 1, MPI_LONG, src , tag, MPI_COMM_WORLD, &stat);
  usleep(Usec);
  if(myrank%2==0)
  MPI_Recv(buf, 1, MPI_LONG, src , tag, MPI_COMM_WORLD, &stat);
  else
  MPI_Send(buf, 1, MPI_LONG, dest, tag, MPI_COMM_WORLD);
  usleep(Usec);
 }
for(i=0; i<Niter; i++){
  if(myrank%2==0)
  MPI_Send(buf, 1, MPI_UNSIGNED_LONG, dest, tag, MPI_COMM_WORLD);
  else
  MPI_Recv(buf, 1, MPI_LONG, src , tag, MPI_COMM_WORLD, &stat);
  usleep(Usec);
  if(myrank%2==0)
  MPI_Recv(buf, 1, MPI_LONG, src , tag, MPI_COMM_WORLD, &stat);
  else
  MPI_Send(buf, 1, MPI_LONG, dest, tag, MPI_COMM_WORLD);
  usleep(Usec);
}

if(myrank==0)
  MPI_Allreduce(buf, rbuf, 1, MPI_LONG, MPI_MAX, MPI_COMM_WORLD);
else
  MPI_Allreduce(buf, rbuf, 1, MPI_LONG, MPI_MIN, MPI_COMM_WORLD);

if(myrank==0)
  MPI_Allreduce(buf, rbuf, 2, MPI_LONG, MPI_SUM, MPI_COMM_WORLD);
else
  MPI_Allreduce(buf, rbuf, 1, MPI_LONG, MPI_SUM, MPI_COMM_WORLD);
```

Fig. 21 The tasks used in experiments. From the top to bottom, allreduce (w/o error), allreduce (w/ data type error), pingpong (w/o error), and pingpong (w/ error), allreduce (w/ operation error), allreduce (w/ data size error)

Table 7 Applications' behaviors and the statuses of error reports

	w/ MUST	w/o MUST
Allreduce w/o error	Completed	Completed
Allreduce w/	Completed	Completed
Type conflict error	Error reports	No report
Pingpong w/o error	Completed	Completed
Pingpong w/	Completed	Completed
Type conflict error	Error reports	No report
Allreduce w/	Completed	Completed
Operation conflict error	Error reports	No report
Allreduce w/	Failed	Failed
Buffer size conflict error	Error reports	Simple error reports

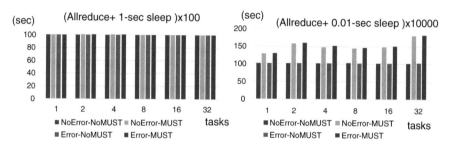

Fig. 22 Execution time when a workflow includes $1, 2, \cdots 32$ tasks executing MPI_Allreduce repeatedly every 1-s (left) and every 0.01-s

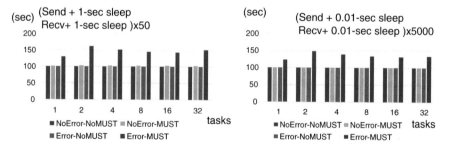

Fig. 23 Execution time when a workflow includes $1, 2, \cdots 32$ tasks executing MPI_Send/Recv repeatedly every 1-s (left) and every 0.01-s

9 Summary

In this chapter, we have presented the mSPMD programming model and programming environment, where several SPMD programs work together under the control of a workflow program. YML, which is a development and execution environment for scientific workflows, and its middleware OmniRPC, have been extended to manage several SPMD tasks and programs. As well as MPI, XMP, a directive-based parallel programming language, has been supported to describe tasks. A task generator has been developed to incorporate XMP programs into a workflow. Fault-tolerant features, correctness check, and some numerical libraries' implementations in the mSPMD programming model have been presented.

References

1. C. Augonnet, S. Thibault, R. Namyst, P.-A. Wacrenier, StarPU: a unified platform for task scheduling on heterogeneous multicore architectures. Concurr. Comput. Pract. Exp. **23**, 187–198 (2011). Euro-Par 2009
2. O. Delannoy, *YML: A Scientific Workflow for High Performance Computing*, PhD thesis, University of Versailles Saint-Quentin (2006)
3. O. Delannoy, N. Emad, S. Petiton, Workflow global computing with YML, in *The 7th IEEE/ACM International Conference on Grid Computing* (2006), pp. 25–32
4. O. Delannoy, S. Petiton, A peer to peer computing framework: design and performance evaluation of YML, in *3rd International Workshop on Algorithms, Models and Tools for Parallel Computing on Heterogeneous Networks* (2004), pp. 362–369
5. T. Hilbrich, F. Hasel, M. Schulz, B.R. de Supinski, M.S. Muller, W.E. Nagel, Runtime MPI collective checking with tree-based overlay networks, in *Proceedings of the 20th European MPI Users' Group Meeting (EuroMPI 13)* (ACM, Madrid, 2013), pp. 129–134
6. T. Hilbrich, J. Protze, M. Schulz, B.R. de Supinski, M.S. Muller, MPI runtime error detection with MUST: advances in deadlock detection, in *International Conference on High Performance Computing, Networking, Storage and Analysis (SC12)* (IEEE, Washington, DC, 2012)
7. T. Odajima, T. Boku, M. Sato, T. Hanawa, Y. Kodama, R. Namyst, S. Thibault, O. Aumage, Adaptive task size control on high level programming for GPU/CPU work sharing, in *International Symposium on Advances of Distributed and Parallel Computing (ADPC 2013)* (2013), pp. 59–68
8. J. Protze, C. Terboven, M.S. Müller, S. Petiton, N. Emad, H. Murai, T. Boku, Runtime correctness checking for emerging programming paradigms, in *Proceedings of the First International Workshop on Software Correctness for HPC Applications* (2017), pp. 21–27
9. M. Sato, M. Hirano, Y. Tanaka, S. Sekiguchi, OmniRPC: a grid RPC facility for cluster and global computing in OpenMP, in *International Workshop on OpenMP Applications and Tools* (2001), pp. 130–136
10. D.C. Sorensen, Implicitly restarted Arnoldi/Lanczos methods for large scale eigenvalue calculations, in *Parallel Numerical Algorithms. ICASE/LaRC Interdisciplinary Series in Science and Engineering Book Series (ICAS)*, vol. 4 (Springer, Dordrecht, 1997), pp. 119–165
11. SuiteSparse Matrix Collection, https://sparse.tamu.edu/
12. The MUST Project, https://www.itc.rwth-aachen.de/must

13. M. Tsuji, S. Petiton, M. Sato, Fault tolerance features of a new multi-SPMD programming/execution environment, in *Proceedings of the First International Workshop on Extreme Scale Programming Models and Middleware SC15* (ACM, Austin, 2015), pp. 20–27. https://doi.org/10.1145/2832241.2832243
14. M. Tsuji, M. Sato, M. Hugues, S. Petiton, Multiple-SPMD programming environment based on pGAs and workflow toward post-petascale computing, in *Proceedings of the 2013 International Conference on Parallel Processing (ICPP-2013)* (IEEE, Lyon, 2013), pp. 480–485

XcalableMP 2.0 and Future Directions

Mitsuhisa Sato, Hitoshi Murai, Masahiro Nakao, Keisuke Tsugane, Tesuya Odajima, and Jinpil Lee

Abstract This chapter presents the XcalableMP on the Fugaku supercomputer, the Japanese flagship supercomputer developed by FLAGSHIP2020 project in RIKEN R-CCS. The porting and the performance evaluation were done as a part of this project, and the XcalableMP is available for the Fugaku users for improving the productivity and performance of parallel programing. The performance of XcalableMP on the Fugaku is enhanced by the manycore processor and a new Tofu-D interconnect. We are now working on the next version, XcalableMP 2.0, for cutting-edge high-performance systems with manycore processors by multithreading and multi-tasking with integrations of PGAS model and synchronization models. We conclude this book with retrospectives and challenges for future PGAS models.

1 Introduction

We have been developing a production-level XcalableMP compiler, and make it available for the K computer's users as well as the users of conventional clusters. RIKEN R-CCS has been carrying out the FLAGSHIP 2020 Project [1] to develop the Japanese flagship supercomputer system following the K computer, the Post-K, formally named as "Fugaku" later, since 2014. In the project, XcalableMP was taken as a parallel programming language project for improving the productivity and performance of parallel programing. XcalableMP is now available on Fugaku and the performance is enhanced by the Fugaku interconnect, Tofu-D. The next section describes the XcalableMP on Fugaku.

M. Sato (✉) · H. Murai · M. Nakao · T. Odajima · J. Lee
RIKEN Center for Computational Science, Kobe, Japan
e-mail: msato@riken.jp; h-murai@riken.jp; masahiro.nakao@riken.jp; tetsuya.odajima@riken.jp; jinpil.lee@riken.jp

K. Tsugane
Fujitsu Laboratories Ltd., Kawasaki, Kanagawa, Japan
e-mail: tsugane.keisuke@fujitsu.com

245

The XcalableMP project has been started from 2008 and the discussion on XcalableMP 1.x has converged. We are now working on a new version, XcalableMP 2.0, targeted for cutting-edge high-performance systems with manycore processors by multithreading and multi-tasking with integrations of PGAS model and synchronization models. In this new programming model, the execution of the program is decomposed into several tasks executed according the dependency between tasks. This model will enable less overhead of synchronization by eliminating expensive global synchronization, overlap between computation and communication in manycore, and light-weight communication by RDMA in PGAS model. We will extend this programming model to combine several kinds of accelerators such as GPU, FPGA, and special-purpose processors with large-scale general-purpose manycore systems. It enables some tasks to be offloaded into the accelerators such as FPGA as well as each core in modern manycore processor. We consider this configuration as a general global architecture of the future system as some part of system will be specialized for high performance and power efficiency. Our programming model will make it easy to adopt the existing computational science program to the new systems.

In Sect. 3, a proposal for XcalableMP 2.0 is presented, followed by retrospectives and challenges for future PGAS models in Sect. 4.

2 XcalableMP on Fugaku

In this section, we report our early experience and the preliminary performance of XcalableMP on Fugaku. The Fugaku is a huge-scale system with general-purpose manycore processors. The node processor is a single chip, Fujitsu A64FX, which consists of 48 cores with 2 or 4 cores dedicated for OS activities, 32 GiB HBM2 memory, with Tofu-D interconnect, and a PCI express controller in the chip together. The Fugaku system consists of 158,976 nodes in 432 racks. The Fugaku is scheduled to be put into operation for public service around 2021. In 2020, the installation is completed and the system partially serves the early access program.

XcalableMP is available as a parallel programming language for the Fugaku, supported by R-CCS team with Fujitsu. C and Fortran are supported as base languages with XcalableMP 1.2 compliant.

We report the preliminary performance of XcalableMP program running on the Fugaku.[1]

We used the following versions:

- Omni XcalableMP Version: 1.3.2, Git Hash: 6d23f46.
- Language specification: 1.2.25.

---

[1]The reported results were obtained on the evaluation environment in the trial phase. Note that the performance is not guaranteed at the start of its operation.

The performance of XcalableMP on the Fugaku is enhanced by the manycore processor and a new Tofu-D interconnect.

2.1 Performance of XcalableMP Global View Programming

We executed the IMPACT-3D, described in Chap. 6, for the evaluation of XcalableMP global view programming in the Fugaku, using up to 512 nodes. The scalability on Fugaku is shown in Fig. 1, comparing to the MPI version. The program is parallelized by hybrid XMP-OpenMP parallel programming: An XMP node is assigned to a node, and 48 OpenMP threads are running within a node. The problem size is $512 \times 512 \times 512$ with three-dimensional block distribution. The compile option is "-Kfast".

As shown in the figure, we found a good scalability in Fugaku, and the performance is better than that by MPI thanks to the optimized XMP runtime for communications in the stencil computation [2].

2.2 Performance of XcalableMP Local View Programming

Fugaku has a customized interconnection, called Tofu-D, which provides hardware-supported RDMA (Remote Direct Memory Access) operations. We implemented the XMP runtime library to make use of Tofu-D for one-sided communication for

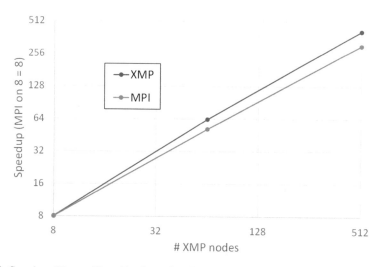

Fig. 1 Speedup of Impact3D on Fugaku and performance comparing to K computer

the XMP local view programming. The library is implemented by using a low-level communication layer, uTofu API [3], provided by Fujitsu.

For performance evaluation of XMP local view programming, we used CCS QCD and NTChem-MINI taken from the coarray version of Fiber Miniapp Suite [4, 5].

To run CCS QCD mini-application [6], eight XMP nodes are assigned to one node, running in a flat XMP mode. The size and conditions are as follows:

- Target data: Class 2 ($32 \times 32 \times 32 \times 32$) (strong scaling).
- Compiler options: -Kfast, zfill, simd=2.
- Timing region: sum of "Clover + Clover_inv Performance" and "BiCGStab (CPU: double precision) Performance" of the built-in timing feature.

Figure 2 shows the speedup of the Fugaku, comparing to the performance of the K computer. The XMP version archives almost same performance of the MPI version. Note that the reason of the performance degradation of the XMP version on the K computer is the overhead of allocation for allocatable coarray used as a buffer for communication. It is improved by removing this overhead by using the uTofu communication layer.

The NTChem-MINI is a mini-application taken from NTChem [7], a high-performance software package for molecular electronic structure calculation. An XMP node is assigned to one node, and within a node, BLAS functions are executed using 48 cores. The size and conditions are set as follows:

- Target data: taxol (strong scaling).
- Compiler options: -Kfast, simd=2.
- Timing region: "RIMP2_Driver" of the built-in timing feature.

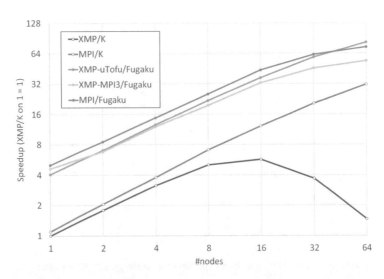

Fig. 2 Speedup of CCS QCD on Fugaku and performance comparing to the K computer

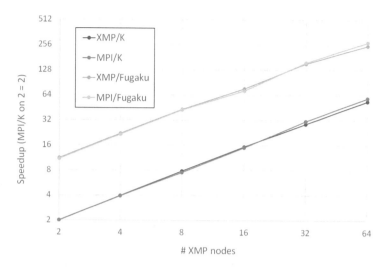

Fig. 3 Speedup of NTChem-MINI on Fugaku and performance comparing to the K computer

As shown in Fig. 3, the XMP versions archive almost the same performance of the original MPI versions.

3 Global Task Parallel Programming

Recently, large-scale clusters of manycore processors such as Intel Xeon Phi have been deployed in many sites from the latest Top500 Lists. In order to program manycore processors, OpenMP is widely used as a shared-memory programming model. Most OpenMP programs are written using work sharing constructs for loops, which involves a global synchronization. However, especially in modern manycore processors, the global synchronization cost for work sharing becomes bigger, and the load imbalance among cores lead to the performance degradation as the number of cores on the processor increases. Task parallel programming using task dependency in OpenMP 4.0 is a promising candidate to facilitate the parallelization for such manycore processors because it enables users to avoid global synchronization by fine-grained task-to-task synchronization through user-specified data dependencies.

We are interested in extending the task parallel programming model to the PGAS model of XcalableMP for distributed memory systems. As well as removing expensive global synchronization, it is expected to enable the overlapping of communication and computation. For XMP 2.0, we propose the global task parallel programming.

In OpenMP, the task dependency in a node depends on the order of reading and writing to data based on the sequential execution. Therefore, the OpenMP multi-tasking model cannot be applied to describe the dependency between tasks running in different nodes since threads of each nodes are running in parallel.

We propose new directives for communication with tasks in XMP, and they enable users to write easily the multi-tasking execution based on XMP language constructs. The tasklet directive generates a task for the associated structured block on the node specified by the on clause, and the task is scheduled and immediately executed by an arbitrary thread in the specified node if there is no task dependency. If it has any task dependencies, the task execution is postponed until all dependencies are resolved. The tasklet gmove directive copies the variable of the right-hand side (RHS) into the left-hand side (LHS) of the associated assignment statement for local or distributed data in tasks. If the variable of the RHS or the LHS is the remote data, this directive may synchronize on data dependency between nodes and execute communication. The tasklet reflect directive is a task-version of reflect operation. It updates halo regions of the array specified to array-name in tasks. In this directive, data dependency is automatically added to these tasks based on the communication data because the boundary index of the distributed data is dynamically determined by XMP runtime system.

We have designed a simple code translation algorithm from the proposed directives to XMP runtime calls with MPI and OpenMP. We have evaluated the performance using block-Cholesky Factorization Program on KNL based-system, Oakforest-PACS. Through the experiment, we confirmed the advantage of task parallelism over the traditional loop-based data parallelism. At the same time, we found the performance problems on communication between multiple threads (MPI_THREAD_MULTIPLE). Currently, we are investigating a lower-level communication API for efficient one-sided communication of PGAS operations in multithreaded execution environment.

Details of the proposal in this chapter are described in [8].

3.1   OpenMP and XMP Tasklet Directive

While OpenMP originally focuses on work sharing for loops as the parallel for directive, OpenMP 3.0 introduces task parallelism using the task directive. It facilitates the parallelization where work is generated dynamically and irregularly as in recursive structures or unbounded loops. The depend clause on the task directive is supported from OpenMP 4.0 and specifies data dependencies with dependence-type in, out, and inout. Task dependency can reduce the global synchronization of a thread team because it can execute fine-grained synchronization between tasks through user-specified data dependencies.

Fig. 4 Syntax of the
`tasklet`, `taskletwait`,
and `tasklets` directives in
XMP

#pragma xmp tasklet *[clause[, clause] ...] [on { node-ref | template-ref }]*
  (structured-block)

#pragma xmp taskletwait *[on { node-ref | template-ref }]*

#pragma xmp tasklets
  (structured-block)

where *clause* is :
  {in | out | inout} *(variable[, variable] ...])*

To support task parallelism in XMP as in OpenMP, the `tasklet` directive[2] is proposed in XMP 2.0. Figure 4 describes the syntax of the `tasklet`,
`tasklets`, and `taskletwait` directives for the multi-tasking execution in
XMP. The `tasklet` directive generates a task for the associated structured block
on the node specified by the `on` clause, and the task is scheduled and immediately
executed by an arbitrary thread in the specified node if there is no task dependency. If
it has any task dependencies, the task execution is postponed until all dependencies
are resolved. These behaviors occur when these tasks are surrounded by `tasklets`
directive. When these tasks are not surrounded by the `tasklets` directives, they
are executed sequentially at the specified node. The `tasklet` directive supports
several clauses for the description of the task dependency. The `in`, `out`, and `inout`
clauses represent the task dependency in a node. When `in`, `out`, or `inout` clause
presents on the `tasklet` directive, the generated task has each data dependency
in a node. The behavior of these data dependencies is same as OpenMP `task`
`depend` clause: flow, anti, and output dependencies.

The `taskletwait` directive waits on the completion of the generated tasks
on each node. Since the directive does not involve the barrier synchronization, the
`barrier` directive in XMP is also required in order to guarantee that all tasks of
all nodes are finished at this point. There is an implicit barrier on each node at the
end of the `tasklets` directive.

In OpenMP, the task dependencies are created according to the order of reading
and writing to data based on the sequential execution in a node. Therefore, the
OpenMP task parallel model cannot be directly applied to describe the dependency
between tasks running in different nodes since threads of each nodes are running in
parallel.

In OmpSs [10], interactions between nodes are described through the MPI
task that is executing MPI communications. Task dependency between nodes
is guaranteed by the completion of MPI point-to-point communication in tasks.
While this approach can satisfy dependencies between nodes, it may cause further
productivity degradation because it forces users to use a combination of two
programming models that are based on different description formats. Therefore,
we propose new directives for communication with tasks in XMP, and they enable

---

[2]There is the `task` directive in XMP, it is different from OpenMP's one.

users to write easily the multi-tasking execution for clusters by only using language constructs.

3.2 A Proposal for Global Task Parallel Programming

In order to support multi-tasking execution for distributed memory parallel systems, we need to perform point-to-point communication within tasks in local task dependency graphs. While XMP provides some directives for communication, many of these are performed collectively, and cause an implicit synchronization among execution nodes. This causes a performance degradation, because tasks participating in communications, such as broadcast, wait for synchronization until all tasks are completed. For XMP 2.0, we propose two directives, `tasklet gmove` and `tasklet reflect`, as shown in Fig. 5, to describe interactions between nodes in tasks by point-to-point communication, for inter-node data dependency. These communications are only synchronized between the sender and receiver of the communication in each task.

These details are as follow:

`tasklet gmove` directive: Although this copies the variable from the right-hand side (RHS) into the left-hand side (LHS) of the associated assignment statement for local or distributed data like the `gmove` directive, it is executed in tasks. The copy operation is basically performed on all execution nodes. However, if the distributed array is specified at the associated assignment statement, only nodes with the distributed array execute the operation in the task. The execution nodes can also be determined by the `on` clause. When the `in`, `out`, or `inout` clause is present on the `tasklet gmove` directive, the generated task has the corresponding data dependency in a node, similar to the `tasklet` directive.

`tasklet reflect` directive: Although this updates halo regions of the array specified to `array-name` as in the `reflect` directive, it is executed in tasks. For example, when updating one side of a halo region for a one-dimensional distributed array on two nodes, these communications are separated into four tasks: the sender of the upper element on node 1, the receiver of the upper halo region on node 1, the sender of the lower element on node 2, and the receiver of the lower halo region on node 2. In this directive, data dependency is automatically added to these generated tasks based on the communication data, because the boundary index of the distributed array is dynamically determined by the XMP

Fig. 5 Syntax of the `tasklet gmove` and `tasklet reflect` directives in XMP

```
#pragma xmp tasklet gmove [clause[, clause] ... ] [on { node-ref \ template-ref } ]
  (an assignment statement)

#pragma xmp tasklet reflect (array-name[, array-name] ... )
              [blocksize (reflect-blocksize[, reflect-blocksize] ... ) ]

where clause is :
  {in | out | inout} (variable[, variable] ... ])
```

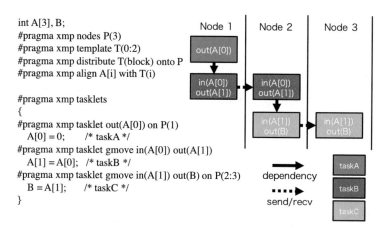

```
int A[3], B;
#pragma xmp nodes P(3)
#pragma xmp template T(0:2)
#pragma xmp distribute T(block) onto P
#pragma xmp align A[i] with T(i)

#pragma xmp tasklets
{
#pragma xmp tasklet out(A[0]) on P(1)
    A[0] = 0;       /* taskA */
#pragma xmp tasklet gmove in(A[0]) out(A[1])
    A[1] = A[0];   /* taskB */
#pragma xmp tasklet gmove in(A[1]) out(B) on P(2:3)
    B = A[1];       /* taskC */
}
```

Fig. 6 Example of the `tasklet` and `tasklet gmove` directives

runtime system. The `chunksize` clause can be matched the task dependency descriptions of users using the dependency generated by the `tasklet reflect` directive. When users calculate an array in block units, such as in the cache blocking technique for a node with data dependency, the user-specified task dependency and generated data dependency for halo exchange may not identically match. By specifying the `chunksize` clause, the halo region is distributed logically to equal-sized contiguous chunks, and data dependencies for the halo exchange are generated automatically by the XMP runtime system based on the specified chunk size.

Figure 6 presents an example of the `tasklet gmove` directive. In this example, array $A[]$ with length three is distributed to three nodes in equal-sized contiguous blocks. This code creates three kinds of tasks. TaskA and taskC are executed on nodes specified by the `on` clause. TaskB is executed on nodes 1 and 2, because these nodes have the specified distributed array $A[0]$ or $A[1]$ in the associated assignment statement under the `tasklet gmove` directive. There is a flow dependency between taskA and taskB on node 1 by $A[0]$. After the execution of taskA, taskB sends $A[0]$ to node 2, which is determined by the distributed array $A[1]$. In node 2, taskB receives $A[0]$ from node 1 in $A[1]$. When the receive operation in taskB is finished, taskC is immediately started, because the flow dependency of $A[1]$ is satisfied. TaskC sends the $A[1]$ to variable B of node 3. Because the variable B is a local variable for each node, the communication destination is determined from the execution nodes specified by the `on` clause.

3.3 Prototype Design of Code Transformation

We have designed a simple code transformation from the code using the proposed directives to the code with XMP runtime calls using MPI and OpenMP. As for a preliminary evaluation, we have made a hand-translated MPI and OpenMP code by using the proposed transformation.

The `tasklets` directive is converted into the OpenMP `parallel` and `single` directives. The execution node is determined by the `on` clause, which is translated to an `if` statement. The `tasklet gmove` and `tasklet reflect` directives are converted into MPI_Send/Recv(), and these MPI functions are executed in OpenMP tasks with data dependency specified by users. In the case that an MPI blocking call, such as MPI_Send/Recv(), occurs in these codes, a deadlock may occur depending on the task scheduling mechanism, from the combination of MPI and OpenMP. To prevent this deadlock, in the actual implementation we used MPI asynchronous communications, such as MPI_Isend/Irecv(), MPI_Test(), and the OpenMP `taskyield` directive, which makes the current task become suspended at the time point at which it is invoked, and may result in switching to different tasks.

3.4 Preliminary Performance

We measured the performance on the Oakforest-PACS [11] systems at at the Joint Center for Advanced High-Performance Computing (JCAHPC) [9], under cooperation with the Center for Computational Sciences, University of Tsukuba and the Information Technology Center, the University of Tokyo. This system has 8,208 computing nodes, each of which consists of an Intel Xeon Phi (KNL) processor and the Intel Omni-Path architecture as an interconnection. In this evaluation, we selected the Flat and Quadrant modes for KNL. While the Intel Xeon Phi 7250 has 68 cores, a 64 core usage per node is recommended in this system. Some cores are used to assist the OS, interrupt handling, and for communication progress. Moreover, in order to avoid OS jitters, only core 0 is set to receive OS interruptions.

We used blocked Cholesky factorization as our benchmark. It calculates the decomposition of a Hermitian positive-definite blocked matrix into the product of a lower triangular matrix and its conjugate transpose. The calculation consists of four BLAS or LAPACK functions, POTRF, TRSM, GEMM, and SYRK, which are performed in block units. Figure 7 shows the Blocked Cholesky factorization code in the XMP tasklet directive.

We compare the performance in two parallelization approaches, "Parallel Loop" and "Task," in MPI and OpenMP. The "Parallel Loop" version is the conventional barrier-based implementation, described by work sharing for loops using the `parallel for` directive and independent tasks using the `task` directive without the `depend` clause. Although this version of blocked Cholesky factorization is applied on the overlap of the communication and computation at the process level, it performs the global synchronization in work sharing. The "Parallel Loop" version of the Laplace equation solver does not include the overlap of the communication and computation. The "Task" version is implemented using our proposed model, based on task dependency using the `depend` clause, instead of global synchronization.

```
1   double A[nt][nt][ts*ts], B[ts*ts], C[nt][ts*ts];
2   #pragma xmp nodes P(*)
3   #pragma xmp template T(0:nt−1)
4   #pragma xmp distribute T(cyclic) onto P
5   #pragma xmp align A[*][i][*] with T(i)
6
7   #pragma xmp tasklets
8   for (int k = 0; k < nt; k++) {
9   #pragma xmp tasklet out(A[k][k]) on T(k)
10      potrf(A[k][k]);
11
12  #pragma xmp tasklet gmove in(A[k][k]) out(B) on T(k:)
13      B[:] = A[k][k][:];
14
15      for (int i = k + 1; i < nt; i++) {
16  #pragma xmp tasklet in(B) out(A[k][i]) on T(i)
17          trsm(B, A[k][i]);
18
19  #pragma xmp tasklet gmove in(A[k][i]) out(C[i]) on T(i:)
20          C[i][:] = A[k][i][:];
21      }
22      for (int i = k + 1; i < nt; i++) {
23          for (int j = k + 1; j < i; j++) {
24  #pragma xmp tasklet in(A[k][i], C[j]) out(A[j][i]) on T(j)
25              gemm(A[k][i], C[j], A[j][i]);
26          }
27  #pragma xmp tasklet in(A[k][i]) out(A[i][i]) on T(i)
28          syrk(A[k][i], A[i][i]);
29      }
30  }
```

Fig. 7 Blocked Cholesky factorization code in the XMP `tasklet` directive

We also show the result of these benchmarks implemented by MPI and OmpSs as "Task (OmpSs)." This implementation is described in the `in`, `out`, and `inout` clauses with the OmpSs `task` directive. The `parallel` and `single` regions are not required in the OmpSs programming model. Except for these differences, this is almost the same as the `Task` version.

We evaluated these benchmarks on the following node configurations. For the Oakforest-PACS system, it is on 1–32 nodes, one process per node, 64 cores per process, and one thread per core. The problem size of these benchmarks is set by a matrix size of $32{,}768 \times 32{,}768$ and a block size of 512×512 in double precision arithmetic. The matrix is distributed by a two-dimensional block-cyclic data distribution in blocked Cholesky factorization.

Figure 8 illustrates the performance and breakdown of blocked Cholesky factorization on the Oakforest-PACS. The breakdown indicates the average time required

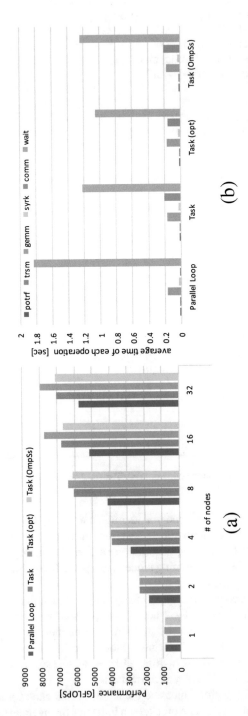

Fig. 8 Performance and breakdown of blocked Cholesky factorization on the Oakforest-PACS system. (**a**) Performance. (**b**) Breakdown at 32 nodes execution

for each operation performed on all threads, because tasks executed on threads differ each time the program is executed. The "wait" in the breakdown represents the waiting time of the thread, including the global synchronization. The "comm" indicates the time from the start of the communication to the end. In Fig. 8a, the "Task" version shows a better performance than the barrier-based "Parallel Loop" implementation. The reason that the "Task" version outperforms the "Parallel Loop" version is that the global synchronization uses a higher cost for the work sharing of loops and among tasks, as shown in Fig. 8b. The relative performance of the "Task" version compared with the "Parallel Loop" version is 123% (Fig. 8).

3.5 Communication Optimization for Manycore Clusters

In the global task parallel programming model, the communication may happen at each pair of tasks between nodes. In order to enable the communication in multithreaded environment, we may use MPI_THREAD_MULTIPLE as the MPI thread-safety level, because tasks executed on threads may communicate simultaneously. We have examined the basic performance of multithreaded communications by using the Ping-Pong benchmark. This benchmark is based on the OSU Micro-Benchmarks 5.3.2 [12] developed by the Ohio State University. we also show the aggregated bandwidth when multiple threads (i.e., two, four, or eight threads) communicate at the same time. Figure 9 illustrates the communication performance on the Oakforest-PACS system. The performance of multithreaded communication with MPI_THREAD_MULTIPLE degrades compared to a single-threaded communication as the number of threads increases. As with the result on the Oakforest-PACS system, the performance of communication on a single thread is better compared to that for multithreaded communication with MPI_THREAD_MULTIPLE. Therefore, the communication performance may be improved if all communications are delegated to the communication thread. To delegate the communications to a single thread, we create a global queue that is accessible by all threads, so that the tasks enqueue the communication requests into this queue and wait for the communication to complete. Meanwhile, the communication thread dequeues the requests for communication to perform the requested communications, and checks the communication completion. The communication thread executes only the communication, and the other threads perform computation tasks.

Figure 8 shows the performance and breakdown of blocked Cholesky factorization with the communication optimization denoted as "Task (opt)." The "Task (opt)" version of blocked Cholesky factorization performs better than the multitasking execution with MPI_THREAD_MULTIPLE. The reason for this is that the communication time decreases compared with the "Task" version, as shown in Figs. 8, because of the use of the communication thread. The relative performances compared with the barrier-based "Parallel Loop" implementation improve to 138% on the Oakforest-PACS systems.

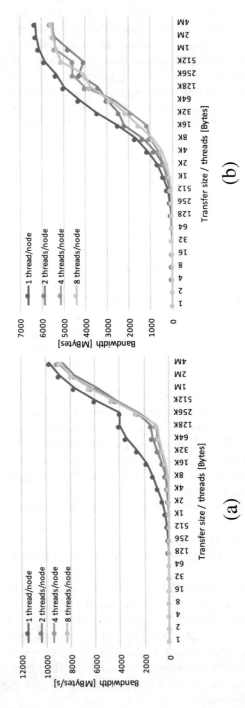

Fig. 9 Performance of the Ping-Pong benchmark on the Oakforest-PACS and COMA systems. (**a**) Oakforest-PACS. (**b**) COMA

4   Retrospectives and Challenges for Future PGAS Models

Since 2007, we have been developing the XcalableMP PGAS language and its reference implementation by the Omni compiler.

In this section, the challenges for future PGAS models are presented with some retrospectives on our project.

4.1   Low-Level Communication Layer for PGAS Model

PGAS is implemented by Remote Memory Access (RMA) providing light-weight one-sided communication and low overhead synchronization semantics. For programmers, both PGAS and RMA are programming interfaces and offer several constructs such as remote read/write and synchronizations.

Remote Direct Memory Access (RDMA) is a mechanism (operation) to access data in remote memory by giving address in (shared) address space. It can be done without involving the CPU or OS at the destination node. Recent advanced interconnect such as Cray Aries interconnect and Fujitsu Tofu of K computer and Tofu-D of Fugaku support remote DMA operations which strongly support efficient one-sided communication.

For the most PGAS runtimes, one-sided communication operations such as Remote Direct Memory Access (RDMA) functions in the MPI are used to implement remote put/get operations in the PGAS languages. Although MPI3 provides several RMA APIs as library interface, the advantages of direct use of RMA/RDMA Operations are as follows:

- Multiple data transfers can be performed with a single synchronization operation.
- Some irregular communication patterns can be more economically expressed.
- The RDMA can be significantly faster than send/receive on systems with hardware support for remote memory access.

We found the multiple data transfers for the stencil computation can be optimized by using a single synchronization operation at the end [13]. As described in Chap. 3, our XMP Coarray were implemented by both MPI and Fujitsu low-level Tofu API. In case of MPI, we used "passive target" mode in MPI one-sided communication. It is noted that the MPI flush operation and synchronization do not sometimes match to implement "sync_images", and the complex "window" management to expose the memory as a coarray. Finally, Fujitsu RDMA interface is much faster than MPI in the K computer.

Other problem is the communication in the multithreaded environment. As described in the previous sections, we found the performance problem of MPI_THREAD_MULTIPLE. As the connection-less semantics of RDMA would be suited to communications in multithreaded environment, we believe that a new design of low-level communication layer would be a desirable solution in near future.

4.2   XcalableMP as a DSL for Stencil Applications

The Domain Specific Language (DSL) is a promising approach to make the programing easy in a specific domain. Many DSLs such as OpenFOAM in CFD are successful.

Many DSLs are proposed to describe the typical stencil computation. On the other hand, we propose the mixed-language programming with XcalableMP in Chap. 5. Using this model, the main kernel of the computation can be written in XcalableMP and other controls, input/output and house-keeping operation are written by other familiar languages such as Python. In this case, a part of XMP is thought as a kind of DSL to write the stencil computation with global view programming.

The advantages of this approach are as follows:

* By using the XMP global view programming model, the stencil computation can be described in a simple loop based on its original sequential program.
* The stencil communication can be done by the XMP optimized stencil communication runtime [13].
* The advanced optimization of the stencil operations is enabled by a set of the directives for the extended stencil optimization such as a loop unrolling and temporal blocking, added in the latest XcalableMP specification, version 1.4 [14].

4.3   XcalableMP API: Compiler-Free Approach

Although many PGAS languages, such as UPC and Chapel, CAF, have proposed, it is hard to say that they are fully accepted by the community of parallel programming. Recently, the libraries supporting the PGAS model, such as OpenShmem [15], GlobalArray [16], even MPI3 RMA, are getting popular for programming some specific applications. Furthermore, many C++ template-based design for PGAS, such as UPC++ [17], DASH [18], are proposed as a compiler-free approach, as C++ template provides powerful abstraction mechanism. This approach may increase portability, clean separation from base compiler optimization, but a problem is that it is sometimes hard to debug in C++ template once a programmer writes wrong programs.

The approach of extending the language given by the support of the compiler, the compiler-approach, may give:

* A new language, or language extension provides easy-to-use and intuitive feature resulting in better productivity.
* This approach enables the compiler analysis for further optimization, such as removal of redundant sync and selection of efficient communication.

In reality, the compiler-approach is not easy to be accepted for deployment and supports in many sites, resulting in the failure of wide dissemination.

We will have a plan to design the library interface for XcalableMP programming model, XMP API, which is aiming to provide the most equivalent programming functions by the set of libraries.

4.4 Global Task Parallel Programming Model for Accelerators

The task-based programming recently supported in OpenMP 4.0 enables to expose a lot of parallelism by executing several tasks of the program in the form of task-graph. To accelerate the task-based parallel program by accelerators such as GPU and FPGA, it is useful for some tasks frequently executed in parallel to be offloaded to accelerators as an asynchronous task executed by accelerators.

In previous section, the global task parallel programming model is presented. The next step will be that this global task parallel programming model is extended to tasks offloaded to accelerators attached to each node in accelerated clusters.

Exploration of new high-performance architectures from programing model's point of view is an important challenge. Future parallel architecture will be more heterogenous having many kinds of accelerators and devices attached to the nodes and directly connected between accelerators by some dedicated interconnect. To program such a complex and heterogenous parallel system, the global task parallel programming model will give a flexible and decomposable model to exploit such heterogenous high-performance architecture.

References

1. *Flagship 2020 Project (Supercomputer Fugaku)*, https://www.r-ccs.riken.jp/en/overview/exascalepj/
2. H. Murai, M. Sato, An efficient implementation of stencil communication for the XcalableMP PGAS parallel programming language, in *7th International Conference on PGAS Programming Models*, Edinburgh (2013)
3. FUJITSU Ltd., *Development Studio uTofu User's Guide* (2020)
4. RIKEN Advanced Institute for Computational Science (RIKEN AICS), *Fiber Miniapp Suite* (2104), fiber-miniapp.github.io
5. H. Murai, M. Nakao, H. Iwashita, M. Sato, Preliminary performance evaluation of coarray-based implementation of fiber Miniapp suite using XcalableMP PGAS language, in *Second Annual PGAS Applications Workshop (PAW)*, Denver, CO (2017)
6. *CCS QCD Solver benchmark program*, https://www.ccs.tsukuba.ac.jp/qcd/ccsqcdsolverbenchmic/
7. *NTChem Overview*, https://www.r-ccs.riken.jp/software_center/software/ntchem/overview/
8. K. Tsugane, J. Lee, H. Murai, M. Sato Multi-tasking execution in PGAS language XcalableMP and communication optimization on many-core clusters, in *HPC Asia 2018*, Tokyo (2018), pp. 75–85
9. Joint Center for Advanced High Performance Computing (JCAHPC), *Basic Specification of Oakforest-PACS*, http://jcahpc.jp/files/OFP-basic.pdf

10. D. Alejandro, A. Eduard, B. Rosa M, L. Jesus, M. Luis, M. Xavier, P. Judit, OmpSs: a proposal for programming heterogeneous multi-core architectures. Parallel Process. Lett. **21**, 173–193 (2011)
11. Joint Center for Advanced High Performance Computing (JCAHPC), *Basic Specification of Oakforest-PACS*, http://jcahpc.jp/files/OFP-basic.pdf
12. *OSU Micro-Benchmarks*, http://mvapich.cse.ohio-state.edu/benchmarks/
13. H. Iwashita, M. Nakao, H. Murai, M. Sato, A source-to-source translation of coarray Fortran with MPI for high performance, in *HPC Asia 2018*, Tokyo (2018)
14. *XcalableMP Language Specification v 1.4*, https://xcalablemp.org/download/spec/xmp-spec-1.4.pdf
15. *OpenShmem*, http://www.openshmem.org/site/
16. *Global Arrays*, https://hpc.pnl.gov/globalarrays/
17. Y. Zheng, A. Kamil, M.B. Driscoll, H. Shan, K. Yelick, UPC++: a PGAS extension for C++, in *2014 IEEE 28th International Parallel and Distributed Processing Symposium* (2014), pp. 1105–1114
18. K. Fuerlinger, T. Fuchs, R. Kowalewski, DASH: a C++ PGAS library for distributed data structures and parallel algorithms, in *2016 IEEE 18th International Conference on High Performance Computing and Communications; IEEE 14th International Conference on Smart City; IEEE 2nd International Conference on Data Science and Systems (HPCC/SmartCity/DSS)*, Sydney, NSW (2016), pp. 983–990. https://doi.org/10.1109/HPCC-SmartCity-DSS.2016.0140

Printed in the United States
by Baker & Taylor Publisher Services